IN THE
SHADOW OF LIBERTY

THE MACMILLAN COMPANY
NEW YORK · BOSTON · CHICAGO · DALLAS
ATLANTA · SAN FRANCISCO

MACMILLAN & CO., Limited
LONDON · BOMBAY · CALCUTTA
MELBOURNE

THE MACMILLAN COMPANY
OF CANADA, Limited
TORONTO

In the
Shadow of Liberty

THE CHRONICLE OF ELLIS ISLAND

BY

EDWARD CORSI

*Former United States Commissioner, Immigration and Naturalization,
New York District*

NEW YORK

THE MACMILLAN COMPANY

1935

INTRODUCTION

Mr. Corsi has written a good book. He describes in an interesting way the operation of immigration inspection, as well as the human side of Ellis Island. Himself, an immigrant, he approached his office with a sympathetic understanding not only of the viewpoint, but the heartaches of the applicant at our doors.

His description of his own landing at Ellis Island is both vivid and touching. In 1907, when the child immigrant Corsi landed at Ellis Island, it happened that I was an interpreter in the Immigration Service at that station. We were then clearing an average of five thousand immigrants a day. That is just twenty-seven years ago. Today, Corsi is the Director of the Home Relief of the City of New York, caring for hundreds of thousands of families.

Ellis Island might have its heart throbs; the rigidity of the immigration laws might have caused many individual injustices and hardships, still America is the land of opportunity. The author's own life typifies that.

F. H. La Guardia

AUTHOR'S NOTE

IT IS with sincere thanks and appreciation that I express to Frank H. Lovette my gratitude for his valuable collaboration. I also owe a deep debt of gratitude to Byron Uhl, Percy Baker, Frank Martocci and other coworkers at the Island for having put life and vigor into this material through their personal recounting of their reminiscences.

EDWARD CORSI

New York
October 23rd, 1934.

CONTENTS

Part IV

Part V

ILLUSTRATIONS

PART I

Chapter I

I BEHOLD AMERICA

THE swelling caravan of immigration reached its record volume in 1907 when the incoming tide brought to America 1,285,349 aliens. I was one of them, a ten year old boy.

My first impressions of the new world will always remain etched in my memory, particularly that hazy October morning when I first saw Ellis Island. The steamer *Florida,* fourteen days out of Naples, filled to capacity with sixteen hundred natives of Italy, had weathered one of the worst storms in our captain's memory; and glad we were, both children and grown-ups, to leave the open sea and come at last through the Narrows into the Bay.

My mother, my stepfather, my brother Giuseppe, and my two sisters, Liberta and Helvetia, all of us together, happy that we had come through the storm safely, clustered on the foredeck for fear of separation and looked with wonder on this miraculous land of our dreams.

Giuseppe and I held tightly to stepfather's hands, while Liberta and Helvetia clung to mother. Passengers all about us were crowding against the rail. Jabbered conversation, sharp cries, laughs and cheers—a steadily rising din filled the air. Mothers and fathers lifted up the babies so that they too could see, off to the left, the Statue of Liberty.

I looked at that statue with a sense of bewilderment, half doubting its reality. Looming shadowy through the mist, it brought silence

3

to the decks of the *Florida*. This symbol of America—this enormous expression of what we had all been taught was the inner meaning of this new country we were coming to—inspired awe in the hopeful immigrants. Many older persons among us, burdened with a thousand memories of what they were leaving behind, had been openly weeping ever since we entered the narrower waters on our final approach toward the unknown. Now somehow steadied, I suppose, by the concreteness of the symbol of America's freedom, they dried their tears.

Directly in front of the *Florida,* half visible in the faintly-colored haze, rose a second and even greater challenge to the imagination.

"Mountains!" I cried to Giuseppe. "Look at them!"

"They're strange," he said, "why don't they have snow on them?" He was craning his neck and standing on tiptoe to stare at the New York skyline.

Stepfather looked toward the skyscrapers, and, smiling, assured us that they were not mountains but buildings—"the highest buildings in the world."

On every side the harbor offered its marvels: tugs, barges, sloops, lighters, sluggish freighters and giant ocean liners—all moving in different directions, managing, by what seemed to us a miracle, to dart in and out and up and down without colliding with one another. They spoke to us through the varied sounds of their whistles, and the *Florida* replied with a deep echoing voice. Bells clanged through our ship, precipitating a new flurry among our fellow-passengers. Many of these people had come from provinces far distant from ours, and were shouting to one another in dialects strange to me. Everything combined to increase our excitement, and we rushed from deck to deck, fearful lest we miss the smallest detail of the spectacle.

Finally the *Florida* veered to the left, turning northward into the Hudson River, and now the incredible buildings of lower Manhattan came very close to us.

The officers of the ship, mighty and unapproachable beings they

ELLIS ISLAND FROM THE AIR, SHOWING THE NEWLY BUILT GATEWAY TO AMERICA.

seemed to me, went striding up and down the decks shouting orders
and directions and driving the immigrants before them. Scowling
and gesturing, they pushed and pulled the passengers, herding us
into separate groups as though we were animals. A few moments
later we came to our dock, and the long journey was over.

A small boat, the *General Putnam* of the Immigration Service, carried us from the pier to Ellis Island. Luckily for us, we were among
the first to be transferred to the tiny vessel, and so were spared the
long ordeal of waiting that occasionally stretched, for some immigrants, into several days and nights.

During this ride across the bay, as I watched the faces of the people milling about me, I realized that Ellis Island could inspire both
hope and fear. Some of the passengers were afraid and obviously
dreading the events of the next few hours; others were impatient,
anxious to get through the inspection and be off to their destinations. I have never forgotten the scene. Impelled they may all have
been, my parents and all the others alike, by a single desire—to make
a fresh start in a free country; nevertheless they were a strange and
motley company. Crowded together upon the little deck of the
General Putnam, each family huddled over its trunks and boxes,
suitcases or bundles wrapped in bedding. Some were guarding
grimy piles of worn bedding wound about with string or rope or
wire. Among the horde of bewildered peasants were some with
their pitiful, paltry personal belongings, all they had in the world,
tied up in old blue or red bandannas, which they clutched anxiously
as they peered over the rail toward the tiny island where their fate
would be decided.

So they had shuffled aboard at the Italian port, forsaking the
arduous security of their villages among the vineyards, leaving behind the friends of their youth, of their maturity, or their old age.
The young accepted the challenge with the daring of youth; the old
pressed forward without a hope of return. But both saw in the future, through their shadowy dreams, what they believed was an
earthly paradise. They did not weigh the price of their coming

against the benefits of the New World. They were convinced, long before they left Italy, that America had enough and more for all who wished to come. It was only a question of being desired by the strong and wealthy country, of being worthy to be admitted.

I was not thinking of all this then, as the boat bore down toward Ellis Island. I was watching our fellow-passengers, some of whom were weeping, some still shouting, others whispering to each other their hopes and fears. I began to pity with something like the confidence of a superior those whose faces showed alarm. Then I heard stepfather tell mother anxiously that we might not be permitted to enter the country—that we might be sent back to Italy.

"What!" I cried angrily. "After we came all the way across the ocean?"

I suddenly remembered that I had heard stepfather say to mother, early in the voyage, that he had spent almost all our money on the second day out of Naples so that mother's passage might be exchanged from steerage to a cabin. I wondered if this was the reason for his sudden doubt.

He confirmed my fears by replying that one could not enter America without some money, and perhaps we would not have enough. Ahead of us loomed Ellis Island, and its buildings of red brick and gray stone seemed to grow more grim every instant.

"Why wouldn't they let us in?" Liberta asked passionately. "Aren't we like everyone else, even without money?"

Mother patted my little sister's curly head. For the first time during the voyage I saw tears in mother's eyes. What sort of world was this, where people were judged by the amount of money they had?

I felt resentment toward this Ellis Island ahead of us, where we could already see many people crowded into a small enclosure. It could not be a good place. It would have been better if we had stayed in our comfortable home in the Abruzzi, back in Italy. To come here made mother cry. I looked around the deck and saw that many women were crying.

Our little vessel coasted into the slip at Ellis Island. The passengers began to move. We moved with them and as we stepped from the gangplank to the land, all silent and subdued, I knew that my parents were thinking as I was, "What is next?"

CHAPTER II

THE ABRUZZI

MY STEPFATHER's anxiety over our lack of money, mother's tears, the dread that we might be rejected, all sent my thoughts back to the native land where we had joined the great caravan of immigration and, boy though I was, I lived over again all the events which had been so largely responsible for our departure.

The Abruzzi was really all I knew of Italy, for it was in the Abruzzi that we had lived, within the natural wall of jagged hills and towering mountains which, due east of Rome, shuts in that rugged land. The Abruzzi is near Rome in mileage, but far distant in all else. There the Apennines rise range upon range, shutting off one high-pitched plain from another, and making strangers of those who inhabit the low-slung valleys and clinging towns and villages.

This wild land of the Abruzzi gave to Italy and the world D'Annunzio, Croce, the Rossettis, De Virgilii, the ancient Ovid and a host of other immortals. Here singers and improvisatori still are heard, shepherds still tend their flocks; witches still practice their magic. No longer do religion and brigandage thrive side by side, but traditions of freedom and courage and romance are stronger here, perhaps, than elsewhere in Italy. Beneath the snow-capped peaks flowers thrive in cloistered gardens which adorn the sheltered enchanting valleys.

That was the Italy I knew and loved, for I was born in the medieval village of Capestrano, midway between Aquila and Sulmona.

8

My background, but still more the career of my father, Filippo Corsi, was to influence me as I grew into manhood.

In his youth my father had become a disciple of the Italian prophet and patriot, Giuseppe Mazzini, and later, when he enrolled in the ranks of liberalism and edited *La Democrazia,* he fought for social and political reform as generations of his ancestors had done before him.

The longing for freedom, not for himself alone but for his fellow men, was in my father's blood. The oppression and injustice which he saw on every side of him, the neglect of the peasantry, their poverty and the apathy of the Crown all combined to urge him on to a career of militant reform which he pursued passionately to his death.

In his newspaper my father waged relentless war on the entrenched classes living at the expense of the peasant. He often took me to mass meetings, where his fiery booming oratory whipped enormous crowds into the frenzy of hero worship. Sometimes these meetings were in halls or theatres; at other times they were in the open squares, or just outside the doors of churches, where my father spoke to random audiences of men and women coming out after the services.

He organized the first farm coöperatives in central Italy, and led in the movement for the unionization of railway employees. His leadership and ideals soon crossed the borders of the Abruzzi and became known throughout Italy. Newspapers reproduced his editorials. The Crown kept its eyes on him.

On press days the townspeople would wait eagerly outside the office for copies of *La Democrazia,* wondering what new denunciation would come from my father's pen. Usually I was there, watching him, as from his six foot height, rugged and aggressive, he greeted the procession of friends and admirers or listened patiently and understandingly to those who came to him with their troubles.

From time to time father took us to Aquila or to Sulmona, the ancient Roman city where mother had been born and where her parents lived. The way led through beautiful mountain-sides and valleys with majestic Gran Sasso or Monte Majella, always snow-capped, in full view. Those were happy excursions, visiting uncles and aunts, and meeting friends of the family everywhere.

Myths and legends surrounded the route to these cities: tales of great warriors, of poets, and of saints who had sought solitude and earthly retreat in the crags and fastnesses upon either side.

"People in the hills were meant to be free," my father said often, and again and again he would dwell on his dream of a free republican Italy. "We may not live to see it," he would tell mother, "but our children will."

But it was impossible for my father's fervor and growing influence to flower in the very shadow of Rome unnoted by the minions of the Crown or the wealthy landowners of the region. Even among the three thousand inhabitants of Capestrano there were doubtless those who viewed with disfavor his revolutionary activities. Yet every effort to block him only spurred him on to greater efforts.

I loved the atmosphere of *La Democrazia* and, though blissfully ignorant of what it all meant, I looked forward to the day when I too should be old enough to write editorials and make speeches. I am sure that no ambition was dearer to father's heart than that Giuseppe and I should carry on where he left off.

"Do you know," he asked me one day, "for whom our village is named?" And then he told the story of John of Capestrano, the fighting lawyer who at the head of forty thousand Christians came to the aid of Hunyadi at Belgrade, stopping the advance of Mahomet and saving all Christendom from the rule of the infidel. "He was a fighter for human rights," father added, "and the Church now considers him a saint."

My father's vigorous crusade for agrarian reform was at its height when the Crown moved to end it forever. One day he came home excitedly crying:

"Giulia! Quick! There is no time to lose! I must leave at once! I will take Edoardo with me and send word from Lugano!"

Chapter III

EXILE

The journey with my father into exile was my first great adventure.

Father's announcement, coming so suddenly, threw our home into excited commotion. While we children hung around, bewildered and half frightened, mother gathered together the few things father and I needed for the journey. Father's warning that the police might appear at our door at any moment made her frantically anxious to have him safely out of the house.

One of father's friends, a close associate who was also a crusader in the liberal movement, stood guard. He was to accompany us. I learned years later in America that both he and my father were heavily armed, for they had resolved not to be taken alive by the police officers of the Crown.

At the last minute my mother clung desperately to us, afraid to let us either go or stay. "Send me word at once, Filippo," she kept repeating. "I cannot rest until I hear. As soon as you send me word, I will come."

Father caught up Liberta and kissed her, then Giuseppe. "Giuseppe Garibaldi," he said, "you are the little man now. You must bring mother and sister to us."

We set off, walking quickly through gloomy, unlighted back streets to the railroad station. The secrecy of this leave-taking, my delight at being permitted to go, thrilled me more than anything that had ever happened to me. I trotted along silently, well aware that I was taking part in an important adventure. But it was not until we had boarded the dingy, almost deserted little train which bore us down its winding grade from the mountains of the Abruzzi that I began to realize something of the significance of my father's flight into exile. Though I was only seven years old, I had sensed the secret in our home—that the police were watching father's political activities. But his sudden leave-taking had been cloaked in a mystery which my brain could not fathom until I heard the story gradually unfold in the talk between him and his companion.

I found that we were on our way to Lugano in Switzerland. There father would wait and watch developments in the liberal movement back home in Italy.

"We must watch—perhaps the police may telegraph," father's friend kept whispering, his dark, big-boned face drawn with anxiety. At each of the tiny villages where the train stopped, both he and my father pulled the brims of their black hats down over their eyes and pretended to be sleeping, their faces hidden. As soon as the train was in motion again they went on with their plans for the future.

I found that the man who was coming with us did not need to remain in exile, but planned to go back to lead the movement during father's absence. He was anxious to arrange matters so that our family might return from exile, fully vindicated.

Finally we reached Gallarate, upon the edge of the most beautiful lake I had ever seen—Lake Lugano. I remember that we ate there while waiting to board the boat which was to carry us across the lake to Switzerland. Previously, on two occasions, we had bought sandwiches from the train window, but here in Gallarate we had our first warm meal since leaving home.

I had never travelled on a boat before, and though it was night I wanted to run about and explore the deck; but father checked me.

"We must not be seen, Edoardo," he warned me, and found seats for us in a dark, secluded corner of the deck, away from the crowd of tourists and vacationists, and the noisy accordion players and violinists, who vied with singers for the approval and pennies of the passengers.

"Remember," said father's companion, "when we cross the line!"

"Yes," father replied, "when we pass the middle of the Lake and the boat flies the Swiss flag instead of the Italian. . . ."

"Then," said the other, "we shall drink to Filippo Corsi, the exile!"

The middle of Lake Lugano was the international boundary between Italy and Switzerland. At that point the lake boats changed their flags, and after that exiles no longer had to fear disclosure of their identity; once on Swiss waters, the agents of the Crown, who habitually rode upon the Lugano boats in search of persons fleeing from Italy, were powerless to arrest them. Often, it is said, fugitives screamed denunciation of the Italian Crown immediately after the Swiss flag was unfurled.

I must have fallen asleep. I do not know how much time passed before I woke to find father's friend shaking me and to hear shouts and laughter from a far part of the deck.

"Corsi!"

"Filippo Corsi!"

"Hurry, Edoardo!" father's friend cried, pulling me to my feet. "The fun! Come and join the fun!"

He took my hand and before I knew what had happened we were in the ship's barroom. There was a great crowd. They were all shouting toasts and holding out their glasses towards my father, who stood smiling in the middle of the room. They were hailing him as a hero. I learned later that even the secret agents of the Crown, none of whom bore him any personal ill will, joined the crowd of his admirers when they learned that he had eluded their dragnet, and lifted their glasses with the others. The violinists and accordion players played faster, and joined with the singers in the song of the Italian liberals. The din kept up until we reached the shore of Switzerland.

There is a quiet sorrow, a deep-seated, earnest melancholy which

afflicts the soul of the patriot living in political exile. At first he
receives a hundred letters a day. Then the number dwindles to
seventy-five—fifty—a dozen—there are even days when no letters
come. He knows loneliness; he tells himself that he has failed, is
forgotten.

Lugano is one of the most beautiful cities in the world. No more
delightful spot could possibly be found by a political leader forced
to seek refuge outside his native land. In two weeks' time mother
came with Giuseppe and Liberta, bringing glowing accounts of the
loyalty of my father's followers. She said they had been holding
many mass meetings, that delegation after delegation had called.
upon her, overwhelming her with offers of assistance. It seemed as
though my father's exile had stirred the Abruzzi as it had not been
stirred in a generation. But the strain of all that father had under-
gone had not been without its effect.

He was tired. The physical toll upon his constitution had been
constant and relentless. He had gone for months without proper
sleep, so devoted had been his attention to the night schools for
adult peasants, the farm coöperatives, the campaigns for the introduction of modern farm implements, and the consolidation of the
many separate units of the republican movement which he had sponsored—all this besides the publication of his newspapers. A physician
had warned him that his heart was bad, and had advised a long
rest.

But there could be no rest in Lugano. In that year of 1903, immediately following the turn of the century, monarchies throughout
Europe were using their mailed fists to crush revolution and the
rising tide of democracy. Russia, Austria, Germany, still being ruled
by the "divine right of kings," were having their troubles with revolutionists. Scores of exiles from these political conflicts had taken
refuge in Lugano. It became the headquarters for so many refugees
that it finally came to be known as the capital of all revolutionary
movements.

Revolutionists from every monarchy in Europe called at our home in Lugano, and there was scarcely a week in which my father did not receive a delegation of his followers from Italy. He completely disregarded the physician's warning, and began to write editorials and pamphlets, sending them by the "underground" route to Italy.

Father had spent nearly all his own money and mother's inheritance on campaigns; but, in spite of our being now in actual want, he often brought less fortunate revolutionary comrades home to dinner. Long after Giuseppe and I had gone to bed we would lie awake to hear his booming voice berating czardom, King Umberto of Italy, or the cruelty and oppression of the monarchy of the Hohenzollerns, Hapsburgs, and other reigning families of Europe, and we would strain our ears for scattered fragments of the conversation which rang forth from the dining room.

Our desperate financial straits bore heavily, of course, upon both father and mother; but exile did not crush my father's virile spirit as it had crushed many who came into our home. Back in the Abruzzi the peasants and shepherds were saying, "Remember Filippo Corsi!"

In Tuscany, the land of father's forebears, but a province in which he had never lived or campaigned, a movement was started to bring him back to Italy in triumph. One night some friends came running up the street. Even before they had reached our doorstep we heard them shouting father's name.

They brought such news as comes to few exiles. A telegraph messenger was at their heels with a personal message for father, but his friends wanted to be the first to announce the good news.

"We salute you, Filippo! It is grand! It is glorious!"

The Tuscany district had elected my father its representative in the Italian parliament. He was no longer an exile. He could return to the homeland under the immunity accorded his office.

That was one of the few times I ever saw my father display his emotion. Tears of joy shone in his eyes. He ran into the house to tell mother, and no news ever so transformed a single household. Then he brought out wine for the messengers. Other visitors arrived, and the house rang with their congratulations. Giuseppe and I capered about, scarcely able to contain ourselves at this sudden change in fortune.

It was decided that father should leave early in the following week, since he wanted to spend a day or two with his parents in Aquila before going on to the great reception that would be held in Tuscany.

Giuseppe and I went to sleep with the wildest visions of a glorious life ahead for us in Rome.

CHAPTER IV

A CAREER ENDS IN GLORY

THE days following the news of father's election to parliament were the happiest we spent in Lugano. My second sister, Helvetia, had been born only a few days before this new tribute to my father's achievements. He had a new and deeper pride in his family. Once again he felt himself a man of action, able to provide substantially for us. We all believed that the face of fortune had once more turned our way.

Father began work at once upon the address of acceptance he was to deliver in Tuscany, and Giuseppe and I loved the moments when he repeated for us bits of that speech. Of course I cannot now remember any of the words he used, but I do recall the spirit. It was a sermon upon the new Italy, the free Italy, the Italy which would bring Italians back into the glory and international prestige of the vanished days when the Italian nation had stood preëminent throughout the civilized world. It became, at the end, a plea for the republic, for the freedom of the crushed and impoverished masses.

Father left Lugano on Monday morning. He was to speak in Massa on Friday afternoon. A throng of the friends he had made in Lugano came to the boat to say good-by and to wish him increasing success in his work for the republic.

I can only reconstruct the events of that Friday from the accounts of my father's friends who attended the ceremony arranged in his honor. By noon more than fifty thousand people had crowded into the public square of the ancient little city which was the seat of his parliamentary district. The city hall and other buildings upon the square were decorated with flags and bunting. The town band played martial music. Prominent political leaders from every part of Italy were there.

When the peasants had eaten the lunches they had brought, and the square was all abuzz with the excitement of waiting, my father appeared upon the balcony of the city hall with the officials and dignitaries of the town and the other guests of honor. I have been told that his appearance before the thousands who had brought him out of exile caused a tumultuous demonstration. Fifty thousand voices shouted their enthusiasm and their pride in him. The crowd surged nearer the balcony.

The chairman of the ceremonies spread wide his arms in a request for silence. As the cheers died down, the young patriot who was to introduce my father came forward. With fiery enthusiasm he eulogized my father's career. Almost every sentence he spoke brought forth a loud burst of applause.

Then my father stood up. No one can really know, or at least put into words, what must have been in his heart—the gratitude, the sense of vindication, the pride, the desire to do much for these people who so appreciated him.

Finally he lifted his hand, his lips moved. He uttered the word "Cittadini!" (Citizens!)

Then his body fell suddenly to the floor. His eyes closed. He was dead.

Chapter V

THE MIGRATION

Our lives had always been molded by father's life; now that he was dead we seemed to have no future. We stayed on at Lugano because we did not have enough money for railroad tickets to Sulmona, the home of my mother's people. The days were long and miserable for all of us. My mother's grief, though silent, was hard for children to watch. Giuseppe and I, child-like, were unhappy because our vivid dreams of the grand life in Rome had burst like bubbles.

Thanks to the loyalty and appreciation of those who were fighting for a free Italy, we survived. The leading members of the movement for the republic were more than kind to my mother. One day she received a present from Italy—a sum of money sufficient for all of us to return, with the assurance of aid that would relieve her of all fear for the future. We prepared for the sorrowful return to Italy.

I do not remember that my mother spoke often during this black period. She devoted most of her time to Helvetia, our newest sister, and stared out of the window. She took care of our wants, and for the rest just looked at us with sad eyes, so that Giuseppe and I, who could scarcely bear her suffering, tried to avoid her glance.

Back in old Sulmona, we were welcomed by the thousands of my father's admirers. We went to the home of my maternal grandparents, but my stay there ended almost as soon as it began. A number of my father's friends came to call upon mother with offers of counsel and assistance. In a few days Giuseppe was bundled off to a boarding school in Venezia. At the same time it was decided that I should go to Aquila, under the protection of one of my father's brothers, who lived with my paternal grandparents. My uncle told mother he would put me in school and look after me as if I were one of his own sons.

Aquila is a lovely little town not far from either Capestrano or Sulmona. I lived there four years. I went to school and was happy, though I missed Giuseppe and my mother. During the years from 1903 to 1907, when immigration to America was at its height, many Italians returned to the little towns in Italy boasting of their success and their ability to gain wealth in the United States. We saw strangers proudly wearing heavy gold watch-chains that we knew had been bought in the New World. Stories of the ease with which money could be earned in America flew through the whole peninsula, and thousands of people, from grandfathers down to small boys like myself, came to center their interests in the wonderful new country. A story is told of a mayor of one of these Italian villages who said, in introducing a visiting dignitary: "I greet you in the name of four thousand fellow citizens, three thousand of whom are in America."

One day, a distant cousin of mine returned from New York and came to dinner with my grandparents in Aquila.

"How stupid all Italy is—not to go!" he said. "Look at me. Here I was nothing. There I made more money than I could spend. It is easy!"

I began to long passionately to go to America.

Toward the end of my fourth year with my uncle in Aquila my mother married again. She had often come to see me and I had gone many times to Aquila, trips which always filled me with the utmost delight. The news of her marriage was unexpected. Her new husband, an ex-army officer whom she had met during his military service in Sulmona, had the same name as my father, and they were distantly related.

After the marriage, mother and my stepfather came to Aquila to take me with them, and although I had been happy with my uncle and grandparents, I was glad to be at home again. Giuseppe was coming back from boarding school. Helvetia could talk. Liberta was eight years old. The new stepfather added solidarity to the family.

During the brief stay of mother and my stepfather at Aquila, I caught the first inkling that they were planning to go to America. My new father had resigned from the army at the time of his marriage. To start life over at any work beneath his caste would have been embarrassing in Italy. America was different. There he could take any sort of employment at first, and no one would think the worse of him. He felt sure of finding something that promised well for the future. Two months later we were on our way.

CHAPTER VI

PATHWAYS OF A YOUTHFUL IMMIGRANT

ELLIS ISLAND in 1907 represented a cross section of all the races in the world. Five thousand persons disembarked on that October day when my mother, my stepfather, and we four children landed there from the *General Putnam*.

We took our places in the long line and went submissively through the routine of answering interpreters' questions and receiving medical examinations. We were in line early and were told that our case would be considered in a few hours, so we avoided the necessity of staying overnight, an ordeal which my mother had long been dreading. Soon we were permitted to pass through America's Gateway.

My stepfather's brother was waiting for us. It was from him that the alluring accounts of opportunities in the United States had come to our family in Italy, and we looked to him for guidance.

Crossing the harbor on the ferry, I was first struck by the fact that American men did not wear beards. In contrast with my own fellow-countrymen I thought they looked almost like women. I felt that we were superior to them. Also on this boat I saw my first negro. But these wonders melted into insignificance when we arrived at the Battery and our first elevated trains appeared on the scene. There could be nothing in America superior to these!

Carrying our baggage, we walked across lower Manhattan and then climbed the steps leading to one of these marvellous trains. We were going, my uncle said, to the upper East Side, where he had rented an apartment in a tenement for us.

On this train I saw a Chinaman, queue and all! It had been a day of breath-taking surprises from the time of our entry into New York harbor, and by the time we started on our journey to Harlem I decided that anything could happen—anything might be true in this strange country.

I liked the din and bustle, the hurrying crowds on every hand, but I could see that my mother was bewildered. They were in startling contrast to the peaceful routine of life back in the Abruzzi. It had never occurred to me that any language except Italian was spoken anywhere, because it was the only one I had ever heard even in Switzerland. Here there were strange tongues on every side. I began to feel dazed and lost, but it gave me a new grip on myself to arrive in Harlem's little Italy and see and hear all about me people of my own nationality.

Our new home was a sad disappointment. We were not strangers to hardship, and our cottage in Lugano had been a contrast to the beautiful home where I was born; but here we found ourselves paying what seemed an enormous price for four sordid tenement rooms. There was, I remember, but one outside window, and this looked down on a dingy street. My mother was discouraged by the sight of the apartment the moment she stepped into it, and she never overcame that repulsion.

Back in Italy, I had seen her sit and gaze for long hours at the quiet beauty of Sulmona's countryside and the towering grandeur of Monte Majella. She loved quiet, and hated noise and confusion. Here she never left the house unless she had to. She spent her days, and the waking hours of the nights, sitting at that one outside window staring up at the little patch of sky above the tenements. She was never happy here and, though she tried, could not adjust herself to the poverty and despair in which we had to live.

My stepfather had no special training except his military service, and had to take employment at manual labor in a piano factory. He earned eleven dollars a week which was barely enough to keep our bodies and souls together. He was brave and did all he could for us, but at the end of three years my mother, who had become ill, went back to Italy. When she could no longer write us, others wrote for her, and she constantly begged me not to forget the ideals of my father. She lived only one year after returning to Sulmona.

I am sure our life on the East Side was typical of the lives of thousands upon thousands of immigrant families. It was a continuous struggle. There were many times when we had nothing to eat in the house. There was one period when my stepfather was out of work for eighteen months.

Those who lived in our tenement had to furnish their own heat, and during the times when there was no money for food or fuel, Giuseppe and I went out into the New York Central freight yards and gathered lumps of coal that had fallen from the cars. On one cold winter day we went there as usual, and crawled under a standing train of cars which had not moved for many weeks. I finished sooner than Giuseppe, and was waiting for him on the other side when suddenly the cars were set in motion. I heard him cry out sharply once, and then there was no sound. The cars moved on, and I saw him lying on the ground, one of his arms torn and mangled and hanging half-severed just above the elbow. Frightened and sick, I somehow got him back to our flat. A doctor came and amputated the arm, and my stepfather had to go out on a borrowing expedition to pay the doctor. Friends induced him to bring legal action against the railroad company, but the lawyer who handled the case managed, in some mysterious way, to settle it for two hundred dollars.

Chapter VII

LIFE ON THE EAST SIDE

When I was old enough for my first job, I went to work as a lamp-lighter, rising at four in the morning to put out the lamps on my route before the noisy movement of the day had set in. Then I would have breakfast and get to school by nine o'clock.

All through my boyhood I worked at various odd jobs, paying my own way through school and at the same time contributing what little I could to the very limited family income. I was in turn lamp-lighter, messenger, and clerk in a telegraph office. The few hours that remained for play, and they were few indeed, I spent in the streets. I enjoyed the excitement, the crowds and the good fellowship of the East Side, and I enjoyed, too, the company of youngsters like myself, many of whom have risen above the handicaps of their surroundings to useful careers in the community.

Down the street on which I lived there was a little brownstone house, which to many in the neighborhood seemed shrouded in mystery. It was a settlement house, which some of our parents feared had been put there to draw Italian children to the Protestant faith. So deeply was this fear impressed upon us that we not only did not dare dream of entering it, but would not even so much as drink out of the W.C.T.U. fountain which adorned its simple entrance.

The day came, however, when we decided to investigate that house and find out for ourselves what it was there for. The gang of boys with whom I played had decided to organize as a club and have a baseball team. The police would not tolerate our presence on street corners and persistently chased us, making it almost impossible for us to meet. We needed a club room, a meeting place where the police could not reach us, and mustering all the courage we had, we applied at the Settlement House.

I remember clearly the day I led my gang into that house of mystery. I was shabbily dressed and embarrassed, but I think my earnestness must have impressed the headworker, for she singled me out of the group and questioned me at length. She wanted to know what I did and where I lived. She explained in terms that we could understand what she and her coworkers were doing in the neighborhood, and smiled understandingly at our suspicions concerning her house. We were admitted on probation. We were not to be rough, or break windows, as other neighborhood boys had done, and we were to have a meeting room and the use of the backyard gymnasium just as long as we behaved.

My admission to the Home Garden, later Haarlem House, marked a decisive advance in my career. It was as if a wide door to America had been opened to me. I caught the spirit of the settlement, entered into its program of leadership and service in the neighborhood, and thread by thread wove my life into it until it became an instrument of my own ideals and purposes and shaped my ambition.

I became the leader of my group. I organized a baseball team and a debating team, and was never so happy as when I could spend long hours discussing neighborhood problems and methods of solving them. It was at this time that the political temper of the country rose to fever heat over the drama being enacted by such men as Roosevelt and Wilson. Roosevelt was the idol of the Italian people generally, and particularly of the Italians in my own district whom he had visited on two occasions, once addressing them in Italian.

I followed Roosevelt and his progressive thought. We organized a Roosevelt Club and received a letter from him expressing satisfaction at the thought that we had chosen to emulate his career and follow his examples. We were very proud of that letter. This active participation in political affairs encouraged my early love of books about history and government, and I read widely in my chosen fields.

Meanwhile my settlement contacts and experiences gave me a new understanding of American life and American ideals. It was a *new* understanding, because until then such dreams as I had had of the land of promise were well-nigh shattered by the grim reality of what I had been forced to undergo. Long before my mother had gone back to Italy both she and my stepfather had realized the futility of their adventure. America had failed to offer its pot of gold. It had offered instead suffering, privations, and defeat. My stepfather's bondage in the piano factory literally crushed him for the rest of his life, even though he managed to carry us through. Moreover, we children missed the open country life of the Abruzzi, much as we loved the novel experiences of the East Side.

Even after my mother died in Italy, friends and admirers of my father's work in the Abruzzi called on us in Harlem. These men with their reminiscences of my childhood encouraged my desire for political service and I began to reach out in my mind for a career that I believed would have pleased my parents.

While active at Haarlem House, I pursued my studies at St. Francis Xavier, the historic Jesuit school on West Sixteenth Street, and later at Fordham, where I obtained my degree in law. These were busy years for me, years of intense activity interrupted only by a brief enlistment in the War.

After graduating from Fordham, I devoted my full time to the work at Haarlem House. The House at that time was too small to meet the needs of an underprivileged neighborhood of more than one hundred thousand people, most of them immigrants. In 1917 we conducted a drive for funds and obtained a new building fully equipped for an effective program of education and recreation. This building is already outgrown.

The House soon became the center of neighborhood life. It aided thousands of aliens on the way to citizenship. It provided adequate recreational facilities for the local children: club rooms, gymnasium, roof garden, summer vacations for tenement youngsters, clinics and classrooms. It sponsored mothers' clubs, classes in English, weekly lectures for the people in the neighborhood, citizenship instruction for grown-ups, social gatherings, neighborhood associations, lectures, plays and numerous similar activities designed to foster a more wholesome tone in the civic life of a heretofore neglected area.

The young men in the neighborhood found in the House a liberal forum for the expression of their social and political views. In coöperation with the staff these young men and women made their influence felt in effecting local reforms. The House fought successfully for better housing in the tenement area, more playground facilities, and clean politics. In time, a machine-dominated, boss-ridden district was converted into one of the most independent and progressive sections in the entire city. In 1924 this district went for La Follette —the only district in the East to do so. It elected Fiorello La Guardia to Congress again and again.

Meanwhile I wrote extensively on political and sociological subjects and talked a great deal on the foreign-born, interpreting to American audiences from my own experience as a new American the needs and problems of my fellow immigrants. In 1923 I was sent to Mexico by the *Outlook* and described conditions in that country to American readers. On the invitation of the New York *World,* to which I was a frequent contributor, I went to Italy and reported on Italian affairs under Fascism from the point of view of one who was at once both an American and an Italian. It was on this occasion that I met Premier Mussolini, who, during the course of an interview lasting fully an hour, failed to utter to a fellow Italian a single word in Italian.

In 1930 I was appointed to supervise the Federal Census in Manhattan. The counting of those who live on New York's East Side has become increasingly difficult with each decade of this government project. Here my knowledge of the foreign-born served me well. We counted hundreds of thousands of immigrants and their children. We found as many as nineteen nationalities in a single block. This gave me my first contact with the Federal Government and it was the beginning of my career in public service.

CHAPTER VIII

A SUMMONS TO THE WHITE HOUSE

ONE morning in 1931 I was at my desk at Haarlem House working on the Settlement budget for the winter program. The telephone rang. "This is long distance," said the operator. "The Secretary of Labor is calling Mr. Edward Corsi."

The voice of Secretary Doak came over the wire. "I wonder," he said, "if you can come down to Washington. I am anxious to meet and speak with you."

I knew that the commissionership at Ellis Island was vacant, and it entered my mind fleetingly that the President might ask an immigrant to accept it. I dismissed this idea at once as too fantastic, and concluded that I was about to be consulted on some local problem. I went down to Washington the next day, and as I sat in the hotel waiting for the time of the interview, I kept wondering just why I had been called.

Secretary Doak received me in his office at the Department of Labor, and greeted me in his informal manner. We talked of many things, but he said not a word of what he had in mind. Finally he looked at his watch, rose from his desk and invited me to go along with him. We walked to the White House.

He took me into the President's office. I had seen President Hoover before, during the campaign of 1928, but now he seemed a greatly changed man. The lines of his face had deepened. His hair

30

was snow-white. He personified in his physical aspect the whole tragedy of the depression.

"Mr. President," Secretary Doak began, "this is the young man about whom we spoke. I am sure we have found the right person."

The President asked me whether I would consider serving the Administration as Commissioner of Ellis Island, if the post should be offered to me. "I think you can clean up the mess down there," he said, "and I know you will try your best."

In spite of my fleeting thought of the day before, I was startled to find myself seriously considered for that important vacancy. I answered that if I were appointed I should consider it a great privilege to serve the government in such a capacity. I said that the problem of immigration and the assimilation of immigrants into American life absorbed me above all things.

Immediately after leaving the President's office Secretary Doak left me standing a moment in the corridor while he went back for a brief conversation with his chief. When he returned he asked me where I was born. I named the town and province in Italy, and he reported it to the President. The interview was over.

As the train took me back to New York I turned over in my mind the significance of that last question. I felt suddenly that my Italian birth was a strong bar in the way of my appointment to the commissionership. I was afraid it was an insurmountable obstacle though just why I could not say. On serious consideration it seemed to me that an immigrant was actually better fitted for such a position than any American-born citizen.

That evening, as I was walking from the Pennsylvania Station up to Times Square, I was attracted by the moving letters on the Times Building. It was quite dark, and they stood out brightly. Following a report of the stock market I saw these words:

"President Hoover to-day appointed Edward Corsi Commissioner of Immigration at Ellis Island."

PART II

Chapter I

BEFORE BECOMING GUARDIAN OF THE GATE

"I CONGRATULATE you, Corsi," a friend said on the day after my appointment to the commissionership. "You've got one of the most important jobs in the country. You'll be helping to *make* America. After all, you know, this nation is only sixty-five per cent Plymouth Rock. The other thirty-five per cent is Ellis Island."

"Maybe," I said. "I'm part of that thirty-five per cent myself. But that's all over. They're not coming in a stream now, only in a thin little trickle. The racial proportions in this country won't change much from now on—not while I'm here, anyway. I'll probably have to send more out than I let in."

Nevertheless, during the three weeks which remained before I was to assume office I found myself thinking about immigration along new lines. My settlement work had, of course, introduced me to innumerable immigration problems. Even as a child I had been keenly aware of immigration as a factor in American development, though this awareness was largely the result of my observation of my parents' and neighbors' adjustments to a new country. I had thought about and studied immigration from an economic and national point of view. Now I began to think about it historically and dramatically. As a historical phenomenon the matter began to take on colossal proportions, and I saw that immigration, and immigration alone, had determined the life-blood of America up to this point, and its reference was not yet finished.

During these three weeks of preparation for my new job I crystallized in my mind several aspects of the matters that I wished to consider logically and in detail. I foresaw that a large portion of my duties would relate to deportation—that is, the weeding out of ugly and sick elements in our national life, and consequently, the vitalizing of that life in general. I should be a sort of physician to the whole country, delegated to cut out the cancers and amputate the infected limbs. I saw that this was not a new and isolated aspect of what is called the "immigration problem," but merely a result of the free and rapid growth of our country, which, if we look at it in the light of true history, had sprung up like a toadstool overnight. So there I was, back to history once more, and it was history I determined to consult in those brief weeks of preparation that were accorded me.

I knew, in a general way, something of the migratory movements that had added race to race to make up the final, and still unstable, sum of America. I wished to make some estimate of what the proportions of these various races had been, and in what order they had mixed with and assimilated one another. Nor was the matter interesting to me merely biologically. America had certain unique social customs and trends of thought. How had these evolved and what had the various races contributed to them?

Every person, black or white, in this country, is an immigrant or descendant of immigrants. The black immigration was largely forced, the white largely spontaneous. The immigrants had entered through many gates, east and west and north and south. Some had come at a time when the labor of extra hands was desperately desired, even prayed for. Others had come at moments when they could not hope to be anything but a burden on the population already here.

The first of these gates was the mouth of the Chesapeake Bay and the James River, down in old Virginia. There, too, an island had been used as a point of settlement by John Smith and those who followed his merry crew. It was selected, probably, for purposes of protection against the Indians. In the years that followed, many gates opened on all our coasts, but the greatest gateway of all was Ellis Island.

For a long time all these gates of entrance had been wide open. Now, as I took office in 1931, practically all but one were negligible, and my duty was to guard that one. I would open it, swing it back upon its heavy hinges to allow the passage of the few who had been carefully selected; then slam it shut and turn the keys again. Oftener than not I would open it to bid good-by rather than to give a welcome.

I should not be given much leeway for decision. I should be expected to enforce strictly the immigration laws which had culminated in the highly restrictive quota act of 1924. Had that law, practically closing our gates, merely represented the congressional sentiment of the hour in which it was passed? Or had it been due to the cumulative experience of many years? Was it, perhaps, the sum total of many previous laws? As a student of law I already knew the answers to some of these questions.

Now, as my second preparatory project, I wished to delve a little more deeply into these laws, to uncover not only their phraseology but their intentions and the reasons for their passage. Many of the hottest battles on the floors of the Senate and the House of Representatives had been waged over immigration. Whenever any state or portion of the country was frightened by the influx of too many members of a particular race or nation, the matter was taken to Congress. And if Congress was genuinely aroused, it could pass a law in a few hours that would have taken several years under ordinary methods of procedure.

Finally, I was interested in the history of the Island itself. Some of our national traditions had been born on its small area; many of our problems had been initiated there. It had in all probability seen many queer "goings on." I found that I knew next to nothing about the little plot of ground where I would spend several years of my life. What was Ellis Island before 1892? I knew, of course, that its history as an immigrant station was fairly recent. Many times on the East Side I had heard old white-haired men say:

"We didn't come through Ellis Island. We landed at Castle Garden."

Others had told me how they were lured to boarding houses where they were beaten or robbed or "shanghaied" to some far off mine or quarry or construction project, there to be delivered to the merciless padrone—all before the days of Ellis Island.

What had been our immigration system in the old days? What had happened at Castle Garden, which is now the New York City Aquarium? What at Ward's Island? or at the Barge Office, located at South Ferry in the vicinity of the Aquarium, and used by federal authorities as an immigration station for two years after the Ellis Island fire of 1897?

I knew without examining the records that Uncle Sam had not always dealt intelligently or humanely with immigrants—that at times they had been treated more like stupid animals than intelligent future citizens. Part of this had been due to the unwieldiness of the enormous masses in which they had presented themselves at our door. Now that the problem of numbers was solved, surely there need remain no question of their welcome. I did not need to study past records to determine how they would be treated under the present régime.

CHAPTER II

GREAT SECTORS OF THE CARAVAN

WHAT we are prone to call the great "wave" of immigration in the latter half of the nineteenth century is only the final one of a series of waves that populated our country with representatives of nearly every race on the face of the earth. Each race in turn grafted on to the developing America a layer of its unique social customs, mental and physical traits, and weak or strong moral propensities.

We have, as basis for this process of racial grafting, the hardy Anglo-Saxon stock that succeeded in planting here the strongest and most permanent colonies during the first glorious period of European colonization. Of all the powers that sent to our virgin country their most adventurous and far-seeing citizens, England managed to hold most truly to her solid tradition in the new wilderness. Instead of a ferment of cultures we had, therefore, a single basic one which later groups could only modify but never absorb. By dint of sending many more colonists than the other countries, England established a body of population which imposed its language, form of government, and opportunities for individual advancement upon all contemporary and later racial groups.

Up to the middle of the nineteenth century, when all the races of the world began the feverish outpouring of hordes of their citizens, thirsty for the opportunities of wealth and advancement which they believed were so abundant here, the various blocks of population in the order of their coming were somewhat as follows:

39

1) The English.
2) The Dutch.
3) The French.
4) The Scotch-Irish.
5) The Germans.

With the beginning of the nineteenth century, new waves of German, Irish and British peoples greatly augmented the percentages of those races already established here. Through it all the English continued to dominate, and all other languages had to give way before theirs.

The middle part of that century saw the change. Then began an enormous migration of Scandinavians and Italians, Swiss and Austrians, Poles and Russians, Spaniards, and Jews of every nationality. The sources of immigration shifted from western to eastern and southern Europe. We received not only new races but new and distinct civilizations. Instead of Teutons there now came Latins, Slavs, the Semitic and Mongolian races. Only at this point did our country become the true "melting-pot" of the world.

It might be well to review briefly the history and experience of each of these groups in their new home and account for their contribution to the new world.

The English came first to Virginia, later to New England. Virginia had a strong commercial tie with the mother country, and this immigration continued in appreciable volume until the Revolutionary War. In New England twenty thousand arrived during the first generation (1620–42), and all through the seventeenth century the English supplied most of the new population of America. Something like ninety per cent of the people of the United States at the time of the first census in 1790 were of British origin, and the proportion still remains very high. English Quakers settled Pennsylvania and English Roman Catholics founded Maryland. William Penn, the founder of the Quaker settlement, was both a humanitarian and a business man; he advertised his dominions back home, so that though Pennsylvania was settled half a century later than the southern and northern colonies, its population soon exceeded theirs.

The Dutch settled New Amsterdam in 1619. They continued to come until 1664, when the city and colony were finally lost to England and became New York. The Dutch then rapidly merged with the English and lost their language. The first recorded immigration of Jews was to a Dutch colony; driven out of Brazil by the Portuguese, these Jews were received by the Dutch government of New Amsterdam.

The French came to colonial America in two groups. The first were the original settlers of the Mississippi. The valley continued French down to 1763, and the descendants of these first settlers are found to-day all the way from Detroit to New Orleans. The second group was composed chiefly of the French Protestant exiles who came after the Revocation of the Edict of Nantes in 1685. These people made a deep impression on America. Though it scarcely seems logical that any but old English stock dominated our development, still one cannot help thinking of the "might have beens." Suppose, for instance, that the Dutchmen had beaten the English in the wars of the seventeenth century, and that one of the hardy Dutch diplomats in New Amsterdam had made a permanent alliance with the French, taking the eastern seaboard from Maine to Georgia as a portion of Holland. With the entire Mississippi in the possession of the French, what might not such an alliance have brought about!

The Huguenots were chiefly manufacturers and merchants, perhaps the most intelligent and enterprising of Frenchmen in the seventeenth century. Few peasants or wage workers came with them to America; the French sent over only their adventurous and educated citizens. It is certainly possible that but for a narrow turn of events our country might have been French instead of English.

In the eighteenth century came the Scotch-Irish and Germans, their combined migration possibly as great as that of the English in the seventeenth century. But the seaboard was already occupied.

They had to move on into the continent, become frontiersmen, and wrest their living directly from the soil as the first coastal settlers had done before them.

The Scotch-Irish came to America from the north of Ireland. They were of a hardy, virile race and contributed to our stock the successful "captain of industry" branch of our present civilization. Originally they are a mixture of primitive Scot, primitive Briton, primitive Irish, Norwegian, Dane, Saxon and Angle. The Puritans did not welcome them, and they settled largely in Pennsylvania, in the foothill regions of Virginia and North and South Carolina, and in Ohio, Kentucky and Tennessee. Many historians believe that the Scotch-Irish had a greater part in the development of what we call our "American type" than any other race.

The Germans began coming at the end of the seventeenth century. German Quakers and Pietists, answering William Penn's advertisement, came to join his colony in Pennsylvania. At the beginning of the eighteenth century, when Louis XIV overran the Palatinate, thousands of Germans fled to England and were encouraged by the English government to migrate to America. The descendants of these people came to be called the "Pennsylvania Dutch." The German population soon spread out from Pennsylvania, north to New York and south to Virginia. A recent calculation gives their number, at the time of the first census, as 293,000 out of a total white population of about three millions.

The Germans who came in the nineteenth century were educated liberals fleeing the despotic government of their country. Many of them were forced out of Germany after the revolution of 1848, in which they took a leading part. They sprang largely from the middle classes of Germany. Later, several severe industrial depressions urged the peasants, too, to emigrate, and many came during the years 1873 to 1879.

The races that began to come after the middle of the nineteenth century included chiefly:

1) The Italians.
2) The Irish.
3) The Austrians and Hungarians.
4) The Scandinavians.
5) The Jews.
6) The Slavs (Jugoslavs and Czechoslovaks).
7) The Poles and Russians.

Except the Scandinavians and Irish, all these peoples belong to the races of southern and eastern Europe, races of ancient traditions and cultures whose contribution is being felt more each day in the building of a new America.

Italian immigration first became noticeable about 1880 and has swollen to high proportions perhaps more rapidly than immigration from any other country. There are roughly 5,000,000 Italians in the United States to-day. In the city of New York alone they constitute one-seventh of the population. The larger portion of our Italian immigrants come from southern Italy. The stream of expatriates is largely a result of economic conditions in the native land.

The Irish started to come a little earlier, about 1840, and were driven to emigration by the economic injustices of England. They flocked to America because of the potato famine, which, by depriving them of their one staple food product, brought them rapidly to starvation. From 1820 to 1900 the Irish contributed to America about four millions of people.

With the other peoples mentioned the facts have been about the same. The several diverse races of Austria-Hungary—Germans, Slavs, Magyars, Latins and Jews—began their heavy migrations in the last decade of the century. Able to earn only a few cents a day as workers on their native farms and in the mines, they hastened here where wages were at least $1.50 a day. They depopulated the forests and left the small farms to go to ruin. Our enormous Jewish immigration arrived from all countries, though during the nineteenth century the Russians sent us about five-sixths of all who came. Besides the Jews, from the Russian territories came thousands of Poles, Lithuanians, Finns and Germans.

The Scandinavians have come regularly since the foundation of our country. A new tidal wave brought us during the nineteenth century, however, about two million immigrants from the northern countries. They have settled in every section of the United States, though not largely in the south.

This little historical review leaves out of account the negro. Coincidental with these major voluntary migrations there is one chapter in our population history which is so terrible that the conventional historian usually passes it by with only a sidelong glance. The black immigration began about 1619, with the sale in Virginia of twenty slaves from a Dutch ship.

The Treaty of Utrecht, in 1714, gave a monopoly of the slave trade to the British and their American colonists. Colonial and British merchants turned West Indian sugar into rum, then traded the liquor on the coasts of Africa for human beings. They sold as slaves in America the barbarians thus purchased. Here the story of the immigrant falls to its point of darkest tragedy. Chattel slavery came near to destroying our civilization; North and South, both being morally responsible, joined in paying the terrible price.

It is a matter of history that each group, after adapting itself to America, wresting a living from the stubborn land, and hewing out a future for its descendants, has resented the coming of other racial groups. The opposition of the older population of America to new immigrants arises from antagonisms as old as our first settlements. Washington Irving, in his "Knickerbocker's History of New York," has made an amusing tale out of the clashes between the Puritanic English and the roistering Dutch. The story of Roger Williams' escape into the wilderness to take refuge with the Indians because he faced persecution in Massachusetts for his religious beliefs surely indicates that the squabbles of the immigrants did not begin on Ellis Island.

The Puritans came to Plymouth Rock and Massachusetts Bay because they hated the Church of England and wished to mould their own form of religion. Later, both Rhode Island and Connecticut were settled by groups of rebels who didn't like the ways things were done in Massachusetts.

Since it was a crime to be a Roman Catholic in England at the time of Lord Baltimore, he and his Catholic friends founded the colony of Maryland as a refuge. Remembering their own persecutions, these Catholic liberals welcomed members of every faith, not excluding Mohammedans or even persons who professed no faith at all. It was not long, however, before opposition forces wrested this territory from the control of the Catholics and excluded every Catholic immigrant from the colony.

Some of these colonizing races have remained singularly pure, in spite of the general tendency toward fusion which has welded the American out of the conglomeration of his forefathers. The city of New Orleans, for instance, was French until 1763, then Spanish until Napoleon took it over forty years later. Being a port city, New Orleans, like New York, has always been a melting-pot; yet the French of New Orleans, like the French of Quebec, have refused to be melted. There is something like tempered steel in these French, which long outlasts the heat of our American crucible.

With our Spanish originals it was the same. In southern California the old mission churches still present their brave façades to the conquerors. Some of the remaining padres occupy the shaded retreats of the mission patios and maintain their language and peculiar culture. In New Mexico, Spanish has remained on a par with English in its legislature and its courts, the only foreign language in America to be so recognized.

We have no racial group that has not produced at least a few outstanding leaders. When Washington was making his intrepid stand during the winter at Valley Forge, his forces were under the command of eight major generals. Of these officers two were English-born; two were Germans; one was French; one was Irish; and two were Americans. General Grant, entering Richmond after the retreat of Lee, was accompanied by a cavalry brigade composed of negroes under an Italian commander. It was a French officer, Duffier, who trained the cavalry of the Army of the Potomac, even as a German, Baron von Steuben, trained the army of Washington until they could attack the enemy's position as well as defend their own.

I am not suggesting that our gate should be opened to more immigrants. Since 1820 there have arrived and been registered a total of more than thirty-seven million immigrants, a number nearly as great as the population of France. These with their increase now number over fifty millions, and they have recast the old American nation into a new image. Economic conditions have now driven us to close the gate and lock it against all the world. We have decided to make a new social beginning by unifying and developing the elements we have at present. Yet the outstanding facts in the history of our immigration are the essential bedrock of our national life.

We would have been limited in national character and mind, as in leadership, had we been all New England Puritans or Virginia Cavaliers. We needed our immigrants from Italy, Germany, Russia, Spain and other parts of the world, their genius and enterprise and loyalty, to mould us into the Nation that we are, and give greater meaning to our institutions and opportunities.

Our intrinsic history through four centuries has been a history of divergent immigrant groups, each lesser element clinging to its own with might and main. Yet always these separate groups have had to surrender to the great united whole, the nation. Separatism, group consciousness, though ever so strong, is always a passing phase.

Ellis Island is only the last act of this long, long drama.

CHAPTER III

AMERICA CLOSES THE GATE

OPPOSITION to the immigrant, and restrictive immigration laws have concurrent histories. Our native American opposition to the immigrant began earlier than most people realize. Thomas Jefferson expressed the fear that too many subjects of the European monarchs might pollute our democracy and so destroy the foundations of our republic. He would admit intelligent artisans, trained to some craft, since we might need their help. It was the peasantry he feared, and the common laborers from the crowded cities of Europe.

Few Americans in the time of Jefferson saw the matter as he did. So long as we had an abundance of free land open to settlement, the American people gave all immigrants a royal welcome. The lonely settler on the frontier wanted neighbors. He who had lands to sell wished as many purchasers as the world might offer. All forms of business enterprise sought to increase the home market for goods. The whole tendency of this country was to grow bigger, and grow we did at a pace which never ceased to astonish those left behind in Europe.

The Germans were welcomed, and the French, though they spoke strange tongues and preserved their peculiar manners and customs.

Quakers, who were persecuted in New England, received as their own the great rich province of Pennsylvania.

When the English took over New York, in the middle of the

47

seventeenth century, they heard the babble of a score of languages in public houses and on the streets. All that was asked of any foreigner was that he pay his own way with work or money. This attitude and policy is nowhere better expressed than in the Declaration of Independence. That document, in its bill of particulars as regards the impatience and tyranny of King George III, contains the following paragraph:

He has endeavored to prevent the population of these States; for that purpose obstructing the Laws for Naturalization of Foreigners; refusing to pass others to encourage their migrations hither, and raising the conditions of new Appropriations of Lands.

Even in colonial times, however, there was a movement against the further importation of negro slaves. The government of King George was accused of assisting in the nefarious traffic and profiting by it.

The first vigorous reaction against the coming of free white people resulted from the great wave of immigration in the middle of the last century. Unfortunately, this movement took the form of a strong religious opposition. The Irish were largely Roman Catholics. The American, or "Know-Nothing," Party nominated candidates in national elections and carried on an intensive campaign of propaganda. It sought the restriction of immigration and, especially, the exclusion of Roman Catholics. The crisis over slavery in the Civil War served to abate this movement, but only for the time. Irish Catholics fell by thousands for the sake of the Union. And on the southern side Father Grady became the beloved poet of the Confederate cause.

This chimerical opposition to the immigrant on religious grounds rises periodically, then for a time fades out of the picture. Before the Civil War it was "Know-Nothingism." Forty years ago it was the A.P.A.—the American Protective Association. Ten years ago it rose again as the Ku Klux Klan. Perhaps the cessation of immigration will help mark the end of religious antipathy.

Another and stronger form of opposition has been voiced by labor unions and America's wage working people generally. Nothing, perhaps, is more natural than the antagonism of the workingman to the foreigner who comes here to compete for his job. In times of prosperity little is said, since there are more jobs than there are hands to do them. When the slack season sets in, however, the trouble begins. With three men and only two jobs, the foreigner is not a welcome guest among the anxious group waiting at the employment office. Strikes and riots against the employment of foreign-born have not been unknown.

Frequently the immigrant workers have taken over the work of whole trades and industries. Once a single nationality holds a majority in any particular line of work, its fellow-immigrants flock to it. Probably this method of employment has the advantage of furnishing a job for the recent arrival, but it bears with it, also, a very great disadvantage. It builds up the local immigrant colony and prevents the worker from entering fully into the life of the new country.

The opposition to immigration sprang from many causes. A satisfactory historical study, psychological as well as statistical, has never been made. The brief summary I offer here presents the matter as I have seen it evolve in the past generation.

The vast majority of Americans had always welcomed immigrants, so they simply continued to do so. America possessed unlimited opportunities for development. The optimistic theory was that every honest man could make a good living, and that any clever man could, if he wished, amass wealth. The earlier migrations were composed of peoples closely akin to the English, and newcomers intermixed and intermarried readily with the older population. The only general reaction was against the importation of negro slaves.

Let us not ignore the idealistic and more generous aspect of this older point of view. The exile for conscience' sake was particularly welcome. The Irish were generally liked because they had fought the British tyrant through the centuries. The "Forty-Eighters" from all countries in Europe came as republicans. If the newcomers were

Protestants, they found a pew awaiting them in any American church. If they were Jews, the American remembered that they had been subjected to Russian tyranny. If the immigrant had no religion at all, that was his business, and his position was amply protected by the constitution and the laws. America's generous treatment of new arrivals became proverbial, and it was a source of wonder and admiration to the common people of Europe.

There was another primary cause for so long keeping the door open. The employing class, by and large, welcomed the immigrants because they furnished labor that was both industrious and cheap. The first thing the immigrant looked for was a job, and he usually had to take one under whatever conditions were offered. In ten years, perhaps in a single year, he joined a union and tried to increase his wages. From his first day on the job, however, he did his bit and kept his mouth closed. The employers were always looking for others like him. Many of them sent their agents to Europe, to contract for workers *en masse*.

It was largely the opposition of American labor that finally secured the passing of two important laws. One provided for the total exclusion of Chinese working people in 1884; the second, in 1885, forbade the immigration of contract laborers. These two laws were but a stiff breeze foretelling the coming storm of American opposition to the policy of the open door.

In the far West the anti-Chinese movement assumed large significance. At many a mining town or railway division point, Chinese were warned to keep moving and be gone before sundown. Here and there a Chinese worker was slain, his body offering mute testimony to the changing attitude towards the immigrant. The American working class was ready to fight the competition of coolie labor to the limit.

Later the same attitude was assumed toward the Japanese and other orientals. In the case of the Japanese, bitter opposition excited in their home country was fully expressed by the policy of the Japanese government. Then, on the Pacific Coast, the young Japanese men began to bring in their brides and Japanese babies began to be born on our soil. The Japanese birth rate in California was shown to be three times that of their American-born white neighbors. The movement for exclusion was no longer confined to the labor unions of the working class. In 1924 a law was passed totally excluding the Japanese.

In dealing with contract labor from Europe, the situation was not so simple. At one time a great English shipping line made a contract with the government of Austria-Hungary. Its terms called for the delivery at continental ports of twenty thousand immigrants to America annually. For this consideration the shipping line paid a regular stipend to the Hungarian government. That government then organized its propaganda so seductively that simple peasants, well established in the villages, sold their properties and left homes where they were comfortable and happy. In America they often found themselves herded into the slums without jobs or other means of decent living. This is but a single instance of the moral perversion of the whole migratory movement.

The law against contract labor was hard to enforce. What, indeed, constituted a contract? The big American employers merely turned over the job of persuading the confiding immigrants to the shipping companies. The dishonest propaganda continued. From these dangerous seeds, sown in the minds of the masses, often grew up a deep feeling of opposition to this country among the immigrants. Indeed, this bitterness still exists in many an alien colony.

From 1885 to 1917 the battle for the literacy test raged throughout the length and breadth of the land. Finally, just two months before we declared war on Germany, the literacy test law was passed over President Wilson's veto. Twice the doughty liberal had hurled this bill back upon Congress, but public sentiment at last forced its passage.

During this generation propaganda for the literacy test led both houses of Congress to take no less than thirty-two votes. Supporters of the test always returned to the conflict, until, in 1917, they finally won.

To the help of the labor unions there came the support of leading newspapers. As one goes over the files of our press the rising tide of native American opposition can be measured. Always couched in courteous language, both editorials and news stories rise in heat as they increase in number. On April 16, 1896, the following story appeared in a leading New York daily:

Small riots that threaten to develop into trouble of a more serious nature are occurring daily among the many immigrants on Ellis Island, and the officials have become so apprehensive, that Dr. Senner yesterday telegraphed to the Treasury Department at Washington, asking permission to swear in a number of special constables to be used in keeping in subjection the unruly aliens. *The Tribune* has already told of the arrival of thousands of peasants, penniless and dirty for the most part, from the Mediterranean ports, and they are continuing to pour in daily. On Sunday the steamship *Bolivia* brought into this port 1,376 of these people, and *Alesia* followed with over one thousand. The *Werra* yesterday brought in 756 and the steamships *Victoria* and *Belgravis* are now on the way here with an aggregate of 2,820 more.

The following news item was printed nearly ten years later (August 1, 1903):

Commissioner Watchorn is considerably exercised over the class of undesirable immigrants now coming to this country. He says there is a large increase in the riffraff class. So far this month 48,000 immigrants have arrived. The riffraff is shown in the largely increased number of deportations. Up to July 27 exactly 1,000 or an average of about 250 a week, have been deported, whereas last year 645 were deported.

The increase in the arrivals is also shown by the increased work of the special boards of inquiry. These boards generally have the dull season at this time, but now are working nearly all the time. Even Sunday they sat until 4:30 P.M. whereas generally on Sunday they stop by noon or 1 o'clock.

The mere facts began to disturb the American majority. The following from another New York daily, as recent as 1920, is coldly statistical. The time for editorializing had passed. The nation had already made up its mind. It was, at this time, moving on from the literacy test to outright exclusion. News items such as this were, doubtless, becoming popular reading in the American press generally:

During last year 290 insane aliens were sent home from New York State institutions to countries from which they came. The immigration authorities deported 147, and 143 were sent back at the instance of Dr. Spencer L. Dawes, medical examiner of the State Hospital Commission.

The foregoing figures were taken from the annual reports of the Ellis Island Immigration Station and the New York State Hospital Commission for the year ended June 30, 1920. A year ago there were 800 deportable insane aliens in the asylums of the State, but this number was reduced to about 500.

The reports which will be issued later, will show that there are 39,000 insane persons in State institutions. There is now room for only 28,000 in the hospitals and sanitariums 'for the proper care and treatment of the victims of insanity,' it is said. Forty-eight per cent of the insane in this State, or about 17,000, are foreign-born. Seventy per cent had one parent of foreign birth. Of the 17,000 foreign-born insane in New York State institutions all except about 500 are not deportable, having been in the country longer than the five year limit for deportation proceedings.

There was another side to these newspaper stories of Ellis Island. Here is a tale of a wholly different tone and color, dated April 30, 1897:

The record of recent years for the number of Irish immigrants landed at Ellis Island in any day was broken yesterday. Seven hundred of them, mostly red-cheeked, laughing girls, were brought there from the steamers *Majestic* and *Servia,* which arrived yesterday from Queenstown. Of these sixty-five per cent had had their passage prepaid by friends in this country.

Three-fourths of the immigrants started at once out of town, most of them going into New England states. The remainder will stay in the metropolitan district. Only some half dozen of the arrivals were debarred from landing.

Now, thirty-seven years later, I wonder what has happened to those seven hundred "laughing red-cheeked Irish girls." How many found the way to their heart's desire? And how long, in the new home, did the laughter last? And the red cheeks?

The rising opposition to the immigrant presented, of course, only one side of the picture. "Full many a flower" of old Europe was "born to blush unseen" in the strange new garden.

One author has given us a curious list of the epithets hurled at the immigrant during this period. This list fills more than a page, and includes nearly every word in the language which could be dug out of the dictionary and shouted by one embittered group of people at another group which it had learned to hate and despise. The immigrants are "lawless, immoral, vicious, criminal." They are "social dregs and rogues; vicious off-scourings," and so forth.[1]

The history of the anti-immigration movement makes a fearful as well as a wonderful tale. We have seen the foreign-born themselves engaged in opposition to bringing in more workers when there was no employment; and the employing class desperately fighting against restrictive legislation. The conflict became at times a chaotic scramble of thoughts, and a babble of tongues. Hate sprang up to a degree which threatened the peace of the country.

On November 22, 1908, Ignace Paderewski, the noted pianist, declared that constant foreign immigration to the United States was threatening the strength and character of the American people. Coming from a Pole, this was a curious statement. Earlier that same year, in May, Professor Lotoslawski, of Moscow University, had predicted that America would have "political indigestion" if it attempted to assimilate its foreign population.

Elihu Root caused much agitation that same year by declaring that foreign immigration had created conditions in the United States similar to those in Rome, when she was overrun by barbarians. On the same day, and coming as a curious coincidence, the liberal minister, Reverend F. H. Wright, said, "Fusion of foreign

[1] "Immigration Crossroads," by Constantine Panunzio.

blood is valuable, especially in preventing national degeneration."
But the controversy waxed to white heat, and Ellis Island was the
storm center.

So vituperative was the criticism of the Island that John H. Clark
of the Montreal Immigration Station declined the appointment as
Commissioner at Ellis Island on May 12, 1909.

The next few years witnessed no abatement of the battle between
those who said, "Send us more immigrants," and those who cried,
"Shut the gates forever!"

In 1914 came that curious book, "The Passing of the Great Race,"
by Madison Grant. To this author the "Nordic" race alone had
created and fostered all the values of western civilization. The ancient Greeks, he held, were "Nordics" because they were brave.
This extraordinary book closed by explaining that the World War
was an effort on the part of the enemies of Germany to destroy the
stronghold of Nordicism.

This issue culminated, however, when our government finally
declared war against Germany. Agents of foreign propaganda had
long been active. With German and Austrian efforts driven underground and with much cause for suspicion, native Americans began
to wonder. The wonder soon turned into distrust. When the Versailles Treaty of Peace was signed, everybody knew that the day of
easy immigration had passed forever. The only questions were
"Who shall be excluded and how?"

The closed gate might never have come but for the deep, underlying opposition to immigration on the part of our rural native
Americans. The farmer and villager in Tennessee or Kansas, as in
New Jersey and Connecticut, had seen New York and Chicago and
Pittsburgh rise, through numbers, to stupendous heights of prestige
and power. The great cities were dominating the country financially,
socially, even politically. What were these great cities but hives of
foreign-born?

These cities in general were described in lurid language as pesti-
lential centers of moral degeneracy. The hinterlands had a majority

and the majority was ready for action. That action took the form of ever more drastic laws excluding the immigrant.

The first "quota" law was passed in 1921. It permitted the coming, annually, of three per cent of the numbers of each national group reported for the census of 1910. Of course this law favored the countries of northern and western Europe and excluded those from the southern and eastern countries. Meanwhile a report was being prepared which permitted quotas to be apportioned according to a method which gave a still greater comparative advantage to the peoples of northern Europe.

This second quota law of 1924 is still in force. It is based upon the numbers of the various national groups present in our population according to the census of 1890. The law originally permitted 15,000 to enter annually, and the proportions were made up according to the 1890 population percentages. Extra allowances now bring the total up to 164,667. Of this total Britain is allowed, together with northern Ireland, 65,721; the Irish Free State, 17,853; and Germany, 25,957. Meanwhile Italy's quota is 5,802 and that of Russia 2,712.

Congress passed the famous bill providing for the quota by a majority of three hundred and eight to fifty-eight in the House and sixty-nine to nine in the Senate. It became a law with President Coolidge's signature on July 1, 1924.

The present depression soon produced its total of millions of unemployed. In the presence of the breadlines, with the terrible burden on private and public charity, even the legal quotas had to be cut off. Last year we received a total of only twenty-one thousand. Eighty thousand more left our shores than arrived here.

CHAPTER IV

ELLIS ISLAND'S ROMANTIC BACKGROUND

NEW YORK, where I had spent all of my life since that October day when our family landed from Italy, is a city of islands. Had Columbus landed at Ellis Island on a summer day he would have found the braves of the Manhattan Indians fishing from its shores, with their squaws and papooses around the tepees and camp fires in the background. And only the Chief of the Manhattans and his favored braves would have been there, for in those days, and for years to follow, it was a retreat of the privileged.

In the days of Peter Stuyvesant, and through the tenure of the second Dutch Governor, Wouter van Twiller, Ellis Island, then called Oyster Island, was a gay and exclusive resort.

At this time, early in the seventeenth century, rollicking young Dutch boys with gleaming shoe buckles, blue pantaloons and bright doublets, took their buxom and tightly-laced Dutch sweethearts to Oyster Island in small boats. There all drank ale and ate roasted oysters, feasting, singing and dancing until the sun went down.

For almost one hundred and fifty years Oyster Island continued to be New Amsterdam's favorite resort for picnics, oyster roasts, clam bakes, and fishing parties. It passed finally into the hands of Samuel Ellis, a farmer of Bergen County, New Jersey.

His strange will, recorded in Abstracts of Wills, New York (1786–1796, page 325), says among other things:

I give to the child to be born to Catherine Westervelt, if it be a son, Oyster Island, commonly known by the name of Ellis Island, with all the buildings thereon.

Whether Samuel Ellis failed to pay his taxes, or the child of Catherine Westervelt was born a girl instead of a boy, or whether New York State bought the Island, is not to be found in any accessible record. The Island became known as Bucking Island and passed a few years later into the hands of the state.

In 1808, however, New York ceded the island to the Federal government. It was then used as a powder magazine and arsenal, doubtless because of the recent experience of the colonies with the British.

The government employees in those days lived on the island, and because of the great stores of powder and munitions kept there it was a fearsome, forbidding place, shunned by all who sailed pleasure craft in the harbor and the residents of the nearby Jersey shore.

But once again the island of changing destinies was due for a new name. In the early spring of 1831, the notorious pirate, Gibbs, was captured and brought to justice. After his trial and conviction, he was taken to Bucking Island with the three associates convicted with him, and there plunged through the trap door of a rudely constructed hangman's gibbet. After that, Ellis Island was called Gibbet's Island.

In 1841 the Federal government commenced the erection of Fort Gibson upon Ellis Island. This harbor defence took three years to build and cost Uncle Sam $5,096. It mounted fifteen guns and required a garrison of eighty men.

Originally the Island comprised an area of but three and three-tenths acres, but the Federal government has increased the area throughout the years by filling in the shallow waters which surround it. The Island, which to-day contains twenty-one acres, is built of soil from all parts of the world, since much of it was formerly the ballast dumped from foreign ships.

Other nicknames, "Gull" Island, "Kiosk" Island, and "Govern-

OLD CASTLE GARDEN, BEFORE IT WAS TRANSFORMED BY JENNY LIND'S TRIUMPH, WAS THE IMMIGRANT DEPOT FOR ARRIVALS IN THE NEW WORLD.

ment" Island have been applied to it at various times, but because it appears reasonable to believe, from the papers of Governor Tompkins, that Samuel Ellis actually conveyed the Island to the state of New York, it must be assumed that the name Ellis was chosen in legal manner for that reason.

In 1890, after the celebrated Supreme Court case in which the Federal government assumed jurisdiction over immigration, Ellis Island was designated as an immigrant station. This caused great satisfaction to the citizens who resided near the Jersey shore, for they had for years feared an explosion of the government powder magazine there. At first there was a demand that the immigrant station be established on Bedloe's Island, but because thousands of American citizens had donated funds for the erection of the Statue of Liberty, following its presentation to the United States by France, the reaction of the donors thwarted that plan.

So it was that on May 25, 1890, the Federal government, having removed all guns, powder and other munitions, formally placed the Island under the supervision of the United States Treasury Department.

Castle Garden, which had already passed nine million immigrants into America under the supervision of the State of New York, also had a colorful background before it became an immigrant station.

It is a coincidence that Castle Garden was first built as a fort by the Federal government. Erected in 1807 and called Castle Clinton, it was manned by soldiers through the War of 1812 and owned by the United States until 1822, at which time it was ceded to the city of New York. About two years later it was leased to private interests and became a place of amusement. Not until 1839, however, did Castle Garden come into prominence as a beautiful and fashionable resort.

French and Heiser were the names of the two proprietors who managed it until 1854, the year before it became an immigrant station.

Walking through it in these times to view the great collection of fish which graces the New York Aquarium, one finds it difficult to believe that it was once a lavishly decorated auditorium containing a stage and six thousand seats, and was considered one of the most beautiful resorts in the world.

Immediately upon obtaining their long lease in 1839, French and Heiser announced a new policy, and in contrast to the honky-tonk tawdriness of the offerings which had gone before them they provided New York with minstrels and music. A company of minstrels, in which were Barney Williams, Billy Whitlock, Dan Gardner and others, was the attraction in 1845 and 1846.

After being closed for renovations in the latter part of 1846 and spring of 1847, the Garden reopened with a stock company.

The outstanding event and one for which old Castle Garden will ever be famous was the triumph of Jenny Lind, the Swedish Nightingale.

P. T. Barnum was her manager. And what a success she scored! After her first concert the demand for seats was phenomenal. The takings of the first day's advance sale exceeded $10,000. She sang six nights and the receipts were $17,864.05; $14,203.03; $12,519.20; $14,266.69; $12,174.74; and on the farewell night, $16,028.39.

Afterward an Italian Opera Company reigned for a season at Castle Garden. Grisi and Mario made their American debuts to an audience of fifteen thousand. Equestrian exhibitions followed in October and November of that year, 1854. In May, 1855, Castle Garden was closed in order that it might be converted into an immigration depot.

With the establishment of Castle Garden as an Immigration Station under the supervision of the State of New York, things began to happen.

The facilities were inadequate for the proper care and treatment of the immigrants who had commenced to arrive in flood-tide numbers. The German revolution of 1848 had started an exodus from that country, while the Irish and Scandinavian peoples were also joining the caravan.

Hospital patients from Castle Garden were detained at Ward's Island in the East River. At Ward's Island riots frequently occurred. Many immigrants escaped by swimming to the Manhattan shore, asking to be arrested and confined in the New York jails, rather than remain there with the insane and, as some charged, in a state of starvation. An investigation on one occasion revealed the startling fact that the bodies of dead immigrants were being used for purposes of dissection.

With this curious and chequered background, the Ellis Island Immigration Station, conducted by the Federal government, commenced to function in the year 1892.

CHAPTER V

I RETURN TO THE ISLAND

ON THE morning of November 1, 1931, I went to Ellis Island to take the oath of office. My wife accompanied me.

No one knew that I was coming, and I had decided to make the trip as any visitor would, asking for a ferry boat pass at the Barge Office in the regular way.

In the twenty-four years I had been in America I had not set foot on the Island since 1907, when I was admitted as an immigrant.

The ride across the harbor, with the Statue of Liberty looming high upon our left, brought back a thousand memories. I thought of the other day when we had come through—of my mother who had entered the country with high hope, but had at last gone back to Italy in desperation to die. That and countless other things which had happened to our family in America passed through my mind.

The sun shone brightly that morning as the ferry coasted into the Ellis Island slip, and groups of deportees were to be seen walking about the enclosed lawn behind the administration building. The place seemed to be a veritable beehive of activity.

No one recognized me as I walked up to the information desk and presented my pass. No name appeared on this pass, and the clerk at the desk asked me a great many questions. Finally I had to tell him that I was the new commissioner. He was somewhat abashed upon that disclosure, directing me at once to the commissioner's office on the floor above. A few moments later I stood in my new office.

In other circumstances I would doubtless have been received by the incumbent commissioner, but Commissioner Day had resigned some months before, and Assistant Commissioner Uhl was on leave. The Assistant Commissioner General, Irving Wixon from Washington, had charge of the Island. The newspapers had been filled for days with the Ellis Island scandal involving the Re-entry Permit Racket. Special agents had been sent from Washington to conduct an investigation and break up the ring which had been charged with taking one hundred million dollars from aliens during the course of this scandal. One racketeer had been killed on Fortieth Street, and an effort was being made to link high officials of the Immigration Service with the gangster.

The moment I entered the office Mr. Wixon informed me that he was hurrying to get a train for Washington.

"We'll have you sworn in," he said, "and I'll leave the Island to you."

The suddenness of it all took me with the greatest surprise. It was like being thrown into the water and told to swim. George O'Donnoghue from the treasurer's office, a notary, was called into the room to administer the oath of office. Thirty minutes later Wixon said good-by, and from that moment I swam.

Before Mr. Wixon's departure, he spoke to me briefly concerning the situation as I was to inherit it.

"The Island is seething with distrust and suspicion," he said. "No one knows where it will end, and even the most loyal of the older employees feel that they are under a cloud."

The morale of the personnel was very low; public confidence in the Island had been shaken. Shortly after my appointment the Republican leader of my district remarked that Ellis Island was such a hotbed of jealousy and intrigue that he doubted if I could last six months.

The first few days revealed that my major problem was to build up confidence. First I had to imbue my men with confidence in themselves and in me, and then rebuild public confidence in the service.

A tour of inspection of the Island gave me my first impression of the men with whom I was called upon to serve. "Old Faithfuls" —many of them twenty and thirty years in the service, each doing a hard day's work at meager pay, and on the whole as honest and reliable a force of men and women as I have met anywhere in public service. These employees were to prove indispensable in effecting the improvements I was later to make.

My job was to stamp out racketeering, and I was deeply gratified when the investigation proved conclusively that only the two minor clerks had engaged in the activities of the racketeers. The rumors of a one-hundred-million-dollar racket proved to be greatly exaggerated.

The tour of inspection was made with Commissioner General Hull of Washington. It was one of my most interesting experiences at the Island.

This first tour of inspection came sooner than I had expected and was purely accidental. Hull happened to be in town and he came over for a visit. I undertook to show him around. I was so green that we almost lost our way about the Island.

We began our tour at the Barge Office. Here we were cordially welcomed by the inspectors of the Boarding Division. These inspectors search incoming ships for stowaways, examine passports, question those of doubtful qualifications and send some to Ellis Island for special inquiry.

Commissioner General Hull and I chatted with various inspectors for a few moments, then hurried on to the ferry boat and journeyed to the Island.

We visited the various divisions of the administration building. This is a huge structure, rather Oriental in appearance.

The building was originally constructed to take care of thousands of immigrants daily. In the heyday of immigration the entire first floor was devoted to the baggage of the arriving aliens. They were examined in the big domed two-story room on the second floor. Much of the space in this enormous room, once densely packed with people, has now been converted into offices.

Once in the building, you go through interminable white-tiled hallways, spotlessly clean but somewhat awe-inspiring and unnecessarily institutional.

The chief divisions of the service housed here are the law, the deportation, the inspection and the registry divisions.

When I went to the Island I found the records scattered over the entire building and too easily accessible. I realized at once the danger of this and the need for greater supervision of files. Today the twenty million records of arrivals have been concentrated in a new room built where a part of the great caravan once waited to learn its fate.

In the course of our inspection, the Commissioner General and I visited the impressive little schoolroom where Mrs. Jean Pratt, a social worker, was teaching a class of tiny tots of many races whose parents were in detention.

In the huge detention room we saw men doing various kinds of handiwork under the auspices of the D.A.R. Some were weaving belts from leather thongs, some making pillowcases from bright-colored cloth, others making shirts. A tailor was making a suit of clothes.

We walked out of the building at the suggestion of Mr. Hull so that we might enter the enclosure where the aliens were taking exercise. They were playing baseball, boxing, and engaging in other games. At the gate a guard accosted us.

"Where do you two think you are going?" he asked none too politely.

"We'd like to come inside," the Commissioner General replied.
"Walk on—nothin' doing," the guard snapped back at him.

He was highly disconcerted a moment later when he learned that he was talking to the head of the Immigration Service from Washington.

When we reported the incident to Superintendent Baker later on, he told us of the time a former Commissioner General, who travelled with a big suitcase and had the appearance of a commoner, was found walking through an Ellis Island corridor and was pushed into a line of immigrants. He is said to have waited there reluctantly until he could establish his identity.

Assistant Commissioner Uhl also told us the incident of an irate deportee pulling the Van Dyke beard of an Assistant Secretary of Labor, who prided himself on his liberal attitude toward the alien.

Our visit to the hospital furnished one of my greatest surprises. I found it large and well-equipped, and certainly a credit to the Public Health Service of the United States.

We entered the dental clinic and came upon a sight both humorous and pathetic. A dentist was in the act of extracting one of the molar teeth of an alien.

"Here it is!" he said smiling, as he exhibited the unusually large tooth. The alien grinned.

It was suggestive of how aliens are uprooted in their native countries and brought to America.

We talked briefly with the dentist and were next conducted to the insane ward. I shall never forget that horrible experience.

When an attendant opened a door, we saw lying prostrate on the floor a man without clothes. He was moaning and muttering like an animal. I turned away, sickened by the sight.

Going through that ward, we talked to an old Englishman who was reading. We did so at the special request of one of the attendants who introduced us.

"Mr. ——," the attendant said to the man, who appeared to be about fifty-five, "I've brought you some visitors, the new Commissioner at Ellis Island and the Commissioner General of Immigration from Washington."

The alien came forward and shook hands as cordially and with as much self-composure as though he were sane. In fact, I was almost persuaded that the attendant was playing a practical joke upon us.

"The very two people I'd rather meet than any others," he began. "If you have a minute, I'd like to explain my cure for the depression. I've got it—the only plan that will save the country."

"What is it?" we asked in one breath.

"Simply this," was the alien's reply, "it's as easy as falling off a log. Take a penny a day from every person in the United States." Turning to the Commissioner General, he hesitated a moment, then continued. "You and the President would head the list. No one would miss that amount and we could use Ellis Island to distribute this amount of money to the unemployed."

"A better plan than many that are being offered," was Mr. Hull's comment as we started to my office to discuss some of the important phases of the work which lay ahead.

My tour of inspection had added immeasurably to my knowledge of the Island. Each person I talked with had been friendly and receptive. Practically all suggested improvements. The tour had led me to visualize many things which I thought I could do. I foresaw in the Island a place of beauty which would grace the harbor and contribute to the new liberal spirit of the country. We were walking back towards the administration building. On the hospital side of the ferry slip were moored a string of yachts and speed boats which the Coast Guard had captured from rum runners. On the other side was the old boat, *Fred R. Moore,* formerly used for the transporting of immigrants from incoming ships, now moored and in disuse.

"Prohibition of liquor" on the one side. "Prohibition of immigrants" on the other.

PART III

CHAPTER I

A PICTURE OF 1907

MANY friends and officials of the Immigration Service called at my office during the first few days after my arrival to take up my duties at Ellis Island.

One day, when the flood of visitors had subsided somewhat, and I was discussing various phases of the work with Assistant Commissioner Byron H. Uhl, the conversation happened to turn to the year 1907.

"Who was here," I asked him, "when I came through the Island?"

"Well, I for one," he replied, laughing. "I'm nearly as old a fixture as the first buildings. I've been in the Service about forty years, you know."

"But an Italian immigrant boy coming through in 1907," I said, "surely wouldn't have seen *you*."

Again he smiled. "We couldn't see the individuals for the crowds we had in those days," he said. "But wait—Martocci! Why didn't I think of him before! He probably admitted your family."

Seeing my eager interest, he explained: "He's the same Italian interpreter we had when you came through the Island. Wouldn't you like to talk with him?"

A few days passed before I had the opportunity to see Frank Martocci. He came into my office and congratulated me in Italian, having already read in the papers of my appointment and my immigrant background. When I asked if he had escorted me personally into this country, he paused reflectively, going over in swift review his many years at Ellis Island. His merry dark eyes twinkling, he ran a stubby hand through his shock of iron-gray hair, which, despite the years, had not thinned. Finally he said:

"Of course I can't remember whether I inspected your family, but I can tell you that the millions of other Italians who came through Ellis Island and now live in America are glad to see you here."

I thanked him and we chatted for some time. Finally I said, "Tell me, what do you remember of the days when I came in? What were the conditions in those days?"

Eyes twinkling, he rubbed his hands together and leaned forward.

"We went to work, of course, from the Barge Office at the Battery. From there the ferryboat took most of the employees to Ellis Island at nine in the morning. Hundreds of other people were always eagerly waiting and clamoring to get on the same boat. These were the friends and relatives of immigrants expected during the day, or already being detained at the Island.

"To get on the boat, these friends and relatives, a mixed crowd of all nationalities, had to obtain passes from the steamship office, and guards used to circulate among them at the Barge Office to make sure that only the proper people had these passes.

"Fortunately or unfortunately—however you look at it—I was a native Italian, knew the language, and had already been in the service a long time. This combination made me a sort of godsend to many of these people, who, recognizing my nationality, would seize me by the coat, by the arm, and even by the neck, and insist on following me everywhere I went, babbling out their problems and pleading for aid. I did my best to keep clear of them in a kindly way, but sometimes I couldn't help but lose my patience. Waiting for friends, brothers, mothers, fathers, or sisters, they looked at me so hopefully, so anxiously, that my sympathy for them was quite a strain on my nerves.

"Once at the Island, we employees had to plunge immediately into our work, for in those terrifically busy days whole boat loads of immigrants were waiting to be inspected every morning. They came from everywhere: from England, Germany, Russia, Italy, France, Greece and other countries.

"At quarantine, inspectors had already boarded the boats to examine the first- and second-class passengers. Those found eligible were landed at the pier. Many less fortunate, who were considered ineligible, were brought to Ellis Island, where they had to undergo the experience of being judged by the immigration authorities on the following day."

"How different the inspection routine must have been in those days," I mused.

"It certainly was," he answered, "I can well remember, for at that time I was in the registry department, assigned to decide the eligibility of aliens to land. To make things run fairly smoothly in that mixed crowd of poor, bewildered immigrants, we would tag them with numbers corresponding to numbers on their manifest, after they had been landed from the barges and taken into the building.

"Here, in the main building, they were lined up—a motley crowd in colorful costumes, all ill at ease and wondering what was to happen to them. Doctors then put them through their medical inspection, and whenever a case aroused suspicion, the alien was set aside in a cage apart from the rest, for all the world like a segregated animal, and his coat lapel or shirt marked with colored chalk, the color indicating why he had been isolated. These methods, crude as they seem, had to be used, because of the great numbers and the language difficulties.

"All the other aliens were passed down a long line and grouped according to their manifest numbers, and the inspection continued. There were twenty-two lines of inspection, as well as a number of side sections where the aliens were grouped according to letters.

"Every manifest held thirty names, but one inspector never got all thirty. Some were detained by the doctors at the medical inspection, and others were held back for other reasons. Those aliens who were passed were told by the principal inspector to follow the line to a point where another inspector sat with his manifest before him."

"And there, no doubt, occurred the essence of the work," I interposed. "You had to question the aliens to find out if they were eligible to enter the country."

"Yes, and that's where most of our headaches began. If, for example, a woman with three children came before the inspector, she was asked her name. Then she had to produce her vaccination card, which the inspector would compare with her name on the manifest and the line number of the manifest. Her age was asked, and again the manifest was consulted. These manifests, of course, had been prepared by the purser or some other official of the ship, so that they were all ready when the alien came before the inspector.

"Before a barrage of questions such as: Sex? Married status? Occupation? Where born? Where last resided? Where going? By whom was the passage paid? Is that person in the United States or not? If so, how long? To whom is the alien going?—the alien would do his best, wondering what it was all about and when and how it would end. These crowds, this pushing, this hurrying to get things done, this red tape, those cards containing he knew not what damning information against him—it was not at all like his peaceful life back in his native country. Would he get along in this new and strange land? Maybe he should never have come. These thoughts must have been in the minds of most of them.

"Well, to get back to the story, every alien was supposed to be asked these questions individually, but naturally, every inspector used his own judgment. If a woman had children, you talked with the children yourself to see if one might be deaf or dumb. One might be, for all we knew, and as a matter of fact, we did find

THE STEERAGE CROWDS AS THEY LOOKED IN 1907. HUDDLED TOGETHER BETWEEN THEIR BOXES AND BALES MASSES OF STRANGERS HURRIED TO THESE SHORES.

cases that the medical officer had failed to discover. These cases we had to refer back to the medical division for action."

"Women presented a special problem, didn't they?" I asked. "Tell me about the procedure in their case. There must be plenty of interesting instances you remember, too, no doubt."

"Yes, indeed I remember some instances," he replied. "A woman, if she came alone, was asked a number of special questions: how much money she had; if she were going outside of New York; whether her passage had been paid by herself or by some charitable institution. If she had come to join her husband in New York or Brooklyn, we could not let her loose on the streets of a strange city looking for her husband. Actually he might have been waiting outside the Barge Office for a week, but the inspector would detain the woman, and her children if she had any, until the husband came for her, for there were too many unscrupulous people preying on the ignorance of the immigrant in those days.

"The woman had to remain in the detention room, where employees looked out for her while she was detained. If her husband were on the Island when her name was called, he would accompany her to the inspector whose duty it was to discharge such persons to their relatives or friends. With the wife safely and happily in her husband's care, the case was closed so far as the immigration inspection went.

"If no callers came for the woman, the person in charge of those being detained had to wire the immediate relative who was expected to call for her. This telegram or other communication also stated that it would serve as a pass to Ellis Island.

"When the person claiming the immigrant called, he or she was first directed to the information division, and then into the presence of the woman, but only after due inquiries by the inspector handling the case, to make sure he or she was the right person. If the inspector saw any discrepancies, or if the names or previous history did not agree, he referred the case to a Board of Special Inquiry, which would hear the case and then make its decision."

"You had quite a bit of trouble with contract laborers, too, I understand, didn't you?" I asked at this point.

"I was coming to that," he answered. "You see, at that time I acted not only as an interpreter but also as a primary inspector. Sometimes there came before me a group all hailing from about the same section in Italy and bound for a single destination, in this country. Of course there might be nothing wrong about this, but if they had contracted to work here before they came over it was illegal, and the primary inspector had jurisdiction to examine aliens as to contract labor.

"In addition, we had a contract labor bureau whose personnel asked the male alien in particular, after he had passed his primary inspection, whether he had come to the United States with a contract for a job. If the alien, who, of course, could not know it would provide difficulties, answered in the affirmative, he would be held for final examination by the contract labor bureau. This also applied to other aliens with him heading for the same address, on the suspicion of being contract laborers.

"It sometimes happened that one member of such a group would produce a letter from a friend or relative within the United States to prove that work had been promised him here. He would willingly sign an affidavit of this, thereby leading not only to his own deportation, but also that of his entire group.

"Although these aliens had final recourse to the Commissioner General of Immigration, most of them were deported. Once, when I was the official interpreter, thirty-four common laborers were deported because one of them was honest about coming here as a contract laborer, and unwittingly involved all the others in his group."

"I understand that besides Italian, you also know German, Spanish, French and Polish," I said, when he paused. "You must have been in great demand, considering the numbers in those days." Martocci nodded, with a weary gesture at the thought.

"Three or four times a week, from nine o'clock in the morning to nine in the evening, we were continuously examining aliens," he confessed. "I thought it was a stream that would never end. Every twenty-four hours from three to five thousand people came before us, and I myself examined from four to five hundred a day. We were simply swamped by that human tide.

"With those who were being detained matters were still worse, for it was almost impossible to provide strict sanitation. I said before that we could not let a woman with her children out on the streets looking for her husband. This also applied to all alien females, minors and others who did not have money, but were otherwise eligible and merely waiting for friends or relatives. We generally had more of this class than we could handle. One Sunday morning, I remember, there were seventeen hundred of these women and children kept in one room with a normal capacity of six hundred. How they were packed in! It had to be seen to be appreciated. They just couldn't move about, and whenever we wanted to get one out it was almost a major operation.

"For example, I was one of the four employees whose duty it was to distribute their detention cards. That day it took us all of four solid hours to distribute the cards to the seventeen hundred people, because, added to the general noise in several different languages, we were simply unable to work our way through the massed crowd. We finally solved the problem by taking our places in the four corners of the room and distributing the cards by shouting out at the top of our lungs the names of the aliens. When they answered we threw the cards as near to them as we could and let them scramble for them."

"You were just talking about sanitation and cleanliness," I reminded him.

"There was no such thing in those days," was his answer. "With so many people packed together under such conditions, it was naturally impossible for them to keep clean, for the clean ones were pressed against aliens infected with vermin, and it was not long before all were contaminated.

"Why, I used to find vermin on myself sometimes. More than once, when I reached home, my wife or some other member of the family would discover with repugnance that I had something crawling over my neck. They were usually found on my left side, a fact which I thought strange till I remembered that when I interpreted before the Board of Special Inquiry, the alien always stood on my left.

"As for sleeping quarters, please don't imagine they were anything like what we have now. Not only were they inadequate, but what we had were not of the best. There were iron bedsteads, which folded like a pocketbook, and these were in three tiers. The aliens who were unfortunate enough to be without beds had to sleep on benches, chairs, the floor, or wherever we could put them. To-day there are usually about two hundred detained every night, but in those days we averaged about two thousand. In the detention room there were never less than nine hundred. It was an endless affair, like filling a trough at one end and emptying it at the other.

"And the feeding of the immigrants! It was a sight, back in those days, and I hate to think of it. One employee brought out a big pail filled with prunes, and another some huge loaves of sliced rye bread. A helper would take a dipper full of prunes and slop it down on a big slice of bread, saying: 'Here! Now go and eat!'

"The poor wretches had to obey, though they didn't know where to go. They moved along, their harassed faces full of fear, with their cards held dumbly in their hands. It was my job to take the cards and put down their names by hand, for we had no typewriters in those days. As I handed them back I said: 'Go downstairs.'

"And down a few steps they would go to a little hut, which they all had to enter. Poor unfortunates, they were worried and nervous, and disgusted with the place. All they got to eat there was prunes or prune sandwiches. Now this may make a novel sandwich for once, but when you have it all the time, morning and evening, evening and morning, it becomes revolting. Even though they were

THE OLD MESS HALL, WHERE OLD AND YOUNG OF ALL NATIONS AND CREEDS MET IN A COMMON CAUSE.

peasants and many of them poverty-stricken, they had never been reduced to such monotony in their food in their own homes."

"Wasn't anything done to better those conditions?" I interrupted. "Couldn't a report or a protest be made on the matter? I'm sure it was not the intent of the law to feed the immigrants, even in those crowded days, so wretchedly."

"It was a case of profiteering. The man in charge of the food was making money out of those poor devils by giving them the cheapest food he possibly could, for, you see, he was allowed so much per capita," he explained. "That was the sort of thing they had to eat from about 1898 on, but in 1907 Mr. Williams, the Immigration Commissioner at that time, changed all that and saw to it that better food was provided, though it still was not so good as it is to-day.

"Speaking of food reminds me of the thirty howling Dervishes we once had on the Island. It was the *Trinacria* of the Anchor Line, from Mediterranean ports, which one bright day brought in the Dervishes: Mohammedan priests who had come from the East to give exhibitions in the United States.

"They were a colorful, bizarre sight in their red fezzes, loose, flowing trousers, soft sandals, and coats of bright blue. They were in the charge of Sheik Maluck, of Damascus, said to be a personal friend of Emin Pasha, whoever he was. An Americanized Arabian, Josef Maluck, managed them while they were in the United States.

"As I remember it, one of the papers announced: 'It is expected that an exhibition will be given in this city.' And it certainly was—right on the Island, for it turned out that they would eat no food over which the shadow of an infidel had passed. This was absolutely forbidden by their religion. Now of course the cook, the employees, waiters, helpers, and in fact everybody connected with the Island were infidels to them. So the serious question arose: What were we going to feed those howling Dervish dancers?

"Fortunately, before they starved themselves, someone had a brilliant idea. 'Why not give them eggs?' We tried eggs, and to these they had no objection.

"These same Dervishes, incidentally, had given another unexpected exhibition on the ship coming over. A queer sort of light showed in the sky one day over the *Trinacria*, and suddenly, without any warning and to the amazement of the other passengers, the whole troop of thirty Dervishes began spinning around on one toe and howling in a way that brought everybody up on deck. I suppose they could howl for food or anything else, when they felt like it."

"You certainly had all kinds coming over in those days," I commented, at the end of this amusing story. "But most of the cases, as I gather, were somewhat sadder. There were quite a number going back, too."

"Plenty. And in the case of aged people it was particularly pitiful," he acknowledged. "You see, in nine cases out of ten, an old person was detained until called for by some relative or friend. At the Island, these poor unfortunates would wander about, bewilderment and incomprehension in their eyes, not even knowing where they were, or why they were being kept. It was touching to see how, whenever they saw anyone who spoke their language, they would ask hopefully: 'Have you seen my son? Have you seen my daughter? Do you know him, my Giuseppe? When is he coming for me?'

"There were times, of course, when all our efforts to locate the immediate relative failed. Sometimes a married woman had come to join her husband, or a young woman to marry her fiancé, and the man could not be located. Perhaps he had died, or moved, or the correspondence hadn't reached him—who knows? In any event, the results were tragic indeed, as I well know from personal experience. There was no way of soothing these heartbroken women, who had traveled thousands and thousands of miles, endured suffering and humiliation, and who had uprooted their lives only to find their hopes shattered at the end of the long voyage. These, I think, are the saddest of all immigration cases.

"Sometimes these women were placed in the care of a social agency which agreed to be responsible to the Commissioner, caring for them or placing them in some appropriate occupation. But if everything possible had been done, and the missing husband or fiancé still could not be traced, the poor alien, despite all her tears, had to be returned to her native country.

"Occasionally cases of this kind did not have the element of tragedy, but were queer and hard to handle. There was, for instance, the second-class passenger from Vera Cruz booked under the name of Alejandra Veles. Boyish in appearance, with black hair and an attractive face, she proved to be, upon examination, despite her earlier insistence to the contrary, a young woman. Vehemently she insisted that her identity had not been questioned before. When Dr. Senner asked her why she wore men's clothes, she answered that she would rather kill herself than wear women's clothes. Perhaps some psychoanalyst can explain it, but she said she had always wanted to be a man and it was no fault of hers that she had not been born one!

"Finally she broke down and pleaded with us not to expose her. Then, being threatened with arrest for her defiance of rules, she sent for a very prominent lawyer of the city, who, it turned out, had received a fund for her support. He identified her immediately, and after having exacted a pledge that the girl's identity would not be revealed, he told her amazing story.

" 'Alejandra Veles' was the daughter of a cultured Englishman who had married a wealthy Spanish woman, and then had been sent to represent his government in the Orient. The girl had been born in the Far East and, when a little child, for some reason or other unhappy at being a girl, she had insisted on dressing as a boy. Although her parents did all they could to discipline her, she would tear her dresses to shreds. She defied all control and finally was allowed to grow up as a boy.

"At the age of fifteen she deserted her parents and started drifting. She came to this country and for two years worked as a hostler in a New York stable, after which she went to the West Indies and bossed men around, nobody ever suspecting she was a girl. Her father, frantic and at his wit's end, had provided this lawyer with a liberal sum for the girl's support. Was there anything else she wanted, she was asked. 'Yes—give me two plugs of tobacco and a pipe.'

"These were given to her, and she was allowed to leave the Barge Office on her promise to leave the country at once. This she did, sailing for England to visit her parents."

"Did she," I wondered aloud, "sail for England in a man's outfit, or dressed as a woman? But I suppose, having seen thousands of cases, she was just another case to you, and no doubt you are already thinking of someone else."

"Right you are," was his response. "I'm thinking of another strange human specimen we once had detained on the Island— José Maria, who baffled all our officials. Until then I had thought that among all of us interpreters we could find someone speaking the language of most every alien. But José Maria was more than our match. He understood none of the many languages we tried on him. Even the Chancellor of the Japanese Consulate, who had a reputation for speaking and understanding almost every dialect of the Orient, and whom we called on for assistance, could make nothing out of José Maria, who looked like a mixture of Japanese, Chinese and Malay. All he ever said to anyone was, 'Me no sabe.'

"There was nothing about his person by which he could be identified. The newspapers got hold of the story and played up its human interest. They even went so far as to offer us suggestions. One paper guessed offhand that the man was Burmese, and he may have been for all we knew, but he was the only one who could tell, and he couldn't or wouldn't.

"In his satchel he had two envelopes, one addressed to 'José Antonio Chins, Rua de Mancel, Rio de Janeiro, Brazil,' and the other covered with Chinese characters which told a lot about a restaurant somewhere, but nothing about himself. He had $1.50 in German

money, and he was heading for Brazil. We never found out anything definite, and my memory is a little vague now as to what
became of him, but I do remember that Dr. Senner decided that,
in sailing from Bremen, José Maria had taken the wrong steamer,
and had landed in New York, when in fact he had meant to take
the boat for Rio de Janeiro.

"There were so many times when an inspector's sympathy was
touched, despite the calloused attitude we were forced to adopt as
a sort of self-protection. After all, we wouldn't have been human
had it been otherwise.

"I remember, for example, the case of an Italian girl who hesitated in answering my questions. Her mother was with her. Although the girl was supposed to be feeble-minded, somehow that
explanation did not entirely satisfy me. I asked her: 'What part
of Italy do you come from?'

"Her answer interested me, for it happened that her town was
right in the district from which I had come myself.

"'Don't you know me?' I said. 'I am your countryman—your
townsman.'

"At these words she brightened up a little, and I was satisfied to
have aroused that faint glimmer of interest. I don't remember
whether or not the case was certified as one of feeble-mindedness,
but one of the doctors present complimented me on the way I had
treated that poor, unfortunate girl."

"Tell me," I said, "do you remember particularly any case of a
man being deported to a country that refused to take him back?
A man without a country is a tragic person."

"There were many such cases, but none more strange or more
tragic than that of Nathan Cohen, who came to us again in 1916.
He was insane, and try as we might we could not establish his nationality. As a result, he was shipped back and forth, again and
again, between South America and the United States.

"Although we had but few facts to go by in this case, we did
manage to find out that he had been born thirty-five years before

in Baush, a little village in the province of Kurland in Russia. As a boy he had left home and gone to Brazil. Three years previous he had landed in America, married, and gone into business in Baltimore with several thousand dollars. All seemed to be going well with him. Then his business failed, followed closely, as happens all too often in life, by other catastrophes. His wife ran away with another man, and Cohen lost his memory and his power of speech, and had to be taken to an insane asylum in Baltimore.

"Now he was a public charge within three years of the time he had first landed in the United States and, under the alien law, had to be sent back to the country from which he had come, by the line which had brought him originally. The Lamport Holt Line was therefore instructed to return him to Brazil.

"The Brazilian authorities, however, would not accept Cohen, and the Argentine, where he was next sent, also refused him entrance. Back he was sent to the United States, which promptly shipped him back to Brazil. Since the steamship company could produce no evidence of his Russian birth, he could not be returned to Russia. Such a situation might be funny in fiction, but in real life it was too tragic for humor.

"At last the Knights of Pythias found that he had joined their order in Jacksonville, Florida. With the help of former Justice Leon Sanders, the immigration authorities were induced to let Cohen land, on condition that he be deported to Russia after the war if he proved to be a Russian citizen.

"So Cohen finally was sent to the sanitarium at Green Farms, Connecticut, as a charge of the Hebrew Shelter and Immigrant Aid Society and the Knights of Pythias. It was there he died.

"Of course it wasn't all tragedy in those days. Now and then bits of humor and comedy drifted in at the Barge Office and on the Island. For instance, there was something about the Italians, especially the women, that would not let them leave their pillows behind. No matter what else they relinquished, they usually brought

Left. French peasant woman with stiffly starched cap and all-enveloping apron. *Right.* African wild man clad in the glory of his own strong muscles.

A VARIED ASSORTMENT OF FOREIGN STYLES

Left. Albanian mountaineers in the picturesque costumes of their calling. *Right.* Russian Cossacks gorgeous in their fierce but colorful uniforms.

along bulky pillows and mattresses. And very often this was just about everything they did bring!

"But whether they were Italian or Russian, Swedish or Spanish, German or Greek, many of the immigrants came in their native peasant costumes—a strange and colorful procession of fashions in dress from all parts of the world. One would think we were holding a fancy dress party, judging by the variety and oddness of the styles. And the gypsies—I mustn't forget the gypsies!

"The Cunard liner, *Carpathia,* brought them in September of 1904, two hundred and eighty of them, in all the picturesque gorgeousness of their various tribal costumes. But what wasn't so picturesque was the fact that forty-eight gypsy children had measles and had to be sent by the immigration doctors to the Kingston Avenue Hospital in Brooklyn.

"This taking of the children was what started things; and what fanned the fire was the fact that several members of distinctive families were taken from the detention room and placed before the Board of Special Inquiry.

"More and more gypsy forces arrived—gypsies from Long Island, New Jersey, and other adjacent points flocked into the Island to meet those detained. Then some gypsy spread the rumor that all the children taken by the doctors had been drowned, and you can imagine what happened!

"At eleven o'clock that night a doctor, who tried to feel a gypsy child's pulse, was attacked by the gypsies as a murderer. This started a riot which could not be checked or stilled, and which raged all night. Every time the gypsies saw anyone wearing an immigration uniform or cap they opened fire, using as weapons anything on which they could lay their hands.

"But at last a way of explaining things was worked out. The next gypsy child who developed measles was sent to the hospital like the others, but the parents were allowed to go along and see how the other gypsy children were being cared for. They brought the news back to the other gypsies, and this was successful in appeasing them. But as long as I live I shall never forget the picture of those gypsy women pulling off their heavy-soled slippers, and sailing into us inspectors and the doctors with fire in their eyes!

"One of the most disgusted men we ever had on the Island was a young Hungarian who, in 1905, had, as he complained, to marry his own wife!

"They were two young Hungarians, and I remember them well, though it was back in 1905 that they got to Ellis Island. They had come from London separately, on tickets bearing different names, and at that time they had said they were cousins.

"Once they arrived at the Island, however, they explained that they were really man and wife, adding that they had bought return tickets for other people, and so had been forced to represent themselves as the people whose names were on the tickets.

"The immigration authorities brought the case to the attention of the superintendent of the Home for Jewish Immigrant Girls, requesting her to become responsible for the girl. She agreed and took the girl to the Home. Later the man appeared with several of his countrymen and demanded his wife. A conference followed, in which they were asked for evidence of their married status. Their explanations, given convincingly, were that they had been too poor to get a wedding ring and that the wedding certificate had been in a trunk which was lost.

"Finally the superintendent said: 'Well, if you're married already, it won't do you any harm to be married all over again. If you will marry here and now, you can go away as you like, but if not, I will have to keep the girl, for in spite of what you say, you have no real proof that you are her husband.'

"The man looked dazed. 'What kind of country is this,' he asked hoarsely, 'that makes me remarry my own wife?'

"He agreed, however, to the proposition, and after a rabbi had been called in they were married again, to the bewilderment of the bridegroom and the amusement of his naturalized friends. The couple went away happy, however, with clear sailing ahead."

"It's good to hear that with all the squalor and bewildered crowds and misfortunes," I said, "a little occasional humor or romance lightened the day's work. Perhaps it would have been unbearable without that."

"Oh, we had plenty of that! It seems to me now as I look back that in those days there were crying and laughing and singing all the time at Ellis Island," he recalled. "Very often brides came over to marry here, and of course we had to act as witnesses. I have no count, but I'm sure I must have helped at hundreds and hundreds of weddings of all nationalities and all types. The weddings were numberless, until they dropped the policy of marrying them at the Island and brought them to City Hall in New York.

"Incidentally, as you may have heard, there is a post at Ellis Island which through long usage has come to earn the name of 'The Kissing Post.' It is probably the spot of greatest interest on the Island, and if the immigrants recall it afterward it is always, I am sure, with fondness. For myself, I found it a real joy to watch some of the tender scenes that took place there.

"There was a line of desks where the inspectors stood with their backs towards the windows and facing the wall. Further back, behind a partition, the witnesses waited outside for the detained aliens. As the aliens were brought out, the witnesses were brought in to be examined as to their rights of claim. If the inspector found no hitch, they were allowed to join each other. This, because of the arrangement of the partitions, usually took place at 'The Kissing Post,' where friends, sweethearts, husbands and wives, parents and children would embrace and kiss and shed tears for pure joy.

"I have shown how the routine was held up and how complications arose when an alien was unable to give the information required of him. When an alien refused to give this information, the complications that resulted were still more serious. Take, for example, the case of Joaquin Nabuco, the Brazilian Ambassador at Washington, who arrived in November 1906 on the White Star Line steamer, *Baltic,* from Liverpool.

"Senhor Nabuco refused to answer the following questions which were put to him by immigration authorities purely as a matter of routine: 'By whom was your passage paid? Have you fifty dollars in your possession? Have you ever been in prison or in an alms-house or in an institution for the care and treatment of the insane or supported by charity? If so, which? Are you a polygamist? Have you come here under the promise, offer, or solicitation to labor in the United States?'

"Although it was explained to Senhor Nabuco that these were certain set questions, the answers to which were required by the immigration laws, he persisted in his refusal to answer, drawing himself up to his full height and saying:

" 'I have answered every question which I believed would add to the necessary statistical governmental information; but these other questions are different. I am not a visitor to this country in the implied sense of the word. I am here as the representative of an-other power, and as such I am to a certain extent the guest of this nation. This is the ground I take, and for this reason alone I re-fuse to answer certain questions. There is no friction over the affair, and I should like nothing said about it.'

"Lord Curzon, the English statesman, was also a passenger on the *Baltic* at that time, and he had answered the same questions, although this did not establish a precedent, for Lord Curzon was not an official representative of a foreign power.

"At any rate, the purser of the *Baltic* reported the matter and the desired information was asked of E. L. Chermont, secretary of the Brazilian Embassy, but Mr. Chermont could not provide it. Again the information was requested of Senhor Nabuco, and again he refused to supply it.

"It was then that Secretary of State Root, upon being unofficially notified of the situation, got in touch with the Department of Commerce and Labor and requested that the courtesies of the port be extended to Senhor Nabuco and his secretary.

"There was talk for some time of an apology being made, and

for all I know it may have been; but under customs regulations,
a country sending a diplomatic representative to this country is
required to notify the Secretary of State in advance, and the State
Department then informs the Secretary of the Treasury, who orders
that the customs laws be suspended in the instance of the incoming
individual. Brazil had not given such notice, and we, as a result,
had received no word to suspend such questions in the case of the
Ambassador."

"You haven't said anything so far about cases involving actual
crime," I interposed. "In the year 1907 something like one million,
three hundred thousand immigrants came through Ellis Island.
You don't mean to tell me that not one of those was a criminal!"

"Oh, yes," he replied smilingly, "we had criminals of all types and
descriptions and from all parts of the world. My most interesting
case was that of Alfano, who was wanted by the Italian police and
who was a menace to my fellow Italians in the city. I mention this
case because my friend Petrosino, one of the greatest detectives New
York has ever seen, had come into it.

"This man Alfano, commonly called Erricone here, had escaped
from Italy under a false name and had come to this country through
France. He had gotten through at the time, for we knew nothing
about his Italian background.

"Now Petrosino, one of the finest men I ever met, had been put
in charge of the Italian squad at Police Headquarters in New York.
His name was anathema to the Italian criminal here, who feared
and hated him. It was my good fortune to have known Petrosino
even before his detective days, and yet, though we had been friends
for many years, he was so tight-lipped he never let out a word to
me about his police activities.

"But the time came when he had to. One day he looked me up
and announced briefly:

" 'Say, Martocci, I've got a fellow down at Mulberry Street who's
wanted by the Italian police—I happened to jump into a reception

his pals were giving for him. His name's Alfano. He says it isn't, but I know it is.'

"Petrosino brought his man over to Ellis Island, where he was locked up pending action by the immigration authorities. But they couldn't deport him—they couldn't do anything—till they had established his identity.

"The prisoner gave us no coöperation whatsoever, for he would not admit his true name. Together with the immigration lawyer, Mr. Govin, I went to consult Alfano in his cell a number of times, but he would not confess who he was. Even before the Board of Special Inquiry, where we had him testify, and at which I happened to be the interpreter, he still refused.

"We had just about given up the affair in desperation when one day, I don't know just why—perhaps out of sheer disgust at the constant hounding of him—he admitted:

" 'Yes, yes, all right. I'm the Alfano you want. Do whatever you want with me.'

"This admission he later made in a sworn statement, and he was deported to Italy where, with one hundred or more, he was prosecuted in the famous Abbatemaggio case. It was the conspiracy of this Camorra for which Alfano, by the way, is now serving a life sentence. And it was Alfano's group which, in 1909 in Italy, killed my friend Petrosino while he was tracking them down. They say sometimes that criminals are colorful or interesting, but Petrosino had more color and picturesqueness than any criminal we ever harbored at the Island."

"Petrosino and his exploits are remembered to this day," I agreed. "We need more men like him."

"Another source of trouble in those hectic days"—Martocci continued, "was the money exchange. Perhaps there was no other financial institution or procedure like it anywhere in the world, and it would have provided a real thrill for those who make antique and foreign money collections.

"Before going out of Ellis Island to the mainland, the foreigner

changed his money into American dollars and cents. There were
so many aliens in those days that even for this we had to line them
up after inspection had been made. A hundred lire, for example,
came to $19.30, and the alien was given a receipt to show that he
had received the right amount in American money for his one
hundred lire.

"The money-changers usually paid in gold. From time to time
a number of immigrants complained of being cheated in the exchange. I don't mean to say that the person in charge was dishonest,
but perhaps an occasional helper was found to be untrustworthy.
We could not place the guilt on any money-changer, and we found
the aliens' receipts correct; but the fact remained that sometimes
the alien did not have his $19.30.

"One day an alien came to me, complaining that he was short
five dollars. Incidentally it wasn't often that an alien knew enough
about the money to know when he was cheated. Another inspector
and I returned with the alien to the money-changer and asked him
for an explanation. The alien, mind you, had just had his money
exchanged by this man, who insisted he had given him the right
amount. The alien insisted just as loudly—more so, in fact—that
he had been short-changed five dollars. Although I suspected the
money-changer, I had no proof and was about to try to close the
matter, when the alien, who happened to be an Italian, after fum-
bling through all his pockets again, reached over and pulled the
missing five dollar bill out of the money-changer's pocket. It was
done so cleverly that to me it seemed a sleight-of-hand trick."

"Tell me, Martocci, how did the War affect the Island?" I asked.
"It changed things, didn't it?"

"It certainly did, for then we had practically no immigration
from the northern countries of Europe. The only immigration
during War days was from the Mediterranean, and a good many
vessels from that area were torpedoed. One Italian ship, the *Ancona,*
was sunk, but fortunately her passengers were saved.

"Finally we had to resort at that time to the inspection and detention of aliens on board ship, because all our accommodations on the Island were taken up by the interned enemy aliens and individual hospital cases brought back from the War. We had, in fact, about two thousand aliens on the Island.

"For persons being detained, these enemy aliens were treated royally. There were concerts on Sundays in the large detention room upstairs. Friends of the enemy aliens came in such numbers that three or four trips had to be made by the Island ferryboat.

"The police department was kind enough, when we held the concerts, to furnish police women in uniform to guard the entrance and exit of the reception room where the concerts were held. It was exceedingly difficult to explain to visitors how they could see the aliens and under what conditions, and arguments were endless. To cap it all, one day one of the police women tried to push me out of the room where I was going to see my chief. How could she know I was not a visitor?"

CHAPTER II

DEPRESSION TURNS THE TIDE

FROM the outset of my administration I realized that the modern problems of Ellis Island were in distinct contrast to those of the flood-tide days.

The depression throughout the country had brought a lengthening of bread lines and those clamoring for municipal relief. The immigration laws provided for the deportation of "public charges" or vagrants under certain conditions. To all parts of the world had gone the news that America was no longer the "land of promise"; it was being rumored and reported by disappointed aliens in writing to their friends on the other side that the "promise" had been deleted from the mythical name which had gained force for two centuries.

In the administration of Secretary Doak at Washington there was a clearly defined policy of deportation. First, he had publicly announced that he intended to rid the country of undesirable foreigners. In some instances, he employed the "anarchist" or radical clause of the law, but he also made a drive against vagrants and the unemployed, as well as those here illegally.

Early in my regime at the Island, New York's Alien Squadron of the Police Department accompanied by ambitious Immigration Inspectors detailed by Secretary Doak to Ellis Island for the grand clean-up, entered a Finnish dance hall in Harlem and locked the doors behind them. The celebrating Finns were lined up against the walls, searched, and surprised by star-chamber proceedings, and all who could not convince the excited officers that they were in the country legally were arrested.

A repetition of the performance occurred at the Seamen's Home on South Street. Seamen, many of whom claimed to be American citizens and some of whom were later released, were jerked from their beds and taken to Ellis Island.

It was my duty under my oath of office to enforce the law. The deportation of admitted and proven anarchists and those here illegally was mandatory and I had no power of discretion in these matters.

But about the time these wholesale deportations began, thousands of persons throughout the country began to turn their eyes towards their native lands. In many cases, where the radical or voluntary deportee left Ellis Island for home with a smile, I was reminded of an instance reported to me by Interpreter McClennan who had been on the Island for many years.

"Two Scots," he told me one day, "both born on the banks of the Clyde, were arrested as anarchists, shortly after we deported John Turner.

"A large number of Poles had arrived in Glasgow about 1910 and 1911 to work in the ship yards. They had preached anarchy to the Scots, many of whom had been converted.

"When the Immigration Service had picked up the two Scots for making radical speeches out West, they were deported. Times were hard in America that year and many Scotchmen wanted to go home. A considerable number became anarchists over night to save passage money. That was the only time we ever had the trouble of trying to disprove that aliens were anarchists."

Under the law of 1917, any alien in the United States less than three years, who can prove that he is destitute, may be deported at government expense. About two hundred applications per month were coming in to Ellis Island from those in this category. In many cities, Detroit for instance, municipal authorities coöperated with immigration inspectors to bring about such deportations.

But these cases were not without their problems, because of the difficulty of obtaining passports for vagrants, no country desiring them, and because many of the aliens had American wives or husbands.

The table below illustrates the changing tide of immigration brought about by the depression:

	1928	1929	1930	1931	1932	1933
Immigration	307,255	279,678	241,700	97,139	35,576	23,068
Emigration	77,457	69,203	50,661	61,882	103,295	127,660

I was to witness during my administration in the year 1932 the actual changing of the tide—the first year in more than a hundred years when more people had left our shores than were arriving in the dwindling caravan.

And instead of humanizing the reception accorded those who came to cast their lots in our country, my problem was to exercise eternal vigilance in order that no injustice be perpetrated in the treatment of the thousands being returned to their native countries, and also those who were saying voluntary farewells. Deportation was the big business at Ellis Island.

Chapter III

AMERICA'S LAST LONG MILE

Deportation problems of every description awaited me from my first day at the Island.

An hour or two before our Christmas concert, I learned that our program, in addition to being broadcast over a national radio network, was to be transmitted by short waves for the reception of listeners in foreign countries.

Broadcasting officials had requested that, when preparing my brief greeting to the several thousand visitors who were expected in our auditorium, I arrange to say something to the international audience.

The hour for the concert was nearing, and already most of the available seats had been filled, when finally I found time to work on the address I was to deliver. Our guest artists from the Metropolitan Opera Company and the National Broadcasting Company were arriving and, of course, I had to greet them. I had not had time to take so much as a look into the auditorium and had spoken to no member of my staff concerning the number of aliens who would be at the concert.

I was finishing the address when a friend came into the office and threw one of the printed programs down upon the desk before me.

"Look at that!" he said in evident astonishment.

I glanced at the line he indicated: "Given by the Fellow Countrymen of those Immigrants who wait at our Gates."

"What is the matter with that?" I asked, surprised at his question.

"Simply this," he whispered. "I've just come from a look-in on the Deportation Division. There are only three immigrants on the Island—but I have just seen the guards march nearly two hundred deportees into the concert room."

For a moment I was perplexed as to what I should say to him, but finally the words came to me. "It's Christmas, after all," I countered. "In that group of deportees you will find every conceivable type of alien—criminals, repatriates, vagrants who became public charges because of the depression. And, moreover, many of them are being sent to the lands of their birth although they no longer have relatives or friends there. I'll venture there are even some who cannot speak the language of the countries they are going to.

"Do you think it will hurt them any to hear the songs of their native lands? Why, it may even do something for them—it may make their going easier and happier."

"I hadn't thought about it that way," was my friend's reply.

But when I faced that audience and the microphone, when I was telling the unseen audience in foreign lands how their countries had contributed to the upbuilding of America, I must confess that I felt a tinge of shame. And over and over the words dinned in my ears, "What a Christmas present! Deportation!"

Now that I am no longer at the Island and can speak more freely, I must confess that the duties of deportation were never very pleasant to me and often very bitter. Our deportation laws are inexorable and in many cases inhuman, particularly as they apply to men and women of honest behavior whose only crime is that they dared enter the promised land without conforming to law. I have seen hundreds of such persons forced back to the countries they came from, penniless, and at times without coats on their backs. I have seen families separated, never to be reunited—mothers torn from their children, husbands from their wives, and no one in the United States, not even the President himself, able to prevent it.

Especially marked was the element of tragedy in the cases of alien criminals. Certainly no one condones the acts of those who waste their lives in crime, and I am strong in the conviction that our doors should be shut tight to those who have shown their inability to conduct themselves as American citizens.

But often I have felt a qualm at signing the deportation order of the alien who came to America as a mere baby and became a criminal in the environment and under conditions in which he was compelled to live in our country.

The old law with regard to alien criminals provided that any alien, no matter how short or long a time he might have lived in this country, who had been twice sentenced to terms of a year or more was deportable. A new law, passed in 1917, provided that aliens here less than five years were deportable if, during that time, they had been sentenced to a year or more in prison.

In one specific case we were trying to obtain a passport from the Polish Consul for a Pole who had come to America when he was two years old. At the age of fifty-two he was being deported for two crimes. A Polish official, commenting upon the request, remarked sagely:

"A two-year-old baby was sent to your country. You desire to send back in his place a fifty-two-year-old criminal."

The last long mile in America for the deportee is the trip in the Revenue Cutter from the Ellis Island wharf to the New York steamship dock where he is placed aboard the vessel which is to transport him back to his native land. And each time that I have seen one of these cutters leave our wharf I have thought of the story of the deposed Queen of Hawaii who was banished after the revolution there in 1892. She went down to the boat of deportation in tears and to the plaintive sounds of her followers singing Aloha Oe. But indeed her fate was more to be envied than that of the deportee leaving Ellis Island, for none is at the dock to sing or say good-bye.

In December of 1933 when the last Kline Deportation Special, the train which leaves San Francisco and crosses the continent picking

DEPORTEES AND REPATRIATES LEAVING THE TRANSCONTINENTAL TRAIN AT JERSEY CITY ON THEIR WAY TO ELLIS ISLAND, TO BE RETURNED TO THEIR NATIVE LANDS AT GOVERNMENT EXPENSE.

up criminals and others who are to be deported, had arrived, I went into the Deportation Division to have a look at those in detention. On that morning I knew about two hundred were being sent out, and I desired to talk with them, for they all knew that as Commissioner at Ellis Island I had had absolutely no hand in having them brought to us.

In the great chamber, which has a tiled floor and barred windows, I saw before me a cross section of all the races in the world. And curiously enough, but as I already knew, I found that many of them were like men condemned to die, praying and crying for last-minute reprieves—clinging to fraying threads of hope. At frequent intervals I saw them approaching the guards with frantic pleas. Few if any of them knew my identity.

"I know a friend of Senator ——," one alien began with emphatic desperation. "If you'll only get word to him he'll save me——"

"I've got to find Guy Lombardo, the orchestra leader," one of them said. "We went to school together as kids in Canada."

"I want to make a bond," declared a young Italian. "It doesn't make any difference about me—it's on my mother's account. Can't you understand? She's sick, I tell you! I've got to stay with her till after Christmas. Oh! This will kill her!"

Up and down the center of the room a young Finn, said to be a hold-up man and narcotic addict, was pacing. He walked perhaps fifty feet, wheeled about and repeated the process at a high rate of speed, never looking to right or left, never speaking or moving a muscle of his face.

And, in strange contrast, over in another corner a placid group of Orientals remained silently apart from all the others, their eyelids drooping, their religion telling them that life is an eternity in which there is time for everything and in which Ellis Island is merely a record of a minute. To the left of them, two Spaniards but recently out of Dannemora prison were weaving fantastic pillow cases. A Javanese seaman, picked up along the New York waterfront for stabbing a comrade, and now fresh from Sing Sing, was spending his time contriving a black and white checkered belt from thin, narrow thongs of leather. At a long table a group of South African stowaways were playing cards and muttering savage gibberish as they played. Sitting nearby, but paying no attention to them, was a youngster with strange glittering eyes. Something about him intrigued me and I decided to speak with him.

"I'm going to Ireland," he answered in reply to my usual question.

"Been here long?" I asked.

"When my parents died in Canada," he replied, "I was a kid. And not having anybody there I just walked across the border. I got a job soon and never thought anything about any papers."

"What did they get you for?" I asked.

"Pinched me one night on the street in Los Angeles," he answered. "Panhandling. But I had to. I haven't had a job since the depression started. I don't know anybody in Ireland. Do you think if I got in touch with the Catholic Church—do you think they might stop this?"

I shook my head gravely. It was a pathetic case. I did not wonder that the boy had panhandled if he had been starving.

Even more tragic than any of the others was the next group I saw isolated from the rest. One of them was a young man in his early twenties, who wore a large black hat, a tan rain coat, and a conspicuous vermilion tie. He sat awhile, then stood up and stared. Next to him was the hulk of a gigantic man who looked vacuously about the room. They and the group huddled around them, all under special guard, were the insane.

I said good-by to the Irish lad. As I walked past the table where cigarettes are sold the guard who was with me spoke to a handsome youngster from Sweden.

"What are they sending you out for?"

"Robbery," the Swede replied hoarsely. "What else could I do? I had nothing to eat."

"Glad to go home?"

"Of course not. I'd rather be in jail than go out like this."

I next spoke with a young English woman and her daughter, both being repatriated, then to a group of seventeen Persians being sent home by the City of Detroit. I chatted briefly with a polished East Indian swindler, and then I saw something on the wall which arrested my attention. It was a perfect drawing of the NRA Blue Eagle. Under it the alien artist had lettered: "We Didn't Do Our Part."

Above the din of conversation the voice of a guard rose:

"Leondruggi! Zeligowski! Smith! Breitenstein! Rostoff! Kalif Said Ali! . . . Get your baggage!"

The roll call was on. It was the beginning of the last long mile in America.

Deportations in wholesale quantities, the purging of the caravan of its undesirables, stories of humor and pathos are by no means confined to modern times. From the earliest days of Federal regulation of immigration and in the first records of those days they are to be found.

In most cases, except the repatriations, aliens are generally found to be humiliated at the deportation procedure. In the case of repatriations, it has usually been the custom for steamships to carry up to ten of these aliens gratis. The consuls generally have limited funds. Vagrants are sent back by the United States at a cost of about ninety dollars each.

To save unfair and unwarranted deportations, a law was passed in 1929 providing that any alien here illegally before 1921, and otherwise a desirable member of the community, might register at the Island and so legalize his status. Many took advantage of this privilege.

Uncle Sam had five boarders in Europe for years. These were insane persons who were legally deported but were not received by their respective native countries. Because it cost less to keep them in Europe, the United States government paid their board in foreign institutions for twenty years.

In the early summer of 1893 a young concert singer from the

musically famous city of Vienna attracted no little attention from Ellis Island. Miss Martha Heur arrived one July afternoon on the *Augusta Victoria*. She was registered for the passage as Mrs. Max Lindenbaum, her alleged husband accompanying her on the journey. In examining her for entry, inspectors became suspicious, and under interrogation she confessed that her real name was Martha Heur and that she was a concert singer from the music halls of Vienna.

Martha had no money of her own and the Ellis Island officials disbelieved Lindenbaum, who vociferously asserted that he would marry her. It was finally decided, after three weeks of publicity for Martha, and the offer of a New York music hall to engage her at a salary of one hundred dollars per week, that she should be deported. Hundreds of those in detention broke into tears as she sang a good-by song in German before guards came to take her to the steamship *Normania*.

I can find only one record of a deportee who ever actually profited to any appreciable financial extent from his stay at Ellis Island.

Miji Cogic, who arrived in pre-War days, actually spent five years and five months in detention at the Island. He reached the Island on August 8, 1914, and was ordered deported because of defective eyesight. But the War prevented his going back to Austria. Since he had to remain at Ellis Island because there was no place to send him, he commenced to work at his two trades, that of tailor and that of barber. What he spent from his earnings was never determined, but he actually saved $495. After he had been deported, Superintendent Baker estimated that because the Austro-American Line which had brought Cogic from Trieste had gone out of business and his expenses could not be recovered in the legal way, Cogic's visit to the Island had actually cost Uncle Sam $2,046.

The old contract labor laws were the direct cause of many pathetic cases of deportation, cases where poor laborers on the other side had mortgaged their homes, borrowed or collected the last available penny of family funds to come to America. Having already been engaged by responsible persons or firms in America at salaries which promised financial independence, the immigrant felt secure in spending his last cent for clothes and passage. For the contract he had obtained was to provide him with a steady job at what he thought were enormous wages. But his dream faded when, upon reaching Ellis Island, the canny inspectors wormed out of him that he had a good job waiting here in the United States. With great pride he perhaps exhibited the actual contract, only to find that it rang the death knell of his hopes to enter the country.

Back in December, 1895, a group of Swiss artists met a fate similar to this. The ship *La Normandie* entered New York harbor at daybreak. A part of its cargo was a shipment of decorative materials consigned from a Swiss firm to an express company.

At quarantine the vessel was boarded by contract labor inspectors. James McKim of the inspection service noted the presence of the second cabin passengers, Otto Webber, Gustave Kauncher, Ludwig Fischer, Jacob Wehland and Pens Doublin. All were from Basle. McKim grew suspicious but gained little by his interrogations. He felt justified, however, in taking the group to Ellis Island.

A subsequent examination disclosed that all the men had been brought here under contract to the Swiss firm which sold the decorative materials to a wealthy American with a home on Park Avenue. The materials had been purchased during a visit to Switzerland with the understanding that the firm send native artisans to accompany them for the purpose of decorating the house.

It was learned that the men were to work for six, eight, and twelve francs per day. But, notwithstanding the evidence which clearly showed the laborers were to toil for a firm not having headquarters in the United States, they were deported.

One can imagine the frustration of those who reach the grim red buildings at Ellis Island and view the farther shore which they will never be allowed to visit. They are confined behind barred windows in the very shadow of the Statue of Liberty. Although their disappointment is understandable, it is difficult to believe that any of them would actually take their own lives rather than be sent home again.

Lorenzo di Renzo could not have known that there was to be a World War when he came to America in July of 1914. And certainly in the light of the events now so well remembered he would not have become a public charge, for jobs became plentiful one month after he killed himself. The young Italian was barely twenty-four, but he had been ordered deported on the grounds that he might become a public charge. The Ellis Island guards had taken him to the French liner *Lorraine* on the night of July 7. On the morning of July 8, a few moments before the vessel sailed, he told comrades that he would rather die than go back to Italy after the vows he had taken to become a success in America. So saying he drew forth a revolver and ended his life.

Perhaps fully as tragic as death have been some of the separations caused by deportation. Old-timers at the Island recall the case of Clara Schmitzky and her two children. Mrs. Schmitzky and her children arrived August 13, 1904. The 13th proved to be her unlucky day.

Frail and weak, practically a dwarf and afflicted with curvature of the spine, Mrs. Schmitzky was unable to pass the medical examination.

While she was in detention, her husband, Maurice, haunted the Island, prowling distractedly about the buildings. The case was appealed to Washington and every effort was made by the Hebrew Immigration Aid Society to prevent a separation of the family. For Maurice Schmitzky had been here nearly two years and had established a home for his wife on Rivington Street in New York.

When Mrs. Schmitzky had been ordered excluded and the order had been affirmed she sat in the "excluded room," nervous but with a brave attempt at dignity. "I look very poorly now," she told one of the newspaper reporters, "because I have had such a long journey, and such a long stay here. But I am really in perfect health." She pushed her two toddlers forward. "You see," she said, "I am perfectly able to bear children."

Less sympathy was evident at the Island for another Russian.

And not even the records can be found, since her name was never made public.

Gabriel Essipoff is the name of the man who was deported with her. He was supposed to be a wealthy merchant of St. Petersburg, now Leningrad. She was the runaway wife of a Russian General. They were sent away from the United States on the ship *La Savoie*.

It was definitely authenticated at the time that the young woman who came with Essipoff on the *König Albert* from Gibraltar in 1906 was not only the wife of a Russian General, but also a close friend of the late Czar Nicholas.

News of the clandestine meetings of the two had reached the ears of the General after their associations in St. Petersburg had become common gossip. And after a quarrel with him, the wife disappeared. When it became known that Essipoff, too, had dropped from sight, the infuriated Russian General started upon a long hunt for the elopers.

They were traced to Paris, Vienna, Berlin, Lisbon and Madrid. The General arrived at Gibraltar a few moments after the *König Albert* had borne them away from those rock-bound shores. And before the vessel was a hundred miles upon its journey the Russian Consulate in New York had received a cable message. Orders were sent to hold the couple at Ellis Island. Commissioner Watchorn received a telephone call and reporters spotted Essipoff reaching the pier of the North German Lloyd at the same time as Nicholas Lodygensky, Russian Consular General.

After a conference in the ship's cabin a tug boat was ordered, and Watchorn, Lodygensky, and a Marine Hospital surgeon escorted Essipoff and the beautiful Russian woman of mystery to the French Line where they were put aboard the *Savoie*.

The Russian Consul refused to give the name of the woman, and Commissioner Watchorn would not discuss the deportation. Such latitude and such a muzzling of the press would never have been countenanced in recent years of immigration administration. And the withholding of the woman's name is in strange contrast to the treatment of those poorer and less fortunate ones who have been apprehended under similar circumstances and given an international brand of shame.

In my own time at Ellis Island the detention case which afforded the most amusement and certainly the greatest degree of satisfaction to certain Americans was that of a noted saxophone player.

It seems that the crime for which this saxophone player was deported (other than saxophone playing) was that of bigamy. And strange to say, when he was first indicted, there appeared in the courtroom to confront him, not just his first legal wife who had brought the suit, but other women, all insisting that they too had entered into the relationship of marriage with the defendant. As was to be expected, he was convicted. On the night before he was deported from Ellis Island, he entertained the others who were in detention quarters at the same time, by walking up and down the floor and playing Victor Herbert's celebrated musical composition: "Ah, Sweet Mystery of Life."

One of the strangest and most pathetic deportation cases to be found in the records was that of a little Russian girl who evaded the law on account of the World War.

Paula Patton, in her native tongue called Pesche Pitum, came to the United States on the S.S. *Bavaria* in July, 1914. She was accompanied by her mother, Ettel Pitum, and the two other Pitum children, Yoine and Riwke. The father, Chaim Pitum, had been in the country two years and was working as a huckster at Olean, New York. He testified in the hearing before a Board of Special Inquiry that he owned a horse and wagon worth two hundred dollars, and a stock of junk worth one hundred and fifty dollars, and that after defraying the expenses of his family to America he had twenty-five dollars in cash.

The child Paula was believed by the examiners at the Island to be mentally and physically deficient, and because of the father's circumstances it was held that she was likely to become a public charge.

The entire family, with the exception of the father, was ordered deported. Prominent citizens of Olean, New York, had vouched for the father.

The mother's brother was engaged in the mercantile business at Olean. While not a wealthy man, he was in comfortable financial circumstances, and readily agreed to make a bond whereby the family, which had come all the way from Russia with high hopes of making a start in the new land, might be admitted. The immigration officials, however, ordered Paula and the others deported on July 9, 1914.

Through the Hebrew Shelter and Immigrant Aid Society, the case was appealed to the Secretary of Labor. The appeal was sustained, it being granted that all but Paula might enter, and an attendant was provided by the Pitums to take the nine year old Paula back to Russia. On July 30 the child was placed aboard the *President Grant* of the Hamburg-American Line. The ship had already put out to sea when a stay of deportation came from Washington, but fate again interceded for Paula. The World War broke out and the *President Grant* was ordered back to port.

On August 6, 1914, the Department at Washington granted Paula's admission under bond on the guarantee that she would be sent out of the country at the end of one year or sooner if directed, and on the further condition that she be placed in an institution.

On December 15, 1914, it was reported to the Ellis Island authorities that the child was attending the public school at Olean. This was contrary to the conditions of her admission and a further investigation was begun.

"Her physical condition," wrote the Medical Inspector of Olean city schools, "has improved very much, and she is doing well learning the English language. The father is an industrious workman and is providing the family with a good home for a laboring man's family. It is clean and neat and the children are well-dressed and seem happy."

But the officer in charge at Ellis Island hewed to the line of duty, and wrote the Commissioner General at Washington on January 14 that Paula was not in an institution and that the other conditions of her bond were not being fulfilled. On receiving the reply from Washington which directed him to proceed, the Acting Commissioner wrote the Illinois Surety Company of Chicago to demand that the conditions of Paula's bond be carried out.

The Surety Company countered with doctors' certificates and statements which insisted that the treatment Paula had received for the past six months had been more beneficial than she could have obtained in an institution for the deficient.

Finally on February 2, 1915, the Department agreed to Paula's remaining at home and declined to take any action upon her bond. The pressure from neighbors and leading citizens of Olean had been fully exerted at Washington. But in July of the same year, the Department requested a new bond guaranteeing Paula's departure in one year. This new bond was executed by Julius Harris, the child's merchant uncle. The last report up to our entry into the World War was made on July 26, 1916, and was to the effect that the child was improving in every way and showed every evidence of the beneficial results of care and education.

No action was taken on the case until the close of the War. On August 6, 1919, however, the child was ordered to submit to a hearing on the ground that she was residing in the country illegally.

Surely anyone can visualize that scene in the Pitum cottage at Olean. Paula was fourteen years old. Her mind and body had improved during the five years in America. There was no question of her becoming a public charge. The very fact that she was afflicted had endeared her not only to every member of her family, but to practically every resident of the little city of Olean. The entire town went "to the bat" for her. It seemed a travesty that she might be snatched from her mother's protecting care and sent back to Russia where she had no relatives or friends—she, who so needed her family. The hearing day found all the Pitums again in distress.

The father was the first to testify. He told of the care which Paula had been receiving and of how she had been provided for in every way. He also testified as to his own financial progress and the sacrifice all were making in the hope that the little girl might be left in America.

"She has no relatives in Russia that I know of," he said. "At the time they came, my wife had two sisters there. One sister went to Germany to live. The other, married to Nuchem Vogel, remained in Russia. They lived in Kovno. Then the Germans invaded Russia; the family removed to a small village. Afterwards the husband went back to Kovno to see whether he could save any of his property. He was not permitted to leave, and the village where he had left his wife and children was entirely destroyed and he never found out what had become of them. He was then sent to Siberia.

"My wife received one letter from him, telling what had happened to the family and asking for help. We sent some money to the address given and a long time afterward this money was returned to us, since it was impossible to locate the man. We have heard neither from him nor his family since. Nor have we ever heard from the other sister, Fanny Lewin, who was in Koenigsberg, ill and in a hospital there. We do not know whether they are living or dead."

"Have you ever declared your intention of becoming a citizen of the United States?" the immigration inspector asked Pitum.

"I am a citizen," was the reply, and Pitum produced his citizenship papers, also evidence to show that he was worth four thousand, five hundred dollars and was applying for a ten thousand dollar life insurance policy.

"She has no one to go to in Russia," he went on pathetically. "She might better be thrown in the ocean. I intend to take care of her and leave things so that she will always have enough money to take care of herself. I wish always to remain here with my family. I have bought Liberty Bonds and War Savings Stamps and am loyal to America."

For the next two years Paula Pitum was Ellis Island's football. Like the sword of Damocles the threat of deportation was a constant shadow over the Pitum cottage at Olean. And at last, in the spring of 1921, the child was ordered arrested for the purpose of being sent back to Russia. On June 9, six days before the order of deportation was effective, the Assistant Commissioner at Ellis Island, in answer to a protest from Olean that Paula's uncle was in Europe and that she be permitted to remain until his return, informed the Pitums that "unless otherwise directed," the order must be carried out.

Allen J. Hastings, Olean attorney for the Pitums, countered by pointing out the section of the law whereby an alien filing a declaration of intention of becoming an American citizen is permitted to bring in children "who will not endanger other persons."

On June 30, Washington stayed deportation and ordered a medical examination of Paula, and on July 21, Washington wired Ellis Island as follows:

"By direction Assistant Secretary re-examination Paula Pitum to be had at Ellis Island. If still feeble-minded deport at once. Attorney Hastings requested to arrange delivery of alien at your port."

July 25, Washington writes "to stay deportation until otherwise ordered even though still feeble-minded."

On August 10, 1921, a medical board affirmed Paula's mental deficiency, but thirteen days later for some mysterious reason Washington wired a release.

Almost two years passed in which nothing transpired. The Assistant Commissioner, on January 6, 1923, wrote the Bureau at Washington reminding it of the release, and asking what disposition should be made of the warrants in the Ellis Island files. On February 17, the Second Assistant Secretary of Labor replied that the warrants should be held because of a bill pending in Congress to legalize the status of a group of defective aliens. On April 10, 1923, the Assistant Commissioner at Ellis Island wrote Washington:

"Since bill failed of passage she should be deported immediately," and on April 23, Washington ordered deportation without further delay. A few days later the child Paula was again brought to Ellis Island.

On April 28, the Department refused to stay deportation proceedings, precipitating such a tempest in Olean as had never before been seen in one immigration case.

The alien's family suggested "sterilization". Congressman Daniel A. Reed intervened, and the Commissioner at Ellis Island informed the irate citizens of Olean that leaving the child in America after reporting others in a similar category would disqualify him as an honest government official.

Mrs. L. M. Homley, one of the Olean neighbors of the child, wrote to Ellis Island:

In the winter her mother broke her arm and Paula kept house, cooked and did everything just as well as anyone could. We have here in Olean a very prominent citizen, who has a daughter that is afflicted the same way as Paula, and if anyone were to say that his daughter were feeble-minded he would be very indignant. Our country boasts of liberty and justice to all, and you as a high official would want to maintain that standard, and see that justice was done for the little girl.

On May 12, 1923, the Pitums obtained a writ of *habeas corpus,* but Judge Francis A. Winslow dismissed the writ. The Pitums on July 20 appealed to the U. S. Circuit Court. But in March, 1924, the order was affirmed with a sixty-day delay of the mandate. On September 13, 1924, the case went to the United States Supreme Court and a writ of certiorari was issued.

On February 18, 1925, the Bureau at Washington directed Ellis Island to leave Paula permanently in the United States under a three thousand dollar bond, a condition being that her surety furnish Ellis Island with a report upon her every six months. And this case has been reported to Ellis Island every six months since that time. All told, the case has consumed twenty years and, to my way of thinking, provides one of the most interesting examples of government vacillation to be found in all the annals of Uncle Sam. But the tragic side is to be found in the shadow which has hung over the Pitum home in Olean.

On first consideration the government may be severely criticized, but it must be remembered that the case was handled by many different people, different administrations and under mandatory laws. In the end justice was tempered with mercy.

CHAPTER IV

LISTENING TO REMINISCENCES

TALKING with members of the executive staff after lunch in the Commissioner's dining room, or riding to and from the day's work on the little ferry boat that plied between lower Manhattan and Ellis Island, I heard many interesting tales from men who had spent most of their lives in the Immigration Service.

Hundreds of stories might be told here, for every outstanding case left behind its memories for those who handled it; but perhaps the three outstanding episodes, which remain in the minds of all who were in the service when they occurred, dealt with neither individual cases nor immigrant groups. Instead, they arose from circumstances and conditions beyond the control of immigration officials. They occurred in the following order:

> The Fire of 1897
> The Communipaw Explosion of 1911
> The Black Tom Explosion of 1916

The fire of June 15, 1897, from Uncle Sam's standpoint, was the most destructive of all the calamities which have befallen Ellis Island. The property loss resulting from the burning of the original buildings amounted to approximately $750,000. Fortunately no lives were lost.

The fire was discovered at 12:30 A.M. There were two hundred persons on the Island, including immigrants in the detention pen, invalids in the hospital, attendants, nurses and watchmen. Five or six boats were always kept at the Island and by quick work all were brought to the Barge Office.

Fire boats and tugs surrounded the Island as soon as the fire was discovered from the lookout of the Harbor Police Station at the Battery, but the thin streams of water they were able to furnish had slight effect upon the Georgia pine buildings.

It is reported that the fire burned and spread as though the expansive landing sheds had been covered with oil, while trails of fire ran along the rain gutters and spread from point to point, licking up and down the trellis work.

New York rushed twenty policemen to keep order among the panic-stricken immigrants, and soon these were followed by thirty reserves.

From all parts of New York, nearby Jersey, and Brooklyn, people gathered to view the great fire. When it was learned that the blaze was sweeping Ellis Island and that all the immigrants were safe, the comment in the crowds was said to be,

"It's a great show—and after all, Uncle Sam can afford it."

The most disastrous loss, more to be deplored than the destruction of the buildings, was the burning of the records. From the immigrants' point of view, however, nothing was so important as the loss of their baggage. All the sixty-one immigrants awaiting examination swore that they had lost in the fire many more dollars than the law requires for entry, and the government simply had to take their word for it. If reports of the contents of this lost luggage could be believed, on that tragic night a boatload of millionaire immigrants were being lodged on Ellis Island.

Losses to the money changers were very great. Of these only one found his safe intact the next morning, and the ten thousand dollars placed there the day before were found to be wet but not destroyed. Other safes throughout the Island had burst.

Not three hundred yards away were government ammunition

ELLIS ISLAND BEFORE THE FIRE WHICH DESTROYED SO MANY BUILDINGS THAT A NEW PLAN FOR IMPROVE-MENT WAS MADE POSSIBLE.

boats loaded with powder. If the wind had been blowing in their direction, the tale told next morning might have been far more terrible.

The newspapers reported many amusing incidents.

A certain Joseph Rozinsky escaped in his underwear, and was seen next day wandering about the Barge Office in a pair of blue overalls, a coat discarded by a priest, and a pair of worn carpet-slippers, all bestowed upon him by the missionaries. Six Hindus, who got away in their gorgeous robes but forgot their shoes, were plunged into the depths of despair, until they were given assorted tan footwear.

A young couple from Leipert, Saxony, were forced to postpone their impending wedding and remain at the Barge Office until they could receive more money from home. Because the groom, a divorced man, had found legal difficulties in the way of his new marriage in Europe, the two had brought over from the old country a trousseau and a complete outfit for immediate housekeeping. All was destroyed, and they sat down woefully to wait for remuneration from their relatives in Saxony.

The New York *World* commented in blistering terms on the liability of the government for the disaster:

"If a private individual or corporation had put up huge buildings of inflammable pine on a little island in the bay, and had kept there as many as three thousand, five hundred persons from all over the earth, public opinion would have risen in its might. But the U. S. Government did it."

Other newspapers took up the cudgels and the federal authorities were thoroughly berated.

On July 1, 1897, two weeks after the fire, President William McKinley went before Congress with a recommendation that six hundred thousand dollars be appropriated to replace the destroyed structures with fireproof buildings. The present structures are the result of his recommendation.

An explosion of dynamite took place at Pier 7, Communipaw, within a few hundred feet of the New York Central Railroad ferry house, on the afternoon of February 1, 1911, shaking New York and New Jersey over a forty-mile radius, causing several thousand dollars worth of damage at Ellis Island, and by a strange quirk of fate narrowly missing the destruction of several hundred immigrants.

An unknown number of men near the dynamite, including members of the crew, were killed and hundreds were injured. Thousands of windows were broken in lower Manhattan and Jersey City, while first examinations at Ellis Island indicated a property damage which could not be estimated.

At noon, men were transferring boxes of dynamite from the boat, *Whistle,* to cars at the end of the pier. The Norwegian ship, *Ingrid,* was discharging a cargo of bone at the same time. Several lighters were moored nearby and more than half of them were destroyed by the explosion.

According to the records, all lower Manhattan was in a turmoil, and the shock was felt as far north as Columbia University. The pier also contained a long train of cars, every one of which was damaged. Two hundred buildings in lower Manhattan were rocked to the point of imperilling their occupants. No licenses had been issued for the moving of the dynamite, and seven officers of the New York Central and DuPont Powder Company (owners of the *Whistle*) were arrested.

Coming as it did, at noontime, the complete destruction of all the immigrants at Ellis Island was prevented. If the explosion had happened thirty minutes sooner or later, the chances are that all immigrants, who had just filed from the big detention room to the lunch room, would have been killed. Immigration was heavy in that year, and it is certain that there would have been many casualties.

It was a clear day, but with the first explosion, muddy rain water swept up from the bay, stains from which never came off the clothing of those exposed to the deluge. The residue showered down upon the Island, and all the hospital attendants and nurses in white uniforms were covered with the black smudge. Iron-framed windows were blown in, and the entire north side of the administration building was also blown inward.

Arms and legs of the crew of the *Whistle* were scattered over the Island after the catastrophe and the grounds and buildings, covered with debris and the effects of the "muddy rain," presented an appalling spectacle.

My secretary at the Island still bears hand scars which were made by flying glass when the window at which she was typing came tumbling in.

Mr. Theis, superintendent of the hospital, in discussing the explosion, recalled that still another explosion occurred in the bay in the late nineties.

"At that time," he informed me, "the old hospital kitchen extended out over the dock. The explosion caused a schooner to break loose from its moorings and the bowsprit of the ship crashed into the Ellis Island kitchen. A colored woman then employed as a cook turned several shades whiter.

" 'Doctor! Doctor!' she cried in panic, 'the ship is in the kitchen!' "

The Black Tom Explosion, however, furnished a night of horror which eclipses any other disaster which ever befell Ellis Island.

This terrific calamity did not cause the loss of a single life on the Island proper, but when viewed in retrospect it assumes the formidable proportions of a holocaust and one wonders at the narrow margin by which the Island itself escaped complete upheaval and demolition.

A series of explosions, occurring on fourteen barges at the piers of the National Storage Company on Black Tom River, New Jersey, a few hundred yards from Ellis Island, began about two o'clock on the morning of July 30, 1916.

The explosions originated in powder and shells which were being stored upon the barges preparatory to being towed down the bay and transferred to a Russian ship which would transport them to Russia for use in the World War. It has since been definitely established by a Department of Justice hearing in Baltimore that the explosions were the direct result of German espionage, and the perpetrator of the deed confessed to it a few years ago. At the time it was believed that sparks from two freight cars caused the ignition of the munitions.

A great pillar of fire lit up the sky, according to press reports of the following day, and thousands of persons hurried toward the neighborhood.

The first explosions caused the wrecking of the National Storage plant and the burning of seven warehouses, together with the shattering of practically all the glass between Manhattan's Battery and Fourteenth Street, and most of the glass in the nearby cities of New Jersey.

The explosions, resembling the sound of big guns, came intermittently and in a succession which lasted several hours. Every available ambulance in New York and Jersey City was rushed to the scene, and an hour later they and the police ambulances had carried dozens of injured persons to the hospitals. Thousands of dollars worth of merchandise, protected only by plate glass windows which had been shattered, was exposed to the looting of vandals.

On Ellis Island proper the panic was unprecedented. According to Superintendent Theis, who was then an assistant superintendent at the hospital and an eye witness of the entire Black Tom tragedy, nothing nearer a "hell on earth" could be imagined.

"About midnight," he informed me, "a watchman, after his tour of duty, reported to the Hospital Superintendent that there was a big fire on Black Tom.

"I got up and looked out of the window at the mounting mass of flames above the four-story brick piers. The whole sky was transformed into an inferno pierced by deafening explosions and the detonation of shells.

"The tide was coming in, and a west wind carried the fire toward the barges moored at the Black Tom wharves. Suddenly I saw that the barges, which had been moored by the usual hemp rope, had caught fire and were exploding as they drifted toward Ellis Island.

Already the Ellis Island windows had been broken, the doors had been jammed inward, and parts of the roofs had collapsed.

"Acting in conjunction with my associates, I hastened to assist in the removal of our insane patients to the tennis courts. We wrapped them in blankets and carried them out into the open air.

"When we had them out of doors, they presented one of the most extraordinary spectacles I have ever seen. As the five-inch shells flared over the Island like skyrockets, the poor demented creatures clapped their hands and cheered, laughed and sang and cried, thinking it was a show which had been arranged for their particular amusement.

"The immigrants became panicky and were finally loaded upon the ferry and taken to the Barge Office amid scenes of wildest disorder.

"We thought for a time that the final explosion had occurred. Then we learned that the barges which had floated against the Island and set fire to the sea wall were loaded with munitions. It was then that we who had to care for the patients first realized to what extent our own lives were in danger. Fortunately the heroism of those who manned the tugs of the Lehigh Valley Railroad saved us. They towed the two flaming barges out to sea, where they sank amid concussions which sounded like the end of the world.

"While the explosions were taking place over this period of several hours, the Island was becoming a depository for flaming debris. The New York Fire Department was on the Island stretching hose and putting out fires at every hand. It was not safe to permit anyone inside the buildings. Then came the second and most terrific explosion of all. It lasted about fifteen minutes and ended the series.

"We bivouacked on the tennis court for the rest of the night, vainly trying to pacify the insane who were disappointed that the show was over. At 7:00 A.M. we cleaned up and returned the patients to the hospital.

"The miracle was that no living thing was injured, except a cat—

Chief Clerk Sherman's office pet—who was cut by flying glass. The roof had been lifted from the administration building and smashed to smithereens. Only the work of the Lehigh Valley tug boats had saved us."

Three hundred and fifty-three immigrants were sleeping in the main building, according to the records, and ninety in the general hospital on Number 2 Island, with thirty-nine in the contagious diseases hospital on Number 3 Island, when the Black Tom catastrophe began. Besides the patients there were one hundred and twenty-five employees on duty. Two nurses and two patients were slightly cut, but not sufficiently to warrant serious concern. The immigrants taken to the Barge Office were not permitted to land and were returned after the explosion was over.

The following day, officials making a tour of inspection of Number 3 Island, found a rabbit owned by one of the nurses sitting on a case of powder, licking his pelt free of molasses which had covered him when a molasses can was overturned as he took flight.

The damage to Ellis Island amounted to seventy-five thousand dollars.

Superintendent P. J. Baker and Assistant Commissioner Byron H. Uhl have been on Ellis Island for approximately forty years. They have had their innings with lion tamers, freaks, fakers, fugitive potentates, radicals, masqueraders, criminals, the insane, and about every other group into which the mighty caravan of immigration has been divided. To hear them recall those flood-tide days was an ever increasing source of interest.

No matter how strange or unusual, there really is nothing entirely new under the sun. Dramatic episodes of the past were invariably reflected, at least in part, in many present-day chapters. Often these stories were merely interesting recounts of unusual adventures, but frequently, they shed a new light on an immediate problem and served as a model for future reference.

Mr. Baker delighted in tales of the problems of administration when thousands of immigrants were coming through the Island daily.

Persons afflicted with cholera, yellow fever, smallpox, typhus fever, leprosy and the plague have been separated from the bulk of immigration at Quarantine (Hoffman's Island) from the earliest days. But idiots, imbeciles, epileptics, the insane and those suffering from trachoma, have been weeded out of the stream only after reaching Ellis Island, and some of these have been detained for months and years before being deported.

The variety of diseases and disabilities among the aliens, some of which are curable, has always presented problems to the administration of the Island. Special foods are required and special care is given, irrespective of the immigrant's chances of ever reaching the farther shore.

At times there have been twenty-five or thirty races in detention at one time. The Italian cares nothing for the dried fish preferred by the Scandinavian, and the Scandinavian has no use for spaghetti. The Greek wants his food sweetened, and no one can make tea for an Englishman. The basis of all Asiatic and Malay food is rice, which they will mix with almost anything. The Chinese take to other foods but want rice in place of bread. The Mohammedans will eat no food across which the shadow of an infidel has fallen. And in big years it has been Superintendent Baker's problem to serve nine thousand meals per day, trying to please all.

Bread was bought at the rate of seven tons a day, both for these meals and for the box lunches formerly sold to immigrants departing for inland points. Those who did not buy box lunches usually found themselves at the mercy of grafters.

"What," I asked Superintendent Baker one day, "is the strangest case in your own recollection?"

"There are so many," he replied, "that it is almost impossible to remember the names and dates of the outstanding ones.

"Once, I remember, a young Italian girl arrived on a French ship.

She announced that she was on the way to her intended husband at Streator, Illinois.

"Of course we detained her until we could hear from her future husband, since Washington was very strict in those days.

"We requested the man in Streator to send affidavits as to his intentions and ability to provide for her. We permitted her to telegraph him under government supervision.

"A day or so after her detention a man appeared, saying he had come for her, and that he was her brother. The case was cited for Special Inquiry in order that a record might be made. It was apparent to me that the man who alleged he was her brother was an impostor, so she was further detained, pending receipt of the affidavits.

"The affidavits were received, and at the hearing she again expressed her desire to join her intended husband at Streator. Everything being in order and according to law, we admitted her. Two weeks passed and nothing had been heard, when a communication was received from the man in Streator claiming that his fiancée had not reached him.

"Since a railroad ticket to Streator had been furnished her, it was easy for one of our officers to trace her journey. He reported a few days later that she had detrained at Buffalo. It was also soon discovered that her ticket had not been used beyond that point. The officer next set out to locate the alleged brother. The man was found in Brooklyn, but he had married the girl the day before. The man in Streator had paid the freight for the other fellow.

"We finally learned that she had met the alleged brother at a steamship boarding house in Havre. He had taken a fast boat after they had fallen in love, so that he might comply with the technicalities of entrance into the country and be on hand to claim her after her own voyage on a slower boat. So far as I know the man in Streator is still waiting for a refund."

Fortunately for Superintendent Baker and Deputy Commissioner Uhl, their problems were simplified by the government policy of concessions. As early as April 11, 1893, we find it recorded that Anderson and Taffey bid $10,250 for the restaurant privilege, and that Frank Scully bid $5,520 for the privilege of keeping the money-changing counters. At that time all the leading railroads sold tickets at Ellis Island, but later this privilege was narrowed down to an Immigrant Clearing House of the Trunk Line Association.

The Trunk Line Association included the New York Central, West Shore, New York, Ontario and Western, Pennsylvania, Lehigh Valley, Erie, Delaware, Lackawanna and Western, B. and O. and the Central of New Jersey. Both the money-changing concession and the Trunk Line Association still operate in the big railroad room at Ellis Island.

In the flood-tide years the railroads got about fifty per cent of their business in cash and the other half in orders from the steamship companies. It was not uncommon for the ticket sellers to take in forty thousand dollars gross per day, which meant that, including the orders from the steamship companies, their day's business had amounted to eighty thousand dollars from tiny Ellis Island. The present joint agent, Benjamin Sprung, who came to the Island as an office boy, has held the job twenty-seven years.

Strangely enough, many of the aliens destined to points beyond New York, never saw the city. They were ferried to Jersey piers and there embarked for their destinations.

What a scene the old railroad room must have presented with aliens waiting all day for their tickets and hours of departure! What jabbering! Twelve men sold tickets at the windows, while linguists worked the floors separating the aliens into groups. The Germans were usually en route to Wisconsin, Illinois, North and South Dakota, there to work on the great northwestern farms.

The Hollanders and Germans always had the biggest families. Superintendent Baker recalls one Dutch family who paid nine full fares, eight half fares, and had three or four children too young to require any fares.

"The steamship companies", he recalled to me, "often advanced ten or fifteen dollars to aliens without money. And I have an idea they got most of it back."

On occasion it happened that women waiting for tickets would have babies born in the waiting room. Hurry calls would go forth to the hospital, and attendants with litters would come and carry them off. Others died in the waiting room; a few were murdered. It cost nine dollars to bury a dead alien.

Only the Jews, of all the races in the world, have a perfect record for burying and administering the last rites to their own dead from Ellis Island.

The railroad ticket business frequently caused repercussions in Superintendent Baker's office. Primarily, it was a concession, and as such was beyond his control except for his responsibility for supervising it along with other concessions in order to prevent or eliminate graft. The office now sells two hundred and fifty tickets a month, but there used to be that number in ten minutes. Each ticket seller had to have a number of languages at his command in order to ask the alien where he or she was going. Agent Sprung, then a ticket seller, could ask an alien where he was going in any language in the world except Chinese or Japanese, two which he could never master.

But the repercussions which fell upon Superintendent Baker were often the result of mistakes made by Sprung's men. Once fifteen Italians bound for Amsterdam Avenue in New York City wound up in Amsterdam, New York. The chief of police of that city wired:

"Get wise at Ellis Island. Fifteen Italians sent here want to go to Amsterdam Avenue, New York."

Sometimes the states were confused, as in the case of a party of Austrian laborers who got to Johnstown, Pennsylvania, when in reality they wanted to go to Johnstown, New York.

Once the leader of a group of Italians walked up to the window to buy a block ticket for himself and companions.

"Where are you going?" the ticket seller demanded in Italian.

"P-p-p-p-p-p-p-p—" stuttered the Italian in consternation and distress. Then he tried it again.

"P-p-p-p-p-poo-poo-poo-poo—"

But that was as far as he could get. Finally he reached into an inner pocket of his coat and produced a typed slip. The name of the town was Punxsutawney, Pennsylvania.

One immigrant in endeavoring to ask for a ticket to Detroit, Michigan, said something which was a variation of Detroit-a-Mich. Charley McCullock, the agent at the window, thought the alien had called him a dirty mick, and resented it.

In those days it cost thirteen dollars for a day coach ticket to Chicago. One morning about ten o'clock an elderly Jew with a flowing black beard and a skull cap arrived in the railroad waiting room with his family. The wife, who appeared to be about his own age, had her hair bound in a handkerchief in typically foreign fashion. There were ten children, and each carried a basket.

Approaching the old man, the interpreter questioned him: "Yiddish? Russian? Deutsch? Italiano? English?" There was no answer. Merely an imperturbable countenance and a shake of the head. At four o'clock in the afternoon the family still occupied the same bench. Finally someone thought of asking the old man if he spoke Gaelic. With a big smile he replied that he did, and the interpreter learned that he wanted to go to Chicago.

George O'Donnoghue, formerly of the Cashier's Office at the Island, which handled financial matters and maintained a depository for alien funds, always had difficulty with orthodox Jews who would not sign for the receipt of their money on holy days. They would wait until after sundown before accepting their money from our office.

"Some aliens were reluctant to admit that they had money for fear of being robbed. It turned out that one Greek, who claimed he had no money, was carrying over five thousand dollars on his person.

"Some would squander the money which relatives had sent to them in our care, while going to their destinations. On arrival they would contend that we had short-changed them, and soon we would receive threatening letters from attorneys. The cash business of our office was as high as five hundred thousand dollars monthly and for a time reached eight million dollars per year."

Individual cases frequently became such national storm centers that great groups of former immigrants interceded in behalf of the detained or rejected immigrant. As a rule the authorities at the Island were without discretionary authority and had to accept the mandate of the Department of Labor. But on occasion these cases were appealed to the President of the United States. For that reason the incumbent of the Presidency usually took great interest in the Island and its personnel.

Presidents Theodore Roosevelt, William Howard Taft and Woodrow Wilson all made personal visits to the Island in their times. Roosevelt arrived on a day so stormy that he had to be taken from the *Mayflower* and brought ashore in the launch, *Samoset,* at that time provided by the government for the personal use of Commissioner William Williams. It is said that President Roosevelt came in his usual breezy fashion with a swinging stride and smile for all. He had lunch, took a hurried excursion through the buildings, and went away.

The visit of President Taft was a bit more leisurely. He came, as did Roosevelt, accompanied by the usual bodyguard of Secret Service men, visited the buildings, peeped in at the immigrants and deportees in detention, and left again.

But Woodrow Wilson actually attended a hearing. It was on a day when a case of national interest was being decided. The press had worked up great sympathy for the immigrant. Accompanied by Mrs. Wilson, the then President-elect with some friends and Secret Service men filed into the hearing room. It is remembered that Wilson listened attentively to the testimony, but showed no evidence of sympathy and made no comment as he was leaving.

In my own time, Mrs. Franklin D. Roosevelt came to the Island shortly after the election of President Franklin D. Roosevelt. She smiled when someone called her attention to the fact that she was sitting under the picture of President Hoover, in my office.

Of all the staff at Ellis Island none is more apt in the unfolding of interesting narratives than Superintendent Theis of the hospital, who described for me the Black Tom Explosion. He tells one experience resulting from the law for the exclusion of those diseased with trachoma, which was passed in 1904.

"This loathsome disease," he told me one day, "was brought back to Europe by Napoleon's soldiers. In the late nineties and early nineteen hundreds there were so many cases of it, and so many deportations, that Congress specified it by name in the immigration laws.

"We discovered that a Hollander, a big powerful man with a large family, the youngest of which was a girl of fourteen, had contracted trachoma on the way over. The destination of the family was a town in Texas, and they had already purchased a ranch there on the recommendation of relatives who had preceded them. Everyone else in the family was well and admissible, and there was no question that any of them, because of their financial circumstances, might become public charges. The family was sent to Texas and the father was deported.

"Several years later a letter was received at the Island from the wife and mother of the children. She stated that she had never heard from her husband again, and bitterly denounced Ellis Island authorities for robbing the family of her husband and making her children fatherless. Our assumption was that the Hollander, during the voyage back, had jumped into the ocean."

Superintendent Theis also provided interesting recollections of the World War.

"On March 1, 1918," he told me, "the hospital was turned over to the Army. A part of the immigration building was turned over to the Navy. Ellis Island was known as Embarkation Number 1. The first wounded American soldiers were brought in one Sunday morning in May—one hundred and sixty-four of them. Many were shell-shock cases. Many were soldiers who had lost limbs or been otherwise maimed. It was horrible to hear them scream and moan. At one time we had six hundred and eighty-seven of them in the hospital.

"After the War, when the 1921 law was passed, we began to get a little of everything that Europe could send us. In 1921 we admitted 16,666 persons to the hospital, everything under the sun, but mostly starved persons who were glad to get something to eat.

"These new conditions caused more trouble than we had during the War. There were often more than one thousand at a time in the hospital, and not having room for all of them, we had to let them sleep upon pallets and at times in tents."

Practically everyone at Ellis Island has some tale about the arrival of freaks for the various circuses of the country. There is the instance of the Siamese twins, one of whom was not speaking to the other because of jealousy over her husband; the microcephalics or "pin heads," and the hydrocephalics with enormous heads grotesquely shaped, most of whom were mentally abnormal and had to be cared for like children. These came under bond for a six months' stay; for the most part they came from Arabia, Egypt, and the swarthy tribes which inhabit the north coast of Africa.

Lion tamers, equestrians, savage Zulus, fat ladies, tattooed wonders and many of the other human curiosities which have entertained under the "big tops" have also had their innings at Ellis Island.

One day last year I looked out of my window, and the scene on the lawn below looked just like Morocco. Four hundred Arabs with their fezzes, all attired in long white robes, were flocking about the enclosure. Among them was a sprinkling of Russians in brighter costumes. It was a contingent bound for the World's Fair.

Many times, when passing the detention room after working late at night, I heard the aliens singing and playing. Although prisoners for the time, they were trying to forget themselves, and I admired their stoic fortitude.

Chapter V

RACKETEERS AND HUMAN CONTRABAND

My EXPERIENCE with smugglers and stowaways began almost simultaneously with deportation problems.

We who live in the United States, whether we be native born, naturalized citizens, or even aliens, take for granted the privilege of being here.

For nearly five years now we have struggled through a depression, witnessing a commercial and social catastrophe which has almost shaken our faith in the fundamentals of Americanism. Both the Republican and Democratic administrations at Washington have come in for their respective avalanches of criticism.

Yet, in the face of all that partisan critics say we have lost, there are thousands in every quarter of the globe who would go to any length to exchange places with us.

I will not discuss the value of American opportunity. But that it is to many the pot of gold at the end of the rainbow I have had deeply impressed upon me during my service at the Island. Sometimes I myself have been forced to shatter the hopes and render useless all the enormous efforts that have been expended in bringing the alien illegally into the country. Older cases out of the past were brought to my attention as I considered those in hand, and sought, where the laws permitted me to decide at all, to make a reasonable and just decision. But of course the occasions when a stowaway or smuggled-in alien can be permitted to remain are comparatively rare; and most of these cases end in tragedy for the immigrant who has in his own heart chosen us for his fellow citizens. At times a note of humor creeps in; more often the elements of crime and exploitation come to the surface.

I am sure that most Americans will be astonished to learn that during a single year of the depression eighteen thousand men and women from foreign shores, debarred from our gates by immigration quota restrictions or for other reasons, sought surreptitious entry and were arrested and turned back.

The figure eighteen thousand is a measure of quantity only. Without an examination of specific cases there could be no conception of the intensity, the burning hopes of success, and the countless personal considerations which impelled these eighteen thousand who failed to reach our hearthstone. From each specific case some of us might gain a truer appreciation of our citizenship.

Approximately five thousand of these "gate crashers" stowed away upon ships, living in many instances for days and nights upon bread and water, voyaging to our ports in bales, crates and boxes, in water tanks, and a strange variety of hidden compartments. Sometimes the international racketeers in charge of the smuggling venture foresaw possible apprehension and capture, and then they threw the alien's living body to the sharks.

One might suppose that the steamship companies would be more vigilant in detecting stowaways, since they are liable to a government fine of one thousand dollars for each stowaway.

Those who did not stow away on ships, that most hazardous of all methods of entry, tried to enter in bales of Canadian hay or crates of Mexican freight. They came concealed in wagons, automobiles, railroad cars, or the airplanes of international racketeers. Some, it is true, merely posed as former citizens at points of entry, and walked across the border amid holiday crowds returning from Cuba, Mexico or Canada. Others affected the disguise of priests or nuns. Then there were those who swished through the night in high-powered launches or speed boats, to seek out lone stretches of coast line or isolated lagoons and inlets.

Guns flashed in the darkness along these wild strips of shore. Sometimes it was the alien who was killed; not infrequently it was the immigration inspector or a member of the Coast Guard.

One case came up during my administration which showed me the depths of misery which men will suffer in the hope of sharing what we accept as a matter of course. This is the story of Nicholas Prazza and his comrades. Their tragedy has such a dramatic quality that it is easy to piece together the events into a logical and poignant whole. It began on the night of July 10, 1933.

The setting is the tropical port of Balboa, in the Isthmus of Panama, amid a great bustle and hurry. The *California* is taking on cargo preparatory to her departure for New York. Scores of singing, sweating, swearing stevedores are rushing up and down the gangplank in rhythmic confusion, while the huge piles of freight upon the dark wharves dwindle as night wears on.

Finally all the wharves are nearly emptied. Midnight is drawing near and the eerie noises are subsiding. Now the empty-handed stevedores shuffle down the gangplank more slowly, mopping their grimy faces with grimier handkerchiefs, their bare backs glistening in the moonlight. They plod wearily toward the few remaining crates and boxes and bulging gunnysacks which fringe the docks, and take them up with an apathy that belies their great physical strength.

Lights appear intermittently upon the great ship. Then her engines throb with a low drone, getting up their first heat for the long voyage ahead. Their sound mingles with the clang of signal bells, and the stevedores arouse themselves to a renewed and final burst of energy.

Removed from this age-old scene of the sea, but by no means apart from it, stand three silent, motionless figures deep in the shadows at the rear of the wharves. They await the word from the seaman who has agreed to smuggle them into the United States.

They wonder whether he will ever come, whether or not they have been betrayed, while the interminable minutes drag slowly by, each contributing to the intensity of their suspense. If he does come, will they succeed in boarding the ship? Otherwise, what will be the consequences? They murmur to each other in tense, excited whispers.

For three years they have awaited the opportunity for this supreme adventure. Each has suffered extreme self-denial, each has stinted to save actual pennies in order to get together the money demanded by the smugglers.

No wonder that Satero Zattos whispers, "If he does not take us, it will be too bad if he ever comes back to Balboa!"

"We can do nothing but trust him," Peter Spiro whispers back.

Nicholas Prazza smiles gravely, but says nothing, for he is a quiet, rather melancholy man. And finally Satero Zattos and Peter Spiro stop whispering.

Satero Zattos thinks of his eight-year-old son, of his wife Elene, both far away in his native Grecian village of Tsemanta. For their sake he has been a peanut vendor in Balboa for three years. He hopes that in America it will be different, that soon he will make enough money to be able to send for them. Elene's brother, Michael, who lives in Massachusetts, will help him, and all will be well. What does it matter that he is risking his life when the reward is success and happiness for all?

Peter Spiro is thinking too. He has two sons, one six, the other nine, and they are with his beloved Anthoula in distant Albania. Staring into the darkness, he pictures the happiness he will feel upon reaching his cousin in New Haven. Perhaps there he will not have to drudge for hours over hot stoves and wash greasy, smelly pans. Perhaps he and his cousin will be able to have a restaurant of their own, with someone else to do the cooking. But anything will do for a while, if later he can bring Anthoula and the little sons to share his success. This is a desperate chance he is taking, but getting to

America, just getting any kind of chance in America, is, in his opinion, worth the sacrifice.

As for Nicholas Prazza, he never talks and no one ever knows what he is thinking about. No one even knows if he ever had a wife, or if he has any relatives anywhere.

Now the last of the stevedores comes down the *California's* gangplank, and the shouts of the crew reverberate across her dim-lit decks.

Suddenly the three men who wait in the darkness stiffen and stare ahead. Two shadowy figures are coming cautiously towards them. There is a low whistle, and the trio advances to meet them. It is the Spanish sailor, Sebastian Rivera, with a companion, Peter Heule.

"Keep quiet," warns Rivera. "Follow us, and hurry!"

The seamen smugglers lead the way up the gangplank, then down narrow iron steps into the curious abyss which is the hold. Through lanes flanked by piles of freight they file in the dim light, until they reach a darker chamber which is oppressively hot and stifling. Sebastian Rivera stops.

"Aquí!" he mutters in Spanish, motioning toward the smokestack casing above the boilers.

He has indicated a small trapdoor in an extremely inaccessible place. It leads to the shafting, and a bolt and nut have been removed in order that it may be opened. Below, and with nothing but scorching iron rods between, are the ship's boilers.

"We will die!" exclaims Satero Zattos.

"Don't be fools," snaps Rivera. "Soon you will get used to it." Before he finishes speaking there is a gentle sway of the ship and acceleration of her engines. She has weighed anchor, and the three stowaways look up in bewilderment. They stare at each other in frightened silence. It is Nicholas Prazza who shrugs his shoulders in futile abandonment and crawls head first through the trap door. A moment later he is followed by Satero Zattos, then Peter Spiro.

Within the miniature inferno they hear the door bang shut behind them. They hear Rivera and Heule reaffix the bolt and nut.

Their three years of waiting are over. They are on their way to America.

It was agreed at the beginning of their negotiations, and at the time they paid him their money, that Sebastian Rivera was to furnish food and drink for the duration of the voyage. Will he comply with his part of the bargain? They can only wait and see. After several hours he brings the suffocating trio a hunk of hard bread and a can of water.

Courageously they suffer the torture of their cramped quarters through the long night and through the next day when Rivera returns with more bread and water. For the most part they have been silent, conserving the strength which they can feel ebbing out of their bodies.

One—two—three—the days pass like so many eternities. On the morning of the fourth day, just as Nicholas Prazza is expressing the fear that all is lost, Rivera comes with the bread and water again. With a mighty effort Nicholas Prazza lifts himself on one elbow and attempts to drink, but he slumps backward before he can take the can from the hand of Satero Zattos.

"Drink, comrade," Satero Zattos urges, helping him up and forcing the can to his lips. "It is too late to give up now."

"I try, but it is no use," says Nicholas Prazza, after gulping a swallow of the tepid water.

"It is noontime," remarks Peter Spiro. "Those are the whistles we hear."

"I hope we shall hear them in New York," replies Satero Zattos.

"Maybe in hell," Nicholas Prazza whispers hoarsely.

All three are silent again. More long hours pass. They are hours of indescribable misery. The quarters of the three have commenced to smell foul and sickening. Nicholas Prazza is breathing heavily, as though in deep sleep.

Through the rest of the fourth night Peter Spiro and Satero Zattos pray. For both it is a nightmare during which they battle to retain consciousness, and literally cling to life. Already Nicholas

Prazza is delirious. The heat from the boilers rises in terrific waves; their water has long since been exhausted, and Sebastian Rivera has not come for almost twenty-four hours.

Suddenly there is a whistling sound, a rattle in the throat of Nicholas Prazza. Satero Zattos bends over him, extending one hand in the dark. He feels Prazza's swollen tongue protruding from his lips.

"Comrade!" he shouts. "Comrade!" But the rattle has ended, and Nicholas Prazza cannot reply. With his death have passed the dreams he had of life in America.

Peter Spiro and Satero Zattos utter hysterical prayers. High above them the noon whistles are blowing. They have but one alternative now, and that is to surrender. Sebastian Rivera has not returned, and it occurs to them that perhaps he does not intend to come back. Who will climb up the funnel shafting, the only outlet from their hole of imprisonment? Peter Spiro volunteers.

This is the official report of the outcome:

From H. Manning,
Chief Officer, S.S. *California.*

To: Captain T. H. Lyon,
Marine Superintendent,
New York, N. Y.

Subject: Finding of Peter Spiro and Satero Zattos, stowaways, and body of Nicholas Prazza, deceased stowaway.
Sir:

Facts pertaining to the above are as follows:

At about 1:00 P.M., on July 16, Mr. J. English, 6th Assistant Engineer, while pacing on the fiddley deck, found a stowaway climbing up the funnel shafting (inside). Mr. English notified Mr. Bishop, Jr., 3rd officer and myself.

Investigation revealed another stowaway and body in the shafting around the bottom of the funnel casing over the boilers. Cross examination of the stowaways revealed that they had contracted with Sebastian Rivera and Peter Heule, firemen on this

vessel to stow them away to New York. Peter Spiro claimed to have paid S. Rivera the sum of $60 in cash prior to boarding the said ship at Balboa. Satero Zattos promised to pay a similar amount to the two firemen on arrival in New York........
....

The time of Nicholas Prazza's death was established by Spiro as he heard the noon whistles.

The doctor examined the body of Prazza, found him to have expired from heat, exhaustion and suffocation, no doubt due to the intense heat from the boilers.

The belongings of Nicholas Prazza were very few. A small pocket book contained $1.65, several small pictures, and a small note book. I mentioned this as there appears some doubt as to the correctness of his name. No written or printed evidence has so far appeared. I have written out the name merely from the hearsay of all his companions, who did not seem to know him prior to the meeting for the purpose of stowing away.

The body of Nicholas Prazza was committed to the deep on July 16, 1933, 0:10 A.M. in Lat. 32-36 N., Long. 77-19 N., with due ceremony in the presence of Commander, Officers, Doctor and other members of the crew.

Rivera #145 and Heule #147, Porto Rican and Hawaiian, respectively, placed in confinement in ship's brig until arrival in N. Y.

The denouement of this tragedy, which grew out of the desire of three poor Greeks to live in America, occurred a few days later at Ellis Island. Peter Spiro and Satero Zattos were held as alien stowaways and arraigned before a Board of Special Inquiry.

At the official prelude to their deportation both begged imploringly for a chance to live in the United States. But the deportation statutes, rigid and inexorable, permitted of no discretion in either of their cases. They were held, however, by their own consent, until trial of the smugglers was completed and both Rivera and Heule had been sentenced to terms of imprisonment.

Many years ago Uncle Sam discovered that there were two distinct classes of smugglers. The so-called "honest" smuggler actually tries to deliver his clients at an agreed location in one of the forty-eight states; but the "dishonest" smuggler is in reality not a smuggler at all. He is an international racketeer who robs his victims and leaves them in the wilderness, or dumps them into the ocean.

It has often happened in the past that smugglers in Canada gave their victims into the custody of Indian guides, who conducted them to some isolated region in the wilderness, told them they had crossed the line, and indicated the direction in which they should proceed. They were not, of course, anywhere near the line. Others took their victims to confederates who held them for ransom if they felt there was any likelihood of such payment.

During 1921, the year in which the per centum quota law was passed, 3,539 aliens were found in places of concealment on inbound ships. In most cases they were being smuggled by members of the ships' crews. Both the 1921 and 1924 laws increased the flow of this particular type of smuggling.

At one time some thirty thousand Chinese students were reported in Cuba, waiting to effect illegal entrance to this country. Prohibition provided another incentive as the increased smuggling of rum had been rendered difficult and the human element afforded a profitable substitute.

An interesting incident occurred on June 5, 1929. The U.S.S. *Republic,* a former army transport, steamed into New York harbor on her return voyage to Bremerhaven.

In the usual manner inspectors from Ellis Island boarded the ship to examine passports.

This particular ship has a long staircase which runs down from her upper to her lower deck. At either side of this staircase on the lower deck there are wooden panels.

It so happened on this morning of inspection that a customs official was in the company of the immigration officers. Although a sign on the wooden panel said, "Fresh Paint", the customs officer happened to see a ray of light between two of the panels. At once he called to two of the immigration inspectors, and the panels were forthwith removed.

Eight Polish men and women, all dressed in the height of fashion and of prepossessing appearance, walked out from beneath the staircase. That they were a trifle embarrassed goes without saying.

The most famous stowaway case in the history of Ellis Island concerned a fourteen-year-old Belgian boy named Michael Gilhooley. Young Michael was so determined to live and make his fortune in this country that he stowed away five times in a year, bouncing back like a rubber ball every time he was deported until it became a dull day at Ellis Island when he did not arrive. Men who have been at the Island many years tell me that he was a lovable boy, a composite of wit and fierce determination inherited from his Irish father, and a sweetness and friendliness perhaps acquired from his Belgian mother, who had been killed by the Germans in the Belgian invasion.

The press of the country made much of the pluck of the boy, and publicized widely his efforts to become an American citizen. After his third entry his story was told in the newspapers of every little village, and the human interest was strong enough to touch everyone who read it.

After each of his arrivals, Ellis Island would be in a furore; there were hundreds of telegrams and telephone calls from persons who had heard of Michael and wanted to aid him in staying here. Motherly women begged for the opportunity to adopt him; wealthy women showered him with gifts; business men, intrigued by his stoical determination, offered to employ him; passengers on the various ships on which he came over appeared at Ellis Island in his behalf.

The year 1919 was the memorable year he chose for his expeditions. When he first arrived, on board the transport *Agamemnon* in a soldier's uniform, he was quickly deported. His second trip was on the *Black Arrow* and again he was deported. The third time he

came on an American transport, the *Santa Paula,* surrounded by ad-
miring soldiers who chose one of their number to appear at Ellis
Island in his behalf. Officials adjudged this man unable to give
Michael the care he needed.

The boy washed dishes and helped the cooks, and so never suffered the hardships of the unwelcome stowaway who has to mop all
the decks or ride in the brig during the entire journey. It was after
his exclusion on this third trip that letters began to pour into Ellis
Island requesting information and offering aid. A characteristic
letter received from a New York business man, said briefly:

"Would like to obtain further information about the possibilities of
my adopting the boy, Michael Gilhooley, so he might obtain a chance
to remain here, so much desired by him, in this great country, which no
doubt he truly loves, and is looking forward to becoming a good citizen
later on. I am 31, single, not wealthy, but I am sure I could give him
a good home. . . ."

A woman wrote:

"Ask him if he would let me be a mother to him, or if he would run
away to become a cowboy."

One said, "I would bring the boy up in his own religion."

A man offered a good home and a good education, stating that his
only reason was that his name was Michael and his mother's name
Gilhooley. A State manager of the Mystic Workers of the World
Fraternal Society of Kansas City wrote:

"The fact that he has shot a few craps does not in any way affect me, as
I do a great deal of Sunday School work and have no trouble taking
those little things out of a boy that has plenty of pep."

I am told that the officials at Ellis Island did not like Mike, and
answered many of the inquiries in a tone not calculated to keep the
beneficiaries interested. Many who wrote in were told that Michael
was obstreperous, rough, tempestuous, and almost incorrigible.

While in France, following the death of his mother who was

killed by a bomb, Michael had travelled through the country with American and French soldiers. He said he had escaped from the Germans. He became mascot of the 26th Regiment of American Infantry, and on his fifth stowaway trip on the transport *Orizaba* he brought into the country a considerable sum of money given him by admiring soldiers.

Mike was about to be deported for the fifth time, when a telegram from Washington informed the officials at the Island that a Mrs. Marion Gilhooley Curry, the wife of a wealthy Cleveland exporter, who lived at the Vanderbilt Hotel, New York, desired to make bond for Michael for a year. She took him with her to the hotel, where he lived in the lap of luxury for a while, driving out each morning with a chauffeur. An amusing incident occurred when the chauffeur was arrested for speeding with Michael, and the two were haled into court where the magistrate demanded full details of the case. The chauffeur explained Michael's origin. "Gilhooley does not yet command the English tongue with fluency," he told the judge, "but in answer to your Honor's question as to whether he may become a public charge, may one explain that he will not? The errand of which this speeding charge is the outcome was an affair which required expedition. We were on our way, Gilhooley and I, to the studio of a moving picture corporation which is about to sign Gilhooley up for a fifty-thousand-dollar contract."

The records at the Island do not show whether the contract was duly signed or not. They do show a little later the boy entered the Clark School, and his reports, which were excellent, were filed at the Island. Some time later the Island was notified that because of illness Mrs. Curry wished to transfer the care of Mike to Mr. Harold Bolster, a Wall Street broker, who took the boy to his country place at Briarcliff Manor, then entered him in Horace Mann School, and finally put him on a farm in Delaware County, New York. Mr. Bolster wrote that he believed farm life would build up the boy's health and prove more beneficial to his "real man's sense" than going to school. When last heard from Mike was still on the farm, and had become, Mr. Bolster wrote, almost self-supporting. His guardian requested information as to how he might assist Michael in getting citizenship papers.

An amusing side of the affair was the brief adoption of the boy by Elsie Janis, who returned him after two days of slang, dice, and all the jamborees that a freckled lad could stir up. Miss Janis also adopted Enrico Cardi, the famous boy war hero, whom she also returned afterwards.

Officials at the Island still laugh when they talk about Enrico. He, too, came in 1919, and for all I know his path may have crossed that of his famous contemporary, Mike Gilhooley. Enrico was sent to America as a cabin passenger on the *Patria,* by the American Red Cross at the instance of an American soldier, Robert Clifford of Taunton, Massachusetts. He arrived here on May 10. After he had landed it was found that Clifford could not make bond for the boy's admission. Enrico had a letter to the manager of the Vanderbilt Hotel from a friend who was interested in him, and who asked the manager to arrange for his employment and education.

Enrico was fifteen. He told a pathetic story of the death of his Italian parents and of his hardships in his home country. He wore the Croix de Guerre, an Italian Service Medal, and the Italian Cross of War. He had fought four years in the trenches, and had been wounded several times. American newspapers made much of his war service, recounting again and again his thrilling story of the night he advanced into the Champagne sector and took three German prisoners single-handed. He had joined the Italian Bersaglieri, fourth regiment, when he was eleven, he said, and was in the trenches steadily until 1916 when the French Seventieth Regiment left there, taking him along as an honorary corporal. Later he fought in the Somme, Champagne, at Verdun and in Lorraine, and was advanced to the rank of sergeant. After he captured the three Germans, his own government sent him the decorations he wore on his arrival here. When the Seventieth abandoned the Lorraine Sector in September, 1918, the "little corporal" was adopted by a detachment of the Fortieth Engineers, United States Army. It was then that he was found by the Red Cross, and upon saying that he would like to go to America, he was sent over.

It was assumed by those who looked into the case that much of Enrico's tale was fact. It was evident that he was a waif in the War, and was a great favorite with the soldiers who picked him up from time to time. Both he and Mike Gilhooley were victims of the War, and both decided in their young minds that America was a New World, not war-swept, not starving, where they could make a fresh start and find someone to help them win a future.

Not all of Enrico's story was true, however, as Miss Elsie Janis discovered after taking him to her beautiful home in Tarrytown, New York. He lived there several months before it was found that his parents were alive in Verona, Italy, and thought it was about time he returned home. As Miss Janis' ward he attended a good school, occupied rooms at the Tarrytown estate, picked strawberries with his benefactress, and learned English. The first intimation that all was not well came when Miss Janis informed Ellis Island that the boy desired to return home after Christmas. She expressed herself more firmly in her letter to officials asking for the return of her bond. "I am sorry we were drawn into this whole thing, not knowing anything about it, thinking the boy was alone and unprotected," she wrote. "He has cost us over twelve hundred dollars and much unhappiness. Therefore please return our bond and the deal is closed forever."

Enrico Cardi departed on January 20 on the S.S. *Giuseppe Verdi.* Ellis Island never heard of him again.

From 1920 to 1930 ships arriving from Europe were alive with stowaways who could not scrape together even the cost of steerage passage to the "golden land." On a January day in 1921, the records show, two steamers arrived from Italian ports each bringing seventeen stowaways. The passengers on one of these boats were put to no little inconvenience, when one of the stowaways developed smallpox. The 130 cabin and 1,335 steerage passengers had to be vaccinated. They were transferred to Hoffman Island for observation, where they were quarantined for twelve days.

All the commissioners at Ellis Island have the disheartening experience of receiving pathetic letters from persons caught in their attempt to enter the country, and I was not exempt. Remembering my own fears as an immigrant, I could not help entering sympathetically into the distraught minds of those who wrote such letters. Yet all I could do was to weigh the various elements of the case, and almost always the scales fell on the side of deportation.

In 1932 I received a letter in Yiddish from a young woman named Rosa Nashelska, who had been caught as a stowaway from Cuba on the S.S. *Virginia*. She had with her a child several years younger than the boy whose picture appeared on the passport. She was being brought in as the wife of one Louis Carmona, a member of the crew, who later turned out to be a smuggler and agent of a house which had offices in Havana and the United States and made a business of bringing in unwanted aliens. The young woman wrote:

I am a young woman grievously wronged by my husband, an American citizen. I met him in Cuba about two and a half years ago and he then promised to bring me over within fifteen days and establish for me a home in America. But as a new law barring me from getting a visa just then went into effect, my husband, after a couple months, discontinued all correspondence and was never again heard from. On my part, I exhausted in vain every effort in my power to get a visa. Now while pleading guilty of entering here illegally, I submit to you as thinking and feeling men, who have many daughters of your own, the following extenuating circumstances.

I am the wife of an American citizen, a respectable married woman, whose reputation as such can be readily ascertained by investigation in Cuba. Under the law I am not admissible into the United States to rejoin my husband to whom I am bound by marital ties, nor can I marry another man unless these ties are properly severed.

I lost all track of my husband, who in effect abandoned and left me stranded in Cuba. And a situation fraught with serious danger looms before me and that is one of an unattached, cast adrift, destitute young woman who is apt to be driven by want to encounter trials and temptations which I dread to face.

In order to extricate myself from that strangling plight and to obtain a divorce from my husband, it was absolutely necessary to find him, and it was for that reason, that I resorted to the only known and available means of coming here. I believe that within a short time I will be able to locate him and have him divorce me. And I, therefore, beg you with every fibre of my being to permit me a stay of three months, under surveillance or guard if desired, to enable me to search out my husband, obtain the divorce and again be in a position to be free and live my own life. After that I pledge myself to leave the country cheerfully at once. If that is not granted I am lost.

Would you bestow upon me that mercy and save me?

Respectfully yours,
Rosa Nashelska.

After her case was investigated I had no alternative except to deport the woman.

The fact that our immigration station stands on an island has not deterred many deportees from making brave attempts to enter without permission. They have swum the icy waters to the Jersey shore in the dead of winter, and a few who have escaped death or capture may be reading this story of their own adventures to-day. When I came to Ellis Island I found memories still alive of a time in 1916 when two young Germans swam, in winter and at midnight, to New Jersey. They were, unfortunately for them, picked up as suspicious characters and brought back to the Island. Luckier, evidently, were the four negro stowaways who made a break for liberty in the summer of 1894, and so far as I could find, were never recaptured.

The problems of smuggling faced by immigration officers have always been tremendous. Even before the quota law went into effect many persons, diseased, infirm, criminal, unfit for active labor, stole into the country by different underground routes. The question of smuggling has always been so intimately bound up with that of the stowaways that no dividing line can be drawn. Nearly all the stowaways who figure in the story of immigration have been helped by some member of their ship's crew or some agent.

After the passage of the quota law, the problem of smuggling across the border became a prominent one. A great proportion of those attempting to enter the country illegally were helped across the rivers that separate Canada from the United States, or driven over the line in sleighs. Some immigrants who feared refusal at the legal ports of entry preferred to enter via the smuggling route rather than take a chance of being turned back.

So long as the undesirable immigrants entering Canada were bound for the United States, the Canadian government gave little heed to the matter. Not long, however, after the passage of the quota law, our government placed a special commission in Montreal, where the smuggling of immigrants was carried on to a great extent, and posted deputies along the border. In ten months the commissioner and his staff turned back over two thousand immigrants who were attempting illegal entrance into our country.

The steamship companies, which have always been under agreement to carry back any immigrant refused admission by the authorities, began to take careful cognizance of the state of health of the would-be American citizens after the quota law went through. They took to making up separate manifests at Liverpool, one for the healthy passengers who could pass the governmental requirements here, another for the thousands of diseased and pauperized who were planning to enter. The healthy passengers were booked for America, the unwanted for Canada, from whence they were expected to buy their way into this country. The vigilant guards on the border turned back so many of these that the Canadians began to be anxious about the future citizenship of their country; they began to make their own plans to keep the "scum" out, and prosecuted all the professional smugglers they could catch.

I have often wondered why these sick and infirm people wished to make the long and hard trip to the New World. It would appear that life to them would seem the same anywhere, and that the dangers and troubles of getting in here ought to deter them from such a hazardous attempt. One of the immigration officials told me that many wanted to reach a place where a poorhouse system existed which would enable them to be cared for and to obtain free medical attendance. They paid huge sums of money to be smuggled in, and I wondered where this money came from. The only plausible explanation, I was told, is that those who have had to care for these people on the other side will pay any amount to get the responsibility of their care transferred to someone else.

Before ever going to Ellis Island I remember reading in the papers the story of a Syrian girl who committed suicide by jumping out of the window of the train that was bearing her to New York to await deportation. The story of the girl in the press of the United States attracted a great deal of sympathy for her, and placed much undeserved odium on the officers who were carrying out the law.

Upon applying at Montreal for a certificate to enter the United States, the girl was examined and found to be suffering from an incurable disease which, of course, prevented her admission to the country. A man who claimed to be her fiancé came from Iowa and told a romantic story of his love for the girl. He had worked hard, he said, to earn enough money to bring her to this country. The immigration officers at Montreal explained simply that if he married her in that city she would then have a legal right to enter the country as his wife. He demurred, protesting that he had prepared a wedding feast at Cedar Rapids and did not want to deprive his friends of the pleasure of assisting at his wedding. The officers suggested that he have a second ceremony after their arrival at home.

So the two stole away one night and were caught trying to cross the river at Detroit. The man was held for a time, and after his release went back home, giving up all attempts to help the girl. She was ordered deported. After her suicide it was found that the fond lover had a wife in Dubuque, Iowa, and was merely earning a bit of extra cash by bringing her across the border. It was also discovered that the girl had previously been deported from New York, and had been sent back by the Canadian route to the United States.

Probably the worst case on record of the way in which immigration agents send undesirable and inadmissible people to this continent to get rid of them, was brought to the attention of the authorities a few years ago. A man named Conrad von Walloghren landed in Quebec and was "steered" into the United States illegally. He tried to obtain admission to a Detroit workhouse, and was turned over to immigration officials who sent him back to Canada. He was a hopeless idiot, who had occasional lucid moments when he remembered incidents of his past life. He had been confined for years in an institution for imbeciles in Belgium. He had been released and shipped from Liverpool to Quebec, with the United States as his ultimate destination.

The smuggling in of cripples, paupers, the sick and the unfit began on a professional scale as soon as the local governments in Europe realized the value of the "dumping" process. As early as 1891 a whole colony of Russian paupers were slipped past the inspectors by some ruse and landed at Pennsboro, West Virginia, where they said they had been told they could find work. The dispatch from Parkersburg stated:

"This is the fourth lot of paupers sent direct to Pennsboro in a few weeks. Other lots of about twenty have been sent to other small places in this state and there seems to be no doubt that a systematic arrangement has been made to ship hundreds of paupers into the country by false promises and by evasion of federal laws."

About 1900 paupers began slipping across the Mexican border. In 1906 a large group of Syrian peddlers suffering from trachoma were sneaked into the country from Mexico, the smugglers receiving twelve dollars a head for their work.

The records of the Island show that in 1901 an investigation was made of all employees, to determine which were in collusion with the stewards of Atlantic liners to admit diseased and other undesirable foreigners into this country. It seems that at the period of the great flow of immigration, many inspectors, and those who boarded the ships, were tempted by bribes to betray their official standing. In 1903 a Russian immigrant, who came as a stowaway and was given a job in the immigrant hospital, confessed that he had long been working in conjunction with allies to get diseased foreigners into the United States. Often the agents at the embarkation points in European countries designated a certain city as a clearing house for the undesirable immigrants of their race, and the aliens were then brought from Canada on sailing vessels or by some other means to the assigned city. Early in the century Portuguese undesirables were found to be cleared at New Bedford, Massachusetts.

The worst wave of this smuggling process was probably over before I went as Commissioner to Ellis Island; but it can never be eradicated. So long as we have a reputation for space and wealth and poorhouses, so long will the crowded and poor and decrepit of Europe and Asia, South America and even Africa long to enjoy the fruits of our advantages. With our gates strongly barred and our borders closely patrolled, most of these cannot get through. Yet they will still make the long trip and suffer the hardships, many of them again and again, on the faint hope that a mere chance will get them through and they will be free to begin a new life here.

PART IV

CHAPTER I

VIGNETTES OUT OF THE LONG AGO

ANYONE who has ever thumbed the pages of an ancient family album can appreciate the interest with which I listened to Ellis Island stories of the days gone by.

I was a stranger to my staff upon becoming Commissioner of Immigration, but with each passing day the loyalty and devotion to duty of those who assisted me grew upon me and endeared them to me.

Out of this comradeship there naturally sprang closer relations. And out of those relations came the accounts of many little dramas, tragedies, comedies and romances, which never failed to interest me tremendously. When I had heard the story of a particular case I sent for its file at my first opportunity, to learn its details at first hand.

Often, I wondered where they had gone—those who came in the caravan. For some came and went, leaving as little trace as an autumn breeze rippling over a wheat-field, or a shadow flickering across a hill side. The accepted ones disappeared into the vortex of the melting pot, and seldom were heard of again at Ellis Island. Yet, in their brief sojourns upon the Island, there are many cases which are remembered. Here are a few vignettes from the mighty caravan, which thundered through Ellis Island before its gates were closed.

Those who remember Marie Casacello say she was beautiful. They say of her what was said of another Italian girl, that "Hers

was the beauty to make an old man young and a young man mad."
Marie Casacello was nineteen when she and her father and brother
left Messina and came to this country.

The family took a house in Brooklyn, and Marie was almost in-
stantly the center of a group of admirers. They vied with each
other for her favor, and the most ardent among them was Francesco, a stone-cutter who also owned a macaroni store or factory.

All seemed to be going as merrily as a marriage bell. But the fact
was that Marie had left behind her in sunny Sicily a determined
lover named Terlazzo, to whom Marie, her father now remembered,
was engaged to be married. What had reminded her father of this
fact was her growing attachment for Francesco—Marie's father
preferred the absent Terlazzo and warned her that she must remain true to him.

In addition to an amazing pair of eyes, Marie had a mind of her
own and she told her father that she preferred Francesco. After all,
her father was only her father; to Marie it was a matter simply between her and Francesco.

Marie unquestionably had inherited her obstinacy from her father,
for at this point he announced that he would go back to Italy and
get Terlazzo, who would know what Sicilian justice demanded
under the circumstances. The old man sailed for Italy. That was
the end of the first act of this Italian drama.

The second act opened in April, 1895, with the North German
Lloyd steamer *Werra* arriving and landing at Ellis Island Giuseppe
and Vincenzo Terlazzo, the two younger brothers of Marie's absent lover. Marie herself went to the Island that day, not to welcome
the brothers, but because she remembered her father's oath. She
was determined to prevent the brothers from being admitted to this
country if she could.

In this mood she was taken before the Commissioner and told
her story. The Terlazzo brothers protested that they had come to
this country as immigrants and not as agents of their brother, Antonio; they said over and over that their intentions were simple and

honest rather than bloodthirsty, and they explained further that they were going to launch out here in the chestnut and fruit-cart business and referred to a compatriot, Frank Chioari, of 116 Thompson Street.

Marie was not convinced and she begged that the two brothers should be sent back to the vineyards and lemon groves of their native Sicily. In the face of her fears, one would have thought that this was Corsica and that a vendetta was brewing.

The Commissioner decided to sleep over the matter. At that point Marie's brother came to the Island and said that Marie was overwrought and that the two brothers Terlazzo wouldn't make any trouble. And Marie had to accept this view of it, for the Commissioner allowed the two young men from Sicily to land.

We must go back to the year 1893 to find one of Ellis Island's greatest treats. It occurred when the steamer *Guildhal* arrived from Alexandria, and Mohamet Nur, the mightiest soothsayer of the Soudan, found that he had lost his book of necromancy.

Against a colorful backdrop of bearded, brown and black Egyptians, Turks, Arabs and Nubians, who had come to assist in representing a Cairo Street at the World's Fair, Mohamet Nur uttered his grievance through an interpreter:

"The unlucky son of Mohamet el Kabir mourns in darkness of perplexity without a lamp unto his feet. Give but a piece of American money to him that his good fortune may return."

Then, as a Bedouin came up, Mohamet said to him in swift English:

"Great joke, that! I made joke, you understand? Show me American cent, I grab him. See? Great joke! I say, good-by."

Mohamet Nur was not the only Oriental ready and willing to accept American coins; some two hundred other children of the desert gathered round him at the Island that day, all of them offering everything from heirlooms to trinkets made on the ship, for coin, and all complaining of their sad straits; but unquestionably

Mohamet Nur, son of Mohamet el Kabir, was the deepest mourner of them all.

Then there came in a missionary. He listened to their laments and, good man that he was, his heart was touched; he went out and got an armful of Bibles and started giving them out to these brothers and sisters of the desert places, to make them glad. He started with Mohamet Nur, giving him a Bible as a substitute for the lost book of necromancy.

The soothsayer of the Soudan thrust the Bible into his hairy bosom. The rest of them saw that the son of Mohamet el Kabir had received a present and they closed in on the missionary from every side. They grabbed every one of his Bibles and then cried out for more. The soothsayer of the Soudan, with a readiness which would have done credit to a visitor at a Ford Exhibition when offered coupons as a chance for a car, went to the end of the line and came through again, to get another Bible.

When the last Bible had been given out, these denizens of the desert wanted to show their gratitude, and Fatima Osmar said that she would dance. This modest, unassuming girl was one of the most famous dancers in all Egypt. She had rings on her fingers and camel bells on her slender ankles. Silk like gossamer was rolled about her. Her perfect body moved under strings of jewels and she was most divinely tall; and as she danced she became a thing of joy and life and speaking, sinuous curves.

How they had ever let her leave Egypt no one could imagine. She had said that she would dance. Ellis Island had never seen anything like that dance before, and I seriously doubt that it ever will again. For that dance must have made the senses take wings. Not differently had Salome danced! Anything that fair Fatima might have asked then she would have been granted!

The appreciation of all was expressed to Fatima through an interpreter. I believe that she and her dance came as close to astonishing Ellis Island as anything in the world could have done.

The year 1933 brought to the World's Fair at Chicago a similar group. But during their stay at Ellis Island no such captivating human interest developed.

If Uncle Sam ever decided to deport the alcoholics from the United States, the chances are there would be world-wide repercussions. But that is exactly what Switzerland did to the United States in the late nineties.

Among the extraordinary affidavits recorded at Ellis Island are those of Emil Kunni, twenty-seven years old and a farmer, and Gustave Kammerer, twenty. Both of these men came from Blauer, Switzerland, and swore that because of their intemperate habits the authorities there gave them thirty dollars in cash and steamship tickets to New York. Their story might have seemed fantastic except for the fact that their appearance fully verified their description. They gave ample evidence of being alcoholics.

Of course they were deported; and the Treasury Department was set investigating the action of the Swiss authorities in shipping their drunkards to this country.

Now and again in those old days came striking, even touching, evidences of the immigrant's faith in us—the faith, for instance, of Bridget Coughrey, a charming young Irish girl from Clifden, County Galway, who landed at the Barge Office in June, 1900, with a shilling in her pocket and not one word of any language except her native Gaelic.

So far as making herself understood, she might have been born without the power of speech. The only interpreter at the Barge Office who understood Gaelic was absent. Young, comely, touchingly earnest, she tried in pantomime to explain, to make the immigration authorities understand what was such an open fact to her.

Then finally an interpreter was found who "had the Gaelic", and Bridget's story came out. She was one of a large family of children and was used to farm work. Her uncle, Patrick Coughrey, living in Pittsburgh, would advance the money for her transportation there, if he knew she had landed, and Bridget trusted the immigration officials to tell him. He was promptly informed, and the pretty young Bridget was kept under safe auspices until her uncle came, proved himself, and took her away.

I doubt if any more appealing group ever arrived at Ellis Island than five little Serbian orphan girls whose ages ranged from two and a half years to twelve.

They arrived under the charge of a Serbian nurse. They were all unusually beautiful and dressed in their picturesque native costumes. They attracted the attention and sympathy of everyone. The American Vice-Consul at Athens was said to have given instructions that one of the five little orphans be sent to his wife in Alabama. The Department of Labor investigated. Assuming that one of the little girls thus found a home, what of the other four?

That was in June of 1916. The Great War had had its part, one assumed, in sending these five children to us. Those who saw them say that they were quiet, gentle, and trusting, obviously accustomed to love and tender care. They constituted another example of the complex responsibilities imposed on our immigration authorities and the Department of Labor, another example of problems far outside the ordinary routine.

As in so many other cases, when the press announced the plight of the Serbian children, scores of volunteers rushed to adopt them, and the immigration laws were finally complied with in the case of all five.

In the old days, when the immigrant got off the Ferry at the Barge Office he was in America; and when he got through the Barge Office, he ran into very serious danger of exploitation. The police did all they could to protect the aliens, but still some got into the clutches of the cheats. Most of the runners for boarding houses were of foreign extraction, and those who were crooks would get the confidence of the aliens by speaking to them in their own language, afterwards luring them to places where they would be held or robbed, or, in the case of women, detained in question-

IMMIGRANTS DISEMBARKING FROM THE FERRY WHICH HAS BROUGHT THEM FROM ELLIS ISLAND TO THE BARGE OFFICE AT THE BATTERY.

able houses where the police had sometimes to be sent to rescue them.

There were instances when the finger of crime moved all too fast for the protecting hand of the law. Such a case was the remarkable disappearance of Isadore Termini from immigration custody in May, 1900.

Although mystery will always surround this extraordinary case certain facts are known. Isadore Termini, an old Italian immigrant, reached New York about May 25. He went to the United States Immigration Station at the Barge Office, and his dead body was picked up in the harbor three days later.

Meantime his son, Calegro Termini, lived in Buffalo, and when, after three days, the father failed to arrive, he consulted Immigration Inspector de Barry at Buffalo about the matter. De Barry found that the old man had been under detention at New York, classed as liable to be a public charge. This seemed strange under the circumstances, for he found also that the Italian had landed with a money order for thirty-four dollars, a ticket on the Erie Railroad to Buffalo, and about sixty dollars in cash.

After several days the old man still had not come, so Inspector de Barry wrote several letters to Immigration Commissioner Fitchie at New York. The Commissioner reported that the immigrant had apparently escaped illegally from the Barge Office, and he intimated that the son's inquiries were a pretext to keep the old man from being found.

Young Termini hired a lawyer who soon found that his father had not returned to his relatives in Italy. Inspector de Barry reported the case to the Treasury Department in Washington. During the investigation it developed that the body of an Italian, evidently Isadore Termini, had washed up on the shore of New Jersey near the coal docks of the Jersey Central Railroad. The description of the missing man, as he was last seen, fitted the body exactly. Two boys fishing off the docks saw the corpse floating. They shouted to a negro who was passing and the body was taken to the morgue.

But when the body was officially identified at the New Jersey morgue, a complete change of clothing had taken place. The shirt and coat had been exchanged for a sweater. Obviously this and the other changes had been made to prevent identification. It was said in explanation that the clothes first found on the body had been given to the negro to pay him for his trouble.

Old Isadore Termini was buried in the garments the crooks had put on him. It was found that the old man's ticket over the Erie Railroad had never been used and his money order had not been cashed. The case remains one which was never solved, and yet it serves to show the lengths to which criminals will go in order to get the immigrants' money.

CHAPTER II

MATCHING WITS WITH JOHN CHINAMAN

OF ALL the enigmas represented at Ellis Island John Chinaman takes first prize. Matching wits with him has always been a task replete with excitement for immigration officials.

Obviously the natural points of entry for Chinese laborers are the ports of the west coast, and it goes without saying that there is a well-organized traffic in Chinese labor, participated in not merely by Chinese but also by Americans.

The willingness of the imported coolies to work for a few cents a day, an amount sufficient to buy lodging, simple clothing, and rice, has constituted an extended threat to American labor ever since American immigration began. Their religion and ancient beliefs, their contempt for western civilization and their resistance to Caucasian assimilation have always been considered as a menace to American institutions. It was common knowledge that the population of China was approximately six hundred million, and that social conditions in the main bordered on degradation. Those Americans not in the racket of trafficking in Chinese labor coined the slogan, "Thwart the Yellow Peril!"

The records show that practically every day, boat loads of Orientals were landed at the ports of Seattle, San Francisco, and elsewhere while Chester A. Arthur was President of the United States.

Responsible delegations from the West journeyed to Washington to besiege President Arthur personally, urging him to demand that legal restrictions controlling the situation be enacted by Congress. It was pointed out that the Chinese in many instances had turned to vice as a means of livelihood; that they were the chief offenders against Federal narcotic statutes, and that many arrests had been made in California with subsequent convictions of Chinese for white slavery. Gradually the national consciousness was being fanned into flames.

The problem presented grave aspects for President Arthur. In the first place, it was a serious matter to offend a sovereign power. How could the United States discriminate? Eminent jurists expressed the opinion that any restrictive laws would be unconstitutional, and contrary to international law. Others decried the idea of setting a precedent, fearing that restriction might be extended to other nations, and that thereby the United States, known throughout the world for its open door and welcome to aliens, might defeat the purpose of its establishment: "A haven of refuge for the oppressed of the earth."

But the tide of public opinion had risen to such heights that action became necessary for President Arthur. He took the matter up with the Chinese government, and in some mysterious fashion was successful in negotiating a treaty which forestalled all international complications. This treaty, formal ratifications of which were exchanged on July 19, 1881, accorded to the United States the right to "regulate, limit, or suspend the immigration of Chinese labor."

But with the ratification of the treaty, the fat was merely thrown into the fire.

The treaty proved to contain many loopholes and great difficulty of enforcement, so on May 6, 1882, Congress passed the Chinese Exclusion Act, which has been so strengthened and amended in subsequent years that Chinese immigration can no longer be said to exist.

One of the first amendments occurred in 1888, when Uncle Sam demanded that all Chinese leaving our shores for their native land be barred from subsequent return except in the cases where the individual possessed either one thousand dollars in American property, a legal wife, one or more children or parents in this country. On May 5, 1892, more teeth were put into the law, when all Chinese were afforded one year in which to register their presence in America. Such registration would guarantee them immunity from arrest. The privilege was later extended to six months, but after that, the ban was on in earnest.

However, the activities of the smugglers of Chinese were so far flung and so clever that the government found it next to impossible to cope with the situation.

Canada was permitting the entry of alien Chinese upon payment of a one-hundred-dollar head tax. Canada got the one hundred dollars, and Uncle Sam got the Chinaman.

According to the 1930 census there are 74,954 Chinese living in the United States. But the number here illegally can never be determined, although they are gradually being apprehended and deported, and a veritable international dragnet guards the circumference of the country against their surreptitious entry.

But as far back as 1882 it became apparent to Uncle Sam's agents that the law was being flouted by every conceivable means. And the Orientals were becoming so adroit that a special Chinese Division of the Immigration Service was eventually established so that the government might better match wits with the canny John Chinaman.

In the *New York Tribune* of October 3, 1901, there was published the following comment upon the cleverness of Chinese disguises:

The average citizen can form little idea of the character of cunning which immigrants, especially Oriental, will resort to in order to deceive the authorities. One of the most novel disguises, which had been adopted extensively for Chinese aliens, is the garb of a priest or clergyman. A party of Chinese immigrants with their pigtails under cover, their slanting eyes disguised by some means, and gowned in robes like those of Montreal monks, is likely to be picked up by Government officers any time in the next few days. Authorities here say that prominent men in various sections of the country are interested in the work of smuggling Chinese into America and allow their agents generous amounts for purchasing disguises. These immigrants are willing to spend from $100 to $500 each to get into the United States.

In Baxter Street, New York, it is said, gowns of priests and clergymen's garments in general are available at $2 or $3 each for this purpose. In other places there are shops that make a specialty of selling Quaker garments. The Quaker disguise was worked successfully last year, until a sharp inspector caught a party of twenty.

For miles along the border east of Vancouver, the smugglers disguise the Chinamen as Indians. When this scheme is followed, the Chinaman is schooled to drop his natural walk and articulate like an Indian. When disguised as priests the Celestials are taught to act the part. Smugglers have been known to drive twenty or thirty Chinamen from 75 to 150 miles away from an immigrant station. This is to obviate the necessity of presenting credentials.

A few months after the foregoing exposé, it was definitely determined that soldiers of the 11th United States Infantry, stationed at Fort Niagara, were engaging in the lucrative Chinese smuggling racket on the Canadian border. On December 27, Private John Brown was arrested and turned over to civil authorities.

Uncle Sam's Immigration Inspectors frequently encountered stern opposition and dangerous resistance from the smugglers. Their escapades would furnish suitable material for a modern detective story. One report from Inspector Thomas D'Arcy which was submitted from his post at Plattsburg on February 5, 1905, is of especial interest.

Although the inspector failed to capture a gang of smugglers and their human contraband, the chase he describes was a hair-raising one from start to finish, and he succeeded in blocking the plans of the "villains". His narrative related the attempt of a notorious smuggler, Frank Castine, to bring a sleigh load of Chinamen over the border.

Word reached Inspector D'Arcy from Douglass Corners of Quebec, on the night of January 30, that Castine and his Celestials had left there for LaPrairie. Hurriedly summoning and arming Inspectors Weeks, Maher, Ketchum and MacGretor, D'Arcy proceeded to Dewey's Corners, where the inspectors had decided to intercept the smugglers and the smuggled. They waited until after two o'clock in the morning before their dogs gave the alarm. The thermometer stood at twenty degrees below zero, and it was necessary to keep the horses moving constantly to prevent their freezing to death.

Finally a huge sled filled with Chinamen came into sight. It was followed by a small cutter carrying one man. The inspectors barred the road and ordered the strangers to halt. Instead of obeying, the two sleds were quickly wheeled around and started back in the direction of Canada. The inspectors set forth in hot pursuit. They raced mile after mile over the snow-covered road, in the words of D'Arcy: "In the teeth of the wind, which nearly blew the breath from our bodies, and the hail of ice thrown back by the heels of the horses, which pelted us like a Gatling-gun bombardment."

Gradually the inspectors gained on the smugglers, and when within calling distance shouted for the fugitives to surrender. But the pursued only replied with curses and whipped their horses the harder. Finally D'Arcy fired his revolver after the speeding sleighs, but the shots went wild. When it was apparent that the fugitives could be overtaken in the next two or three hundred yards, the man in the small cutter, who later proved to be Castine, seeing the danger, resorted to a desperate ruse. Rising to his feet he deliberately overturned the cutter in the middle of the road. A minute later D'Arcy and his men were sprawling atop of Castine and his wreck. Castine was captured but the Chinamen escaped.

The immigration records indicate that every restriction imposed upon John Chinaman has increased his cunning and added to the desperate methods he is willing to employ to gain entrance to the country.

To adequately appreciate the weird, innate cleverness of the Chinaman, and the shrewdness necessary to combat it, certain factors must be borne in mind; then concrete cases may be analyzed with better understanding.

Let us assume that a Chinaman is arrested and that his case

reaches court. He is invariably accompanied by a host of witnesses, all of whom tell an identical story. They knew him in San Francisco. On certain points their memory fails completely. Their most frequent rejoinder to the interrogation of the prosecuting attorney is, "I cannot remember." In the event the lower court rules against the defendant, the case is invariably appealed, often all the way to the Supreme Court at Washington. None, however, lacks funds for defense, the money being provided by the strange invisible empire of which all are a part, the interlocking membership of clans and tongs in the Chinese Chamber of Commerce with headquarters on Mott Street in New York.

The immigration inspector has a few tricks of his own, and experience has taught him not to terminate an investigation too readily.

"Take a walk!" he commands John Chinaman.

The Chinaman complies. And upon this little performance has frequently hinged the Oriental's fate, even though the walking test cannot be taken as proof positive.

If he is a native Chinaman, he usually lifts his feet in perpendicular fashion. If American born, he kicks his feet forward in the genuine Yankee manner. This interesting test is predicated upon the theory that the Chinese who have worked in their native rice fields, have worn sandals all their lives and have formed the habit of lifting their feet in perpendicular fashion.

Secondly, the Chinaman has the best memory of any race in the world. This assertion requires little proof, when it is considered that the Chinese language has no alphabet, that it is a picture language containing more than ten thousand pictures, each picture a separate word. The remarkable memory of the Chinaman has been his chief weapon of defense against the "man hunters" of the Chinese Division of Ellis Island, which I am convinced, number some of the cleverest detectives in the world of law enforcement.

Since Ellis Island has no direct supervision over the Border Patrol, the chief work of its Chinese Division is the prevention of illegal

EIGHT YOUNG CHINESE STOWAWAYS LANDING AT THE BATTERY AND IMMEDIATELY APPREHENDED FOR ILLEGAL ENTRY INTO THE UNITED STATES.

entries by Chinese into New York harbor and the metropolitan area, and the apprehension, of course, of those found in New York City illegally. New York being the mecca of Chinese in the eastern part of the country, it is natural that the Chinese Division at Ellis Island has its never-ending problem.

It takes but a few hours' coaching to teach a Chinaman how to replace another Chinaman on a ship's crew. The alien stowaway can board the ship, go to the galley, laundry or elsewhere and immediately make himself at home. He will know where to find all the tools or cooking utensils, and can learn whatever is required of him at a moment's notice. Clever passport forgeries, the difficulty of discriminating between the photographs of Chinese, and various modes of artifice contribute to the immigration inspector's difficulties. In numerous cases the alien has been apprehended after officers of ships have been completely deceived. One Chinese stowaway was recently discovered while shining brass in the Captain's cabin. He had been the Captain's trusted servant all the way from Singapore.

Pathos and humor mingle indiscriminately in the annals of Chinese smuggling.

For example, when an alien suspect is being investigated, he will immediately exclaim:

"Me slitizen! . . . Me born San Flancisco!"

Upon further questioning, he invariably fixes the time of his birth prior to the San Francisco earthquake, which of course destroyed all municipal records. Incidentally, it has been jestingly estimated that each Chinese mother in San Francisco must have had three hundred offspring to prove these calculations correct.

"What school did you go to?" demands the inspector.

The answer is readily forthcoming. The Chinaman can even remember the name of the teacher, the street where the school stood in San Francisco, and a variety of other information all of which has been carefully committed to memory. In all probability he has owned a pre-earthquake map of the city. However, he has no papers of identification. Upon that score he is vague and expresses complete ignorance.

In the days when Canada admitted them in wholesale quantities upon payment of the Canadian head tax, it was not uncommon for sailing vessels to pick up entire boat loads of Chinese at a Canadian port and attempt to land them at some harbor or point upon the American coast. At times the smugglers were frightened by the approach of strange vessels or learned that they were about to be detected. Overboard went the Chinamen. More tragic still are instances where the smugglers made no effort to land them, merely taking them a few miles out to sea from the port of embarkation and dumping them mercilessly into the ocean. These practises finally led to payment only after safe delivery inside the country.

On one occasion a boat load of Chinese was being brought into New York harbor. Suddenly with success in full view, an immigration cutter was seen approaching. The smugglers, in a frantic effort to do away with the evidence, began to throw the Chinese into the harbor. But strange to say, the pacific Chinese turned the tables on the smugglers, and threw every one of them into the water instead. They were picked up eventually in small boats, and the vessel manned by the untutored Chinese sailors was finally boarded and taken in command.

Why John Chinaman will risk death to get into the United States for the doubtful privilege of ironing shirts in a cellar laundry, or washing dishes in the cubby-hole kitchen of a chop suey restaurant is a mystery incapable of solution, unless the answer is that anything is an improvement on the unwholesome conditions in the Orient. I was never more impressed by this fact than recently when a Chinese citizen, who had returned to his native land on several visits, came back to this country accompanied by a band of nineteen alleged sons. Three of them were clearly ten years older than the "father." Curiously, these returning Chinese Americans profess a ratio of sons to daughters which approximates fifteen to one.

In my own time at Ellis Island we had duplications not only of the old practises but many novel efforts of the Chinese to circumvent Uncle Sam's rigid restrictions. The case of Chen Chee is one that I can never forget.

Inspectors of the service in the New York area had for a long while been watching certain sections of Brooklyn, in the belief that Chinese aliens were more likely to frequent the resorts of their fellow countrymen there than the more public resorts of Mott and Pell Streets, which are the main arteries of New York's Chinatown.

One March afternoon in 1933 a Brooklyn apartment house, where, it had been previously determined, large numbers of Chinese were used to gathering and playing cards, was raided. True to expectations, the detectives found the card game going on in a small apartment on one of the upper floors of the building. Arrests were made at once, but in the confusion, one of the Chinese escaped. Two hours later, standing in the snow, attired only in his pajamas and with bare feet, he was discovered on the roof.

"Me slitizen!" he asserted vigorously to the man who had found him. "Me born San Flisco!"

"Then what are you doing up here in your pajamas when it is freezing?" the inspector asked, undoubtedly amused by the Chinaman's answer.

"I come takee sun bath," said the Chinaman.

"What?" demanded the inspector. "A sun bath when the roof is covered with snow?"

"It is my custom," retorted the alien blandly and with utter composure.

The inquiry which followed failed to shake the Chinaman's story. He offered to provide the usual witnesses in corroboration and immediately announced his desire to appeal to the courts. It was learned a few days later that he had engaged counsel. Meanwhile the following letter came to Ellis Island:

Flatbush Avenue, Brooklyn
March 8, 1933.

To Mr. Carsi,
Immigration Commisher,
Ellist Island.
Dear sirs:

I writing this line to let you know the truth of the poin, you remenger your men arrested the china man Henry Mar Sow on 5th inst. last Saturday in apt no Flatbush Ave. Brooklyn you success for this right man, I know very weel bacause I live near him the same day morning about 7 a. m. I standing out door Saw your men go in he house he home be too much room he hearing your men ask for Henry Mar Sow he run out roof after your men arrested him at roof, your men carry him out I saw it right man, no matter what name he say I know this right man your success Sirs.

Henry Mar Sow himself came from Trinidad, B.W.I. by smuggle since Aug. 1930. He doing contractor for bringing Chinese from Trinidid B.W.I. try to send he back to China to fight with Jap.

All above to be very truth by god believe me Sirs.

yours truthly,
Joam.

At a subsequent hearing Chen Chee testified under oath that he was a laborer of the Chinese race, but that he was not in possession of documentary evidence showing him to be lawfully in the United States. He claimed birth in San Francisco, but did not know exactly where in San Francisco he was born. He said that he did not know his mother's name, as he was told that she had died when he was very young. He could not remember who told him this. He testified that he did not remember the full name of the man who brought him East at the age of about five years, and that he did not know whether any one living could swear that he was born in the United States. He also testified that he had never heard of Trinidad, that he had been living on the bounty of friends, and also depended upon them for a place to sleep. He said that he had no money, and that he had once worked as a relief waiter, in various restaurants.

But when questioned by his attorney on July 21, in the court of the United States Commissioner Epstein, the defendant seemed to have in some way acquired information as to his birthplace, the name of the street, number of the house, etc. He had also learned the name of his mother, and had changed his mind as to occupation and places of work. He produced witnesses, none of whom were members of his Clan, the Mar, and these corroborated his story.

In rebuttal the government submitted the following from the Consul at Trinidad, B.W.I.:

Chen Chee is the correct name of a Chinese who, under the name of Edward Marso or Edward Chong Marsow, which he used in Trinidad, was convicted in Trinidad on February 4, 1930, of being in possession of raw opium, and fined 150 pounds Sterling, which he paid, and that record of the said conviction, (a record of which was submitted with the aforementioned evidence), is in Criminal Register No. 94, page 203, Trinidad, B.W.I. This evidence also shows that when the said Chen Chee, under the name of Marsow, applied for a Section 6 Merchant's Certificate, which was denied by the U.S. Consul at Trinidad, on April 8, 1929, he, the defendant, testified that he was born in Hong Kong, China, on September 10, 1900.

But for the tip-off letter which enabled the government to get the finger-prints, photographs and evidence against Chen Chee, his case would have been air-tight. Needless to say, his counsel and witnesses were rather confused when confronted with the proof.

These tip-off letters, frequently attributed to clan or tong enmity, have proved invaluable in the apprehension of Orientals illegally in the United States. Considering the fact that the Chinese Chamber of Commerce with headquarters at 30 Mott Street, New York, remains the capital of the Celestials' Invisible Empire in the United States, and that no Chinaman is ever lacking in funds or witnesses to defend his case, it is curious that such betrayals should be perpetrated.

During my last month at the Island I received two such documents that were particularly amusing. The first purported to come from the Grace Steamship Line. It was as follows:

Dec. 1, 1933.

Dear officer

I let you this port address.................Grand Street
     apt. 4 floor
The Chinese men not passport up there. Please send officer
Ask him for best time up there
SUNDAY P.M. 2
Week day morning best time.

          Yours very truly
From Grace line S.S. Co.
          Agent

The other letter was printed in pen and ink:

GENTLEMEN

This is to INFROM you that a Chinese NAME HO CHUN at
...............Bridge Street, Brooklyn, N. Y. is UNCITIZEN. I just
enclose here with his photo. Beg to asking you send police or your men
there find and deport him to China to fight JAP.
                              Yours citizen
                              A. C. SOLOMAN.

But for tip-off letters and accidental stumbling upon evidence or
blunders upon the part of smugglers it is almost impossible for
the government to cope with this highly organized racket in its
present force. Sometimes these letters come written in Chinese similar to the following:

局長大人先鑒啟者如欲狗拿不良女子局

及片烟可到本埠　街尾　門牌該処

並有華人數名無紙居美祈望

先生前往拿獲撥回原籍是荷

溫龍千 上

TRANSLATION

Most Illustrious Headman:

If you want to meet evil women go to the laundry at 1 Place this city. There also you will find opium and the Chinese who have no passports. Deport them.

WOON LUNG GON.

Dear Immigration Office

I just to report I am expell to immedill sent you men to ketsh bed Chinemen wot no passport in lunre & 1 street

本國人

In addition to his stoicism and his uncanny memory, another factor interlaced with the weird religion of the yellow man accounts for much present-day smuggling. He is a reliable liability. He pays his debts—because his religion paints a damning picture of the next world for those who leave unpaid monetary obligations behind.

So it happens that he is a good risk all the way from Cuba, and at nightfall in Matanzas it is not unusual to see a tri-motored plane roll out of its hangar, pick up two muffled figures who scramble quickly into the cabin, and immediately take off into the clouds.

Morning finds the same plane landing in a deserted New Jersey cow pasture. A waiting furniture van backs up to the side of the plane and the same two muffled figures get into the back of the van. The driver closes and locks the back doors of the van and heads toward Philadelphia. An hour later the furniture truck enters a warehouse, and in another hour two shy young Chinese boys walk out the front office of the warehouse, and so far as anyone knows, they are American citizens.

The truck drivers have received fifteen hundred dollars from the owner of the warehouse, and the young Chinese are free to go wherever they will. The owner of the warehouse has even advanced the young stowaways living expenses until they can find employment. He knows they will pay him back, and with interest. And the secret of the transaction is that both of the young Chinese will be afraid to face their ancestors in the next world if by chance they have left this earth owing any money. If their surviving relatives are unable to pay, then the amount will be paid by their friends or fellow clansmen.

A tragedy in connection with Chinese aliens occurred in recent years when one of the ships of the Prince Line was lost at sea. It contained more than one hundred Orientals who had been deported from Ellis Island, and recalled to old-timers of the service the incident in which a truck-load of tea boxes unloaded at an address on Mott Street in New York's Chinatown proved to contain a score of dead Chinese, who had not survived their desperate effort to enter the country.

Yet it seems that as often as a tragedy occurs in the handling of John Chinaman, some amusing happening succeeds it.

Last year an extortion case was reported to Ellis Island by Louis Sing, a legal resident of the country and a respectable laundryman on Amsterdam Avenue in New York. As I recall the facts, Sing related that one morning he was visited by a white man and a Chinaman. The Chinaman introduced the white man as an inspector of the Immigration Service, who was calling to examine Sing's citizenship papers. The papers were produced, and found by the white man to be out of order due to various technicalities. Sing was informed that for the payment of two hundred dollars he could have the papers validated. When Sing protested that he did not have that amount of money on the premises, Harry Lee, the Chinaman, announced to Sing that he would be arrested then and there.

The fear of arrest threw Sing into such a panic that he immediately dug up the last penny in the laundry treasury, a sum approximating sixty dollars. He paid over the money on condition that he would not be arrested, and agreed to have the remainder ready the following morning. His visitors departed.

The next day Sing, true to his agreement, had the rest of the money, but only the Chinaman, Harry Lee, returned. This naturally aroused Sing's suspicion and he refused to make the payment. Harry Lee left the laundry and did not return.

Several days later, Sing, through his connections with the Chinese Chamber of Commerce, made inquiries and learned that he had been made the "goat" by an extortionist. In recollecting the appearance of Harry Lee, Sing recalled that he had a peculiar, livid scar upon his forehead. Upon further inquiry, he verified the identification. The extortion was reported to Ellis Island.

Working through the police of New York, Inspector Zukor, in charge of the Chinese Division, learned from Albert Huang, an extortionist, who had been arrested previously and was being held for civil trial, that Harry Lee was his room mate. Early the following morning Detective Curry of the New York Police, and Inspector Zukor went to the Bronx flat where Huang had lived with Lee prior to his arrest.

Inspector Zukor knocked on the door.

"Who is it?" came a voice from within.

"Compie!" replied Inspector Zukor, which when translated means "detective," or literally, "hidden shield."

The door was opened and there stood a Chinaman with a livid scar on his forehead. A white girl was vainly endeavoring to conceal herself under a ragged bed covering. Lee was arrested and taken to a waiting taxicab, which conveyed the Inspector, Detective Curry and their captive to Sing's laundry on Amsterdam Avenue.

It was about eight o'clock in the morning. New York's rush hour was in full swing.

The cab pulled up in front of the laundry, and Inspector Zukor with the aid of Detective Curry, forced Lee to accompany them. The entrance of the trio produced a scene of mad commotion. Sing, seeing the Chinaman who had filched the sum of sixty dollars, commenced to scream and gesticulate. The crowds hurrying by the window paused, then hurried on. Someone reported to the policeman on the corner that the laundry was being held up. Detectives and patrolmen arrived a moment later, their guns trained upon Inspector Zukor and Detective Curry. It took some time for Inspector Zukor and the detective to explain and to confirm their identities.

One of my last recollections of Ellis Island is of a shipload of coolies, who had been working for the British Government in one of Great Britain's insular possessions and were detained overnight, just before Christmas in 1933, preparatory to their departure by rail for San Francisco.

While waiting for supper they became inquisitive about the bowls standing on the table. This particular group had never before tasted or seen sugar. The head man asked an attendant what it was and received an explanation. He tried some in his tea, some more on his bread. A moment later his face was rippling with smiles. He screeched the good news down the long table to his companions who all joined him in sampling the sugar. In two minutes the bowls were emptied and the coolies were asking for more. The bowls were refilled and as quickly emptied again. In three more meals at the Island, the coolies "killed" three sacks of sugar and left for San Francisco with an unexcelled appreciation of the hospitality of Uncle Sam.

I had many dealings with John Chinaman—sad ones, exasperating ones and others which still bring smiles whenever I recall them.

But my experience at the Island taught me that Kipling was right when he wrote: "Oh, East is East and West is West, and never the twain shall meet." John Chinaman will always remain for me anthropology's greatest enigma.

CHAPTER III

THOSE "BAD, BAD RADICALS"!

I

THE Government seemed curiously "red"-conscious about the time I was sworn into office. Hence I was plunged immediately into the unpleasant business of dealing with alleged radicals, from my first day on the Island.

In the matter of "reds", the Immigration Law is very explicit. The law of 1918 excludes:

I   Aliens who are anarchists;
II Aliens who advise, advocate, or teach, or who are members or affiliated with any organization, association, society or group that advises, advocates or teaches, *opposition to all organized government*;
III Aliens who believe in, advise, advocate, or teach, or who are members or affiliated with any organization, association, society or group that believes in, advises, advocates or teaches: (1) *the overthrow by force or violence of the Government of the United States or of all forms of law*, or (2) *the duty, necessity or propriety of the unlawful assaulting or killing of any officer or officers* (either of specific individuals or of officers generally) *of the Government of the United States or of any other organized government*, because of his or their official character, or (3) *the unlawful damage, injury or destruction of property*, or (4) *sabotage;*

To the above paragraphs there are added others which include membership in organizations in any way addicted to the above practices or which raise money for these purposes.

Such is the famous "anti-red" law of our immigration service. The enforcement of that law has caused much discussion throughout the whole country. Also it has been accused of causing some acts of outright injustice by public officials. From time to time we have had "red" scares in this country, followed by periods of debate by more or less inoffensive persons in various cities and sections.

When I read the law I began to wonder why there had been, after all, so much perplexity with regard to its enforcement. It did not take me long to discover the colorful person who had taken refuge in the woodpile. My most important case helped to create, I believe, a new technique at Ellis Island.

That case represented the application of a very simple policy in the matter. Before describing it, however, let me take a moment to present the fundamentals of this matter in what seems to me to be their true light.

Why has there been this endless battle with the "reds" at Ellis Island? Has a mountain been made of a molehill?

Here is the law. If an alien anarchist arrives at the gate, he is to be excluded. If a member of an alien organization who proceeds to foment organized crime under the guise of political propaganda is discovered among us, he ought to be expelled. However, nothing in the whole content of the law from which we have quoted indicates that the accused is to be denied the protection of our laws while he is a resident among us. No department at Washington, not even the Department of Justice, is permitted to hang a man without trial. Just why the officers of a department have in the past been permitted to arrest aliens, put them in jail, and expel them from the country without "due process of law", I have never been able to understand. It is apparently possible for an agent of a department to enter a man's house and arrest him, take him to jail, to Ellis Island, thence to be sent to the country of his birth, because of his political opinions. This man may leave behind him a wife and a group of American-born children who are citizens. Forever separated from him, they may become public charges.

The various drives against the "reds" and all the injustices connected with them seem to spring from two causes: One is the craving of the "reds" themselves for publicity. The other, I am persuaded, is a strong desire for martyrdom. All causes, good or bad, tend to produce both genuine martyrs and those who fake their way to publicity and notoriety. In our own country one who has the reputation of a martyr can always go on the lecture rostrum, syndicate articles for the popular press, and write a book.

We Americans may as well admit that we love a bit of sensation. It must be a thrilling experience to a hitherto unknown working man to find himself the center of public interest—hated on one side, admired and praised on the other—for the nine days that such an affair usually holds the public attention.

All my experiences in this connection culminated in a single case. It happened toward the end of my period of service and concerned the entrance of the famous French writer—Henri Barbusse.

M. Barbusse was a private soldier in the French army during the World War. He wrote a famous book entitled "Under Fire." This was one of the first books and one of the best exposing the realistic horrors of modern warfare. Barbusse had been a socialist, and after the War he became a communist. There is nothing to show that he ever advocated violence as a policy. His record was that of an altogether worthy citizen of the Republic of France. Of course, the communist party in France is a lawful organization with numerous representatives in the Chamber of Deputies. However, the course of events hurled this same Barbusse into the circle of my day's work at Ellis Island.

Various organizations in this country, including the communists, had united in arranging an anti-war conference. The communists, as well as the socialists, are an international organization. So are most of the churches, the League of Nations societies, and the international society of postage stamp collectors. The international char-

acter of the communist organization is not at all illegal according
to the laws of this country. Socialists and communists attend international meetings just as do the international members of the Bap-
tists Alliance and the international Chamber of Commerce—much as
good Catholics go to Rome. To our average "red-baiter", however,
this international attitude of mind on the part of the radical constitutes an unforgivable sin. Consequently, according to the logic of
this position, when a foreign socialist or communist, as well as an
anarchist, seeks to come to this country, he should be rigidly excluded.

On September 29, 1933, my secretary interrupted routine business
to announce a telephone call:

"We are holding Barbusse for you."

"And who is Barbusse, and why are you holding him?" I asked.

"Why, don't you know? Barbusse is a red."

So again the fat was in the fire. In an hour I had all the available
facts before me on my desk.

The radical organizations had arranged a conference which included a large public meeting to be addressed by distinguished
speakers, both native and foreign. The purpose of the conference
and public assemblage was to discuss the subject of peace and war;
to advocate the former and oppose the latter. Of course this topic is
popular, and a crowd can usually be assembled to hear it discussed.

What the communist groups now desired above all else was that
Barbusse should be held up at Ellis Island. It would be best of all
for their meeting if he were put in a cell, given bread and water,
and put through the "third degree." In that case a crowd of outraged innocents would have hired a boat, landed on the Island, and
bombarded the door of my office. Of course, they would have taken
care to have the moving picture men on hand. Then, had I acted as
I might have, I would have called the police or perhaps had a company of regular troops come over to Ellis Island. Tear-gas bombs
would have been thrown and numerous demonstrators would have
fallen down pretending they were dying or already dead. They

would have been lugged off the field of battle before the barrage of movie cameras. The next day another boatful would come, and the process would be repeated. All this would appear on the screen from Maine to California; also in Paris, Moscow, Shanghai, and numerous other places.

The professional "red-baiter", whether paid or serving as a volunteer, has a most curious attitude toward the groups he looks upon as enemies. To him the word "reds" mistakenly include the progressive Western farmer-senators, the "brain-trusters" at Washington, and perhaps the Quakers and other pacifists. The more extreme radical is an equally obtuse fanatic.

A typical Union Square communist speaker regards everybody who disagrees with him as either ignorant or vicious. To him the ignorant are the ignorant poor; and the vicious are the vicious rich. The radical, like the reactionary, has created his own world out of his narrow personal experiences and petty opinions.

When the Barbusse case stared me in the face, I again reviewed the law involved. The fanatics might rave and the public mind might ramble on the subject. The law, however, left no doubts. Was Barbusse an anarchist?

The record said, "No." Barbusse was a communist—that is, a member of a party here, as in France, organized according to law and under the protection of the law. There was no record of his ever having said or written anything that brought him under the categories of those who were to be excluded.

I picked up the telephone and called the officer who was holding Barbusse.

"Is this ——?" I asked.

"Speaking."

"You are holding a man named Barbusse—a Frenchman recently arrived."

"Yes, we are holding him."

"Let him go," I said.

"What is that you are saying, sir?"

"I say let him go. Let him out. Dismiss him. See that he gets on the boat for Manhattan immediately, please." Then I hung up.

That was the end of the Barbusse case. Barbusse spoke at the meeting and his statements were those one might expect from a soldier who had been wounded in battle, and from an artist who had written some very fine books.

II

This whole subject of the exclusion of foreign radicals constitutes a long and troubled history. As I spent much of my limited spare time in those days reading backgrounds of history, I left the job with more of this matter in mind than I had taken to it. I tried to get a perspective on the whole game as it had been played in the past. There were some things I felt should be improved for all times. However, as I wished to begin the reforms, I needed to be sure of my ground.

It seems that one of the first organized attempts in this country to exclude immigrants already *en route,* because of the beliefs they held, was made by the Reverend Cotton Mather in New England's early days. We must remember that Massachusetts Bay Colony was, at that time, a theocracy. Its government was, presumably, inspired by the teaching of the Bible.

It is well known to any American who has taken a high school course in American history that the Puritan settlers of New England strenuously opposed the immigration of any who disagreed with them. The history of the Spanish Inquisition, being an oft-told tale, has come to stand for an idea. It is the general idea of murdering somebody who doesn't happen to agree with you. Cotton Mather must have been such a zealot.

This is the letter he wrote:

Sept. 15, 1682.

To Ye Aged and Beloved, Mr. John Higginson,— There be now at sea a ship called *Welcome,* which has on board one hundred or more of the heretics and malignants called Quakers, with W. Penn, who is the chief scamp, at the head of them. The General Court has accordingly given secret orders to Master Malachi Huscott, of the brig *Porpoise*, to waylay the said *Welcome* slyly as near the Cape of Cod as may be, and make captive the said Penn and his ungodly crew, so that the Lord may be glorified and not mocked on the soil of this new country with the heathen worship of these people. Much spoil can be made by selling the whole lot to Barbadoes, where slaves fetch good prices in rum and sugar, and we shall not only do the Lord great service by punishing the wicked, but we shall make great good for His Minister and people.

Yours in the bowels of Christ,
Cotton Mather.

When this country was first settled, we have been shown, there was much hatred because of religion. The Constitution of the United States removed this subject from political controversy. How much we owe to that one paragraph of the Constitution which follows:

Congress shall make no law respecting an establishment of religion, or prohibiting the free exercise thereof; or abridging the freedom of speech or of the press; or the right of the people peaceably to assemble and to petition the Government for a redress of grievances.

The first part of this paragraph settled the subject of religious rights for us, we hope, for all time. Regarding the second half of this paragraph we cannot be so sure. For the last two hundred and fifty years the subject of religion has been causing less and less excitement in the world; and the subject of politics and government has caused more and more excitement.

The boiling crucible of Ellis Island, during the past generation, presents a chapter of this history which every American may well read and reflect upon.

I went back over the record and discovered the famous case of John Turner in 1903. Turner was an English anarchist of the "philosophical" sort. To me the term "philosophical" anarchist has always seemed a contradiction of terms. It appears to me to be about as philosophical to abolish the multiplication table as for a civilized people to abolish all government. Leo Tolstoi, of course, was the spiritual father of the philosophical anarchists of that period.

The other sort of anarchist advocates violence as a means of realizing his ideal society. These are crack-brained bomb throwers and those who advocate bomb throwing. The two types of anarchists are like two varieties of mushrooms found growing side by side in the same pasture or woodland. One is harmless and edible; the other is fatally poisonous. Similarly, all intelligent persons, I think, should strive to see the difference between the mind of a Leo Tolstoi and that of an anarchist like Czolgolsz, who murdered President McKinley.

Leo Tolstoi simply carried our Jeffersonian democracy to an extreme. Using the phrase, "The less government the better", he argued for no government at all. If his theory were sound, then no government at all would yield the perfect form of society. However, no liberal American or Englishman would deny to anyone the right to hold whatever views he considered true. Genuine tolerance and intelligence permit freedom of belief above all else.

The case of John Turner is interesting to us, since he was the first alien ever deported from Ellis Island because of the opinions he held.

On September 16, 1903, the Commissioner General of Immigration, Mr. Frank T. Sargent, received a letter from the chief of the secret service at Washington that "John Turner, a notorious anarchist and labor agitator, is to sail from the other side on Saturday, October 3."

This was Turner's second trip to this country. In 1896 he had addressed a hundred meetings here, mostly of trade unions. Samuel Gompers, President of the American Federation of Labor, had given him a general letter of introduction to the labor unions and had himself actually presided over a large gathering in Indianapolis.

Turner's record showed him to be primarily a trade union organizer. He held his anarchist "philosophy" precisely as other trade union organizers held their religious beliefs. The New York *World,* which interviewed him while he was imprisoned on Ellis Island, described him as a "mild-mannered man" who "held that instinctive morality should be the only government" and who opposed and disavowed the use of all violence as injurious to "equality of liberty for all."

Turner later, in a published statement, declared that the basis of his philosophy was his belief that everybody ought to "live up to the highest he can conceive of—rejecting organized force to compel others to conform." He continued, "Imagine my surprise when placed under arrest. It had nothing to do with anything I had said or done. The warrant had been issued in Washington before I'd spoken in public. . . . Over twenty armed men and a lot of secret-service officials were employed to effect it."

Had Turner been left in peace, as was Barbusse, his addresses would have faded into thin air almost as soon as they were spoken.

Turner in jail became infinitely more powerful than Turner on the lecture platform. At a great public meeting in Cooper Union, the following names appeared among the vice presidents and sponsors in defense of his lawful admission to the country: Samuel Seabury, Carl Schurz, Oswald G. Villard, Charles Sprague Smith and Felix Adler. These liberal thinkers were willing to voice public protest against persecution for freedom of thought. The arrest made Turner an important figure and put him on the front pages.

Despite the defense and the able counsel that were retained, the Federal Circuit Court sustained the action of the Department of Commerce and Labor at Washington. When the case was appealed to the Federal Supreme Court, the decision of the lower court was affirmed. Turner was deported. Before the Supreme Court the case was argued by Clarence Darrow. This was one of the first important labor cases in the distinguished jurist's career. It was this decision of the Supreme Court which opened the way for the general policy of inquisition and exclusion so closely followed for a generation.

III

On December 21, 1919, before dawn of the day when the sun hung at its lowest point of the year, there slipped out of New York harbor a ship which went by the strange nickname of the "Soviet Ark." Its passenger list was composed of the names of two hundred and forty-nine prisoners who were being deported to Russia. They were nearly all said to be "reds."

This motley crowd had been rounded up and shipped from almost every section of the country. Some of them were Russian immigrants who, while lawfully admitted, were members of obscure Russian societies. Some of these societies had "constitutions" or by-laws in which some phrase was so construed by the authorities as to come within the scope of the immigration law provisions for exclusion. For six months Ellis Island became a deportation prison.

Slowly the "Soviet Ark" (S.S. *Buford*) rolled and tumbled across the Atlantic. When it passed from the North Sea to the Baltic through the German Kiel Canal the prisoners were all locked below deck and doubly guarded. It was feared one or more might leap ashore and throw himself upon the mercy of the German people and government. The Baltic Sea once crossed, the prisoners were landed in Finland and thence marched through a forest in the dead of winter to the Russian border. There they were turned over to the authorities of the newly organized U.S.S.R.

Let us suppose that one of these outcasts makes his way again to this country, as indeed some of them are said to have done. Suppose that such a one, perchance, goes sight-seeing in the City of Washington, and strolls out to look at the palace which serves as the Russian Embassy. In that event he will now see fluttering in the breeze the red flag of the U.S.S.R. Perhaps he sees a limousine drive up, and notices that it bears the insignia of the Government of the United States. A lackey opens the door and out steps the Secretary of State himself. Our erstwhile passenger on the "Soviet Ark" sees Mr. Secretary Hull enter the portal of the Embassy. He sees the door swing open and the Secretary grasp the hand of the Ambassador, who is an accredited representative of the Soviet government of Russia to the United States of America.

When I began my work at the immigration office, as I have said, Secretary of Labor Doak was in the midst of his drive against alien labor. There was also a roundup of foreign working people, and again Ellis Island was the main rendezvous for those being deported. Let me hasten to emphasize the fact that the purpose of this effort was vastly different from that of the Department of Justice at the close of the World War. The more recent roundup and deportation of aliens was merely an effort to discover and expel those who had illegally entered the country. Here was a situation of great difficulty; one which required care and tact, understanding and something also of the milk of human kindness. Let us take a very typical case:

A sailor from a foreign merchant ship visits a relative on a farm in New England. He is legally ashore, but he illegally overstays his time of leave. His farmer brother or uncle asks him to lend a hand with the harvest. This sailor comes to find himself very happy on the American farm, and the work agrees with him. He falls in love with a neighbor's daughter. In three months they are married, and in twelve months they are the parents of a child. Meanwhile, the sailor has drifted along, accepting his good fortune as it comes to him. He is young, healthy, and not slow to take advantage of luck, when it rises up in his way and looks him in the face.

This man is now a householder on American soil. He has planted his own crop and awaits the harvest. Every day, on coming in from the fields or from the milking, even before he opens the door to his home, he hears the voices of his wife and baby. Then, one day, he returns and finds—an officer of the law. The remainder of the story can be left to the imagination.

IV

The baiting of the "reds" during the War and post-War period is one of the most extraordinary chapters in the recent history of this country. It developed perhaps as part of the war psychoses.

The fact that the government had abolished the I.W.W. by breaking up its organization and arresting all its leaders—that fact seemed to escape the notice of the reactionaries, who were now on the hunt for more "reds" to devour.

During the year 1919 the issue became one of acid bitterness. The episodes of sending bombs in the mails were sufficient to stir anger in anybody's heart. Quite evidently some of the "reds" had gone outright insane. At least one bomb, sent to a member of Congress, when opened by the servants of his family maimed some of them for life. From that day forth, hosts of neutral-minded Americans were stirred to righteous wrath. As this wrath grew into rage, a particular object on which it could be spent was demanded to satiate the popular passion. While public anger was mounting, the criminals actually attempted to blow up the home of Attorney General Palmer of Washington.

It must ever be regretted that those who committed the crimes were not apprehended and punished. The laxity in our criminal legislation, and in the administration of criminal law, was never so clear as at that time. When it was seen that the criminals were going to escape the clutches of the law, the whole nation seemed to become a frantic mob. It did precisely what the mob always does—upon being denied the rightful object of its anger it seized upon the innocent instead of the guilty in order to satisfy its lust.

The mind of our country, all the teeming life of our one hundred and twenty-seven millions of Americans, has now moved on fifteen years from this time. It all seems long ago. Some Americans are naturally radicals. Others are conservatives. These groups of opposites are quite sure now to grow in numbers and strength. Those who, like myself, try to keep to the middle of the road—we who actually try to see things as they are and hold the balance—note with concern the growing desperation of the forces on the right and on the left. Just because these two extreme forces are developing, and because they have more and more a tendency to clash and to lose their heads—for that reason the history of the deportations of 1919–20 has much to teach us in the living present.

In this extraordinary history the fates acted strangely towards persons as well as towards our country as a whole. There was at that time in the office of the Assistant Secretary of Labor at Washington a man named Louis F. Post. Post was a liberal of the old school, a stalwart American, whose general point of view was that of Thomas Jefferson and Abraham Lincoln. He sought only to do his duty as a worthy public servant.

Two years after Mr. Post left his office, he published a history entitled "The Deportations Delirium of Nineteen Hundred Twenty." That volume tells the whole tale by placing fact after fact in due course.

The introduction to Mr. Post's book was written by Mr. Moorfield Storey, the distinguished Boston jurist and humanitarian.

"We cannot always control the violence of the mob," says Mr. Storey, "but we can at least insist that the men who are charged with the enforcement of the law shall not take the lead in breaking it and in ignoring the fundamental principle that every man is presumed to be innocent until he is proved guilty, and until his conviction is entitled to all the protection which the law gives to an innocent man."

The immigration service was then, as now, entirely under the direction of the Secretary of Labor. However, when Attorney-General Palmer undertook his drive against the "reds" he received special appropriations from Congress. He had under its authority a veritable army of war-time secret service agents and he used that force to the uttermost.

The final numerical record is one which all Americans must for a long time to come look back upon with certain misgivings. Dur-

ing the six months from December 29, 1919, to June 30, 1920, no
less than five thousand warrants were issued for deportation arrests.
The actual arrests followed in about three thousand cases.

V

Who was the most interesting radical ever to pass, eastbound or
westbound, through the gates of Ellis Island?

The answer permits no arguments. For human interest, one person stands out—Emma Goldman.

This extraordinary woman is now in her sixty-fifth year. The
reading of her autobiography indicates that she has lost none of her
fine power of self-expression; nor, in the least degree has she
changed any of her radical opinions.

In our study of Ellis Island the sensational career of Emma Goldman furnishes the central theme. Around this theme there gathers
in my mind a strange history, the history of the changing thought in
America, during the past sixty years, due to radical European movements. We see violent explosive thoughts generated in the minds
of the great European revolutionists of that period. These thoughts
and the revolutionary movements which followed them have cir-
cled the world like cyclonic storms. We see these storms, again and
again. They come as clouds holding in leash their thunderbolts.
These storms have broken about us in so many different ways, and
with such peculiar and divergent effects upon our public mind
and lives, that their history is sometimes quite baffling. I am convinced that the best way to define the effect of European radical
thought on America is to see it reflected in the mind of a single
individual.

In the year 1886 some unknown clerk in the immigration service
at Castle Garden registered the name of a Russian immigrant Jewish girl. She was then seventeen years of age. Nothing in the appearance of this child or in her demeanor singled her out from the
day's run of babbling crowds that moved in and out of the immigra-

tion station. Once safely landed, she proceeded direct to Rochester, New York. In her autobiography she has given us her own inimitable account of that day's events.

In Rochester Emma Goldman lived with relatives and, like most Russian immigrants, worked in the clothing trades.

Then, three years later, she came to New York. The first evening she looked up a friend, a young Russian medical student. He took her to dine at that university of radical thought—the café where there gathered the revolutionary "intelligentsia." It was a primitive café, of the sort found in New York's Greenwich Village. Within a few days the distinguished radicals were pointed out to her, the intellectual radicals of half a century ago. They included Ambrose Bierce, John Swinton, Huneker, and others. In later years Huneker was to become one of the greatest American literary critics; Bierce's stories are classics to-day. Curious it is that in America the young radical "intelligentsia," who forgather in these places, always seem to produce so many distinguished and conservative intellectual stars of the generation that is to follow.

Thus Miss Emma went out to her first radical meeting.

The man who took her to that meeting she had observed gobbling an enormous beefsteak at Sach's on the occasion of her first visit. It was none other than Alexander Berkman, her life long friend and paramour.

That first radical meeting marked the turning point of her life. The orator was the famous anarchist leader, John Most. Berkman pointed out two others whose names were just as distinguished in the radical circles of New York in those days. They were Sergius Shevitch, an exiled prince who had become editor of the German Socialist daily of New York, and his wife, the famous Countess Helena von Racowitza. Countess Helena had taken part in one of the great love affairs of history and the tragedy that led to the death of her distinguished lover, the brilliant Ferdinand Lassalle. Now, nearly half a century later, Emma Goldman describes in her autobiography the cold and appealing face of this strangest of all aristocratic beauties. She never became a radical. In her mind she remained what she was born, a conservative; while in her heart she loved in succession two of the extreme revolutionary socialists of the age. Now she was keeping house for Shevitch, her lawfully wedded husband —cooking ham and cabbage and making coffee in a Hoboken flat.

We come here upon one of the secrets of the power of radicalism in our lives. The uneducated working girl or boy will go to a public meeting and find himself face to face with persons of fine culture and intellectual distinction. This has been true from Moscow to San Francisco. And it is as true to-day in Bombay and Peking as it is in Chicago or London. Radicalism has its positive side. The radicals, in their social relations, customarily practise what they preach. Indeed it has been pointed out again and again that modern radicalism uses the power which was inherited in the early Christian church. To the submerged worker at these gatherings this movement is so thrilling, not only because it prophesies the changed social order of equal rights for all in the living present, but also because it gives intellectual and cultural opportunities which are not to be despised.

So Emma Goldman heard John Most speak. His eloquence enthralled her.

What was the vibrant thought that moved out of the queer perverted brain of Most, through his rapier-like tongue, into the avid mind of the immigrant girl?

This was the idea: that the poor shall strike against the rich and bring them down—not through kind words and teaching, but by fierce blows of terrorism and death. Social government itself, as well as the property system, shall be destroyed. So shall the toiling masses enter into Kingdom Come.

Most's social philosophy was the fruit—doubtless, the very natural fruit—of long oppression and of the suppressed rage of those whose emotions run away with their thoughts. Emma Goldman accepted his philosophy. In the course of the thirty years that elapsed between her first evening at the feet of John Most and the dull gray morning when, from the deck of the "Soviet Ark" she saw the shadows lift from the winter sea, she received no essential instruction on the nature of government and on the laws of social progress. This woman, so honest in all she was and said and did, represents as none other in Europe or America the infant of rebellion in the inexperienced and backward masses in the repressed countries of Europe. The mind of this extraordinary individual is a key to an understanding of that submerged majority of humanity which has accepted new and more frightful tyrannies in place of the old that have passed away.

John Most fell in love with Emma Goldman, and Emma Goldman fell in love with Alexander Berkman. Most's face was deformed and ugly. He seemed to be denied whatever he wanted in life. When he couldn't have Emma Goldman, he grew to hate her and even abused her and her friends.

Emma Goldman, like many another radical, set about to teach her fellow men. She whose language was originally Yiddish and then classical German, now learned English. One reads her writings and marvels at the pure and vibrant style. Emma Goldman read a great many books. She read Dostoievsky, Bernard Shaw, and Anatole France. But Karl Marx? Certainly not. To her Karl Marx was a conservative compromiser, an advocate of political trimming. His writings were to be classified with the Episcopal book of prayer and the Constitution of the United States. Usually the anarchists read only regular anarchist literature; just as the loyal Bolshevists to-day read Lenin but turn up their noses at the recalcitrant Trotsky. It is the old bigotry of the church sectarians all over again. Here a line shall be expurgated. There a whole literature must be condemned to the flames. Cotton Mather and John Most are as alike as two circles inch and inch in diameter. One was drawn in the seventeenth century, the other in the nineteenth. That is the difference.

Many assert the brilliance of the American career of Emma Goldman. Most Americans admire a fighter. Emblazoned on the banner of this remarkable woman are the words, "No surrender." Her circle of friends came to number many persons of distinction and influence. The loyalty she found among these friends never decreased because of her position. She claimed free speech under the Constitution and the law. When one of her speeches sent the poor feeble-minded Leon Czolgolsz out to do his terrible deed, she disclaimed responsibility. The fact that inciting the crime comes within the scope of our criminal law, that her case was essentially one demanding investigation by a prosecuting attorney—that fact she never understood.

There came at last the American declaration of war against Germany. Emma Goldman had cried out against the Spanish-American War, but that war was the affair of a summer holiday, and nobody cared. Most of our university professors, including the President of Harvard, opposed it. In the World War, as in every other great war, our country heard, to its heart's core, the sound of the drum.

For thirty years Emma Goldman had poured out her emotions upon America. Now America, too, had turned emotional, and it proceeded to pour out some of its emotionalism upon that entire breed who had voiced their revolutionary message through her flashing eye and bitter tongue. The War did not suffice to take up all the slack of this emotionalism. The day of the armistice came and went, and it left unsatiated the war hunger of back-country America. Quickly the national hatred turned from a defeated Germany and lashed itself into a rage against all forms of radicalism and all sorts of radicals. Victor Berger of Milwaukee was a conservative socialist. Senator La Follette was a Republican Progressive. Federal Judge Landis of Chicago, in sentencing Berger to jail and prison, said he regretted that he could not have him shot. A popular writer of fiction wrote an allegory intimating that La Follette would be forever ostracized and despised by all Americans.

A year passed and found the prison cells in Ellis Island packed to overflowing. On December 21, 1919, all nations stood at attention in silent salute to the flag that had been unfurled in battle during the great War. The sailing of the "Soviet Ark" marked the final victory of this country over its enemy in Europe.

There is a last word to this history. The S.S. *Buford* came into port on the far coast of Finland. When the two hundred and forty-nine prisoners came to the Russian border, they received the cheers of the strange martial movement. Emma Goldman, as she crossed the frozen river from the forest of Finland to the forests of Russia, declared "this is the greatest day of my life."

Emma Goldman had been deported as an alien anarchist. Her father was a citizen of the United States, and her husband was a former citizen of the United States whose citizenship had been revoked upon the grounds that it had been obtained by false statements. Since the husband was not present and therefore unable to defend the revocation proceedings, there is grave doubt as to their regularity. Emma Goldman had made one voyage abroad after obtaining her passport as the wife and daughter of American citizens. On this journey there was no question of the regularity of her status.

But her life in America had been a long series of strifes, arrests, crusades and more arrests. Alexander Berkman, with whom she had been in love, had served a long term in a Pennsylvania prison. When he reached Ellis Island he appealed his case to the United States Supreme Court. The appeal was denied. Emma Goldman also had the right of appeal. She refused to exercise that right. Suffering the tortures of severe toothache at Ellis Island, realizing that Berkman was doomed to deportation and that the deportation would undoubtedly be to Russia, she got through the days somehow and waited.

Nothing of transcendent importance occurred at Ellis Island during her stay there prior to the hearing which brought about her deportation order.

At that hearing she arose and read the most defiant statement ever hurled into the teeth of the United States Government. With her own permission, it is herewith reproduced:

At the very outset of this hearing I wish to register my protest against these star chamber proceedings, whose very spirit is nothing short of a revival of the Spanish Inquisition or the more recently defunct Third Degree system of Czarist Russia.

This star chamber hearing is furthermore a denial of the insistent claim on the part of the government that in this country we have free speech and a free press, and that every offender against the law—even the lowliest of men—is entitled to his day in open court and to be heard and judged by a jury of his peers.

If the present proceedings are for the purpose of proving some alleged offense committed by me, some evil or anti-social act, then I protest against the secrecy and third degree methods of this so-called "trial." But if I am not charged with any specific offense or act, if— as I have reason to believe—this is purely an inquiry into my social and political opinions, then I protest still more vigorously against these proceedings, as utterly tyrannical and diametrically opposed to the fundamental guarantees of a true democracy.

Every human being is entitled to hold any opinion that appeals to her or him without making herself or himself liable to persecution. Ever since I have been in this country—and I have lived here practically all my life—it has been dinned into my ears that under the institutions of this democracy, one is entirely free to think and feel as he pleases. What becomes of this sacred guarantee of freedom of thought when persons are being persecuted and driven out for the very reasons for which the pioneers who built up this country laid down their lives.

And what is the object of this star chamber proceeding, that is plainly based on the so-called anti-anarchist law? Is not the only purpose of this law and the deportations *en masse* to suppress every symptom of popular discontent now manifesting itself throughout this country, as well as in all European lands? It requires no great prophetic gift to foresee that this new governmental policy of deportation is but the first step toward the introduction into this country of the old Russian system of exile for the high treason of entertaining new ideas of social life and industrial reconstruction. To-day so-called aliens are deported, to-morrow native Americans will be banished. To be sure, America does not yet possess a suitable place like Siberia to which her exiled sons might be sent, but since she has begun to acquire colonial possessions, in contradiction of the principles she stood for over a century, it will not be difficult to find an American Siberia, once the precedent of banishment is established.

The anti-anarchist law confuses the most varied social philosophies and isms in order to cover with the same blanket, so to speak, every element of social protest, so that under the guise of this single law, striking steel workers or railroad men, or any other class of workers, may be corralled wholesale and the most active of the strikers hurried out of the country, in order to serve the interests of our industrial kings.

Collective bargaining for the workers is now an admitted right, recognized by the highest officials of the land and accepted by the most reactionary elements. Yet when the steel workers of this country after a quarter of a century of desperate struggle for the right to bargain collectively, have mustered enough spirit and cohesion to enter into a struggle with steel barons for that fundamental right, the entire machinery of government, State and Federal, is put in operation to crush that spirit and to undermine the chance of establishing humane conditions in the industry where conditions have been worse than those which existed under the most brutal feudalism. The workers in the steel industry have expressed no particular social philosophy. They are certainly not on strike for "overthrowing the government by force or violence," yet the anti-anarchist law is used as a means to reach out for these simple, hard-driven, hard-pressed human beings, who have endangered life and limb to build up this devouring monster—the Steel Trust.

A reign of terror has been established in the strike region. American Cossacks, known as the State Constabulary, ride over men, women and children; deputies of the Department of Justice break into the strikers' homes, violating the sacred Anglo-Saxon tradition that a man's home is his castle and may not be entered except by due Warrant of Law, and to add the finishing touch to this picture of American "freedom," the Immigration authorities, the men of your department, take the strikers off secretly, and order them deported by such proceedings as I am being subjected to to-day, without having committed even the slightest offense against American institutions save the one that is the greatest crime to-day—the right of the workers to life, liberty and the pursuit of happiness—a right that was made in America and not imported by those hated aliens.

A commission appointed by your department finds that eighty per cent of the wealth of this country is produced by these aliens themselves or the sons of these aliens. In return for this, they are hounded and persecuted as enemies.

Under the mask of the same anti-anarchist law, every criticism of a corrupt administration, every attack on governmental abuse, every manifestation of sympathy with the struggle of another country in the pangs of a new birth—in short, every free expression of untrammelled thought may be suppressed utterly, without even the semblance of an unprejudiced hearing or a fair trial. It is for these reasons, chiefly, that I most strenuously protest against the despotic law and its star chamber method of procedure. I protest against the whole spirit underlying it— the spirit of an irresponsible hysteria, the result of the terrible war and the evil tendencies of bigotry and persecution and violence which are the epilogues of five years of bloodshed.

Under these circumstances it becomes evident that the naked purpose of all these repressive measures—chief among them the anti-
anarchist law, is to aid the capitalist's *status quo* in the United States.
Vain is the pretense that the safety of the country or the well-being of
the American people demands those drastic Prussian methods. Nay,
indeed, the people can only profit by a free discussion of the new ideas
now germinating in the minds of thinking men and women in society.
The free expressions of the hopes and aspirations of a people is the
greatest and only safety in a sane society. In truth, it is such free expression and discussion alone that can point the most beneficial path for
human progress and development. But the object of deportation and the
anti-anarchist law etc., is the very opposite. It is to stifle the voice of the
people, to muzzle every aspiration of the voice of labor. That is the real
and terrible menace of the star chamber proceedings and of the tendency of exiling and banishing everyone who does not fit in the scheme
of things our industrial lords are so eager to perpetuate.

With all the power and intensity of my being I protest against this
conspiracy of imperialist capitalism against the life and liberty of the
American people.
October 27, 1919.

The years were not entirely unkind to Emma Goldman. But let
us hear from her own lips what she thinks of Ellis Island. In February of this year, she came out of her retirement in France, obtained the special permission of the United States Department of
Labor to enter the United States for a lecture tour of three months
and arrived in New York after an absence of fifteen years. During
the final week of her visit, surrounded by relatives and friends in
her suite in the Fifth Avenue hotel, she recounted for the purpose
of this volume, her actual going into exile.

"I enjoyed writing pamphlets in those days," she said, "but I was
so afraid my writings would be taken from me that I waited until
everyone had gone to bed at Ellis Island, and when they were
sleeping, I got up, turned on the light and wrote.

"On the night we were taken away I was writing a pamphlet on
deportation at 2:00 A.M. I did not dream that we would be going for
several days. In fact, I had spoken with Superintendent Baker and
others, telling them that we would like to know a day or two before
our deportations in order that we might send for our clothes and

personal belongings. You see—many of us had been jerked up wherever we were found, and not permitted to communicate in any manner with our relatives until after we reached the Island.

"Many of the poor working men were taken in their work clothes without so much as a chance to get changes of underwear, and not even at the last were they permitted to remove their savings from savings banks. I believe the savings of the entire lot amounted to something like sixty thousand dollars.

"As I said, I was writing the pamphlet when a rap sounded on my door. It was one of the coldest nights of the year. I hurriedly hid the manuscript I was working upon and went to the door.

"An official said: 'Get your things together—you're being taken to the deportation boat!'

"Those who were sleeping were pulled from their beds. We were marched between two long lines of soldiers with loaded guns to the cutter. We had to stand in the freezing cold. When two hours had elapsed we reached the *Buford*. Two hours later we were heading out to sea, and none of us knew where we were being taken.

"Everyone was ill from the cold. Some had fever. Some even had grippe."

Miss Goldman then proceeded to describe the congestion on the *Buford,* how insufficiently the majority of the deportees were fed, and how all were constantly guarded by the soldiers.

"A soldier stood outside my cabin at all times," she said. "I was sorry for him standing there in the cold. He was ignorant of what it was all about, merely acting in line of duty. One day I pushed a camp stool out to him. 'Why don't you sit down?' I asked.

"'Why should you give me a camp stool?' he returned.

"I explained to him my feelings. Something about it must have gone the rounds of the other seventy soldiers, for one of them came to Alexander Berkman on Christmas Eve and said: 'This thing is getting on our nerves—it doesn't seem right. Say the word and we'll throw the damn Captain and Colonel overboard. You'll be in charge of the ship, we'll go with you wherever you want to go.'

"Berkman explained that he was not a navigator and that ended what might otherwise have been a mutiny.

"We reached Finland without knowing where we were, having crossed the Baltic sea which was still underlain with German mines. We were placed in sealed cars on a Finnish train, each door manned by a guard, just as Trotsky went through Germany.

"Perhaps this was because the deportees organized a strike on ship because of the food. The strike had been settled by allowing our own bakers, etc., to do the work. To cap it all, the guards looted the train before we got out of Finland and took most of our personal belongings.

"We were received in Russia with military honors. It was a grand ovation. None of us knew for sure that we were nearing Russian soil until we were so informed. The Russians in our party fell down to the ground and kissed the snow. The band played. We were cheered. It was magnificent."

Acme.

Underwood & Underwood.

A NOTED ANARCHIST GOING AND COMING.

Left. Emma Goldman being escorted to Ellis Island, December 5, 1919, "for immediate deportation." *Right.* The sixty-four-year-old radical returning after a fifteen-year exile for a ninety-day visit to the United States, as she crossed the border from Canada on February 1, 1934.

CHAPTER IV

ROYALTY AND FAKERS IN THE CARAVAN

I

WHATEVER else our much-criticized democracy may have done to earn the tirades that have been poured out upon it from time to time, it has never violated the spirit of the Constitution by a worship of titles, crests, and family trees.

The body and backbone of our country—our farmers, our working class, our great middle class, our official group—these have never expressed either awe or envy of the titled representatives of European houses who have walked our streets and made their homes in our hotels.

The "Four Hundred" of our cities have, I am sure, paid excessive honor to some of these highborn personages; and they, who hold the power in our country because of their wealth, have recognized that blood, as well as money, gives prestige in Europe, and have paid their respects accordingly.

In the main, however, the proud possessors of these symbols of pageantry in older countries have been neglected, and many of them have felt injured, on coming here, because of our general lack of interest in their royal accoutrements. It is a quality of our inheritance, this indifference to signs and symbols.

Among the hordes of peasants and merchants, unskilled laborers and artisans, beggars and paupers, which for forty years have streamed through Ellis Island, now and again these princes and countesses from the Continent have strayed. Some of them have not seemed any less "lost" than the poor illiterates, to whom the New World was an enormous whirlpool with no end or beginning and in which it seemed probable they would eventually sink. To the royal visitors, the detention seemed to have prison significance, and they have fumed and stormed in the best quarters the Island affords, while their personal affairs were being investigated and their stories made public to the world.

It seems to me that in the past we have shown too much zeal in catching these wearers of the cloak of royalty in our immigration net. Most of them have never intended to pay us more than a fleeting visit; they have come on business, out of curiosity, or to pay social calls. Perhaps some have come to seek out, with subtlety and tact, American brides whose fathers are pearl-button, or suspender, or automobile-tire kings. We have called too much attention to their presence here. We have used our democracy as a weapon to allow us deliberately to offend them. And in so doing we have given ourselves a reputation for puritanism and prudishness abroad.

On one occasion our over zealousness in holding a lady of title on Ellis Island stirred up an international crisis that scared the authorities at Washington into solving the impasse with sudden action, for which they never afterwards gave a reason. It did not happen during my commissionership, but it is not so long out of memory but that its reverberations still guide policies on the Island and in Washington. No one would like such a situation repeated.

This episode occurred in 1926. Vera, Countess of Cathcart, five years divorced from the English Earl of Cathcart, was taken off the S.S. *Carmania* by immigration inspectors on February 11. She was held a prisoner on Ellis Island for ten days, while her name and story buzzed over the tea tables of two continents. And finally she was released on an order telephoned late at night from Washington, unexpected and never explained.

The affair began when Countess Vera, planning a visit to New

York in the course of which she hoped to persuade one or another of the Broadway producers to buy a play called "Ashes of Love," innocently marked a "D" on her official questionnaire after the question inquiring about her marital status. This signified that she was divorced, and not either married or single. Consequently the inspectors watched for her. They were on the trail of something.

The *Carmania* arrived with the Countess aboard, small, slim, attractive, brunette. An inspector boarded the ship, looked at her papers. "You are divorced," he commented.

"Yes," replied the little countess candidly.

He must have remembered something about her, though they said later at the Island that nothing had been planned in advance.

"You'll have to come with me to Ellis Island," he told her.

She was in a rage. "What for?" she demanded. "I have done nothing in my life that I am ashamed of! It is an outrage, my being held here."

Her friends crowded nearer, indignant and sympathetic. Nearly everyone on the boat, by the time it arrived here, was her friend. Reporters flocked about, and she gave them a generous hearing.

"By the by, why have you a Statue of Liberty?" she asked ironically. "We couldn't see it, coming up the harbor, because of the fog. But what is the use of seeing Liberty if they are going to treat me as a criminal? If it is because I am divorced—well, I understand that there are twenty-five thousand divorced women in the United States."

The Countess was travelling with Lady Frances Huntington and Mrs. Gordon Carr. She said she planned only a three or four weeks' stay, and would return to England in March to marry Ralph Neale, a British playwright. It was chiefly a social visit, but she had brought her play along to dispose of, if opportunity offered. She had no intention of living in America, and had a properly certified visa to that effect.

The question involved was one of "moral turpitude," the old cat'spaw in the law, which had barred so many aliens other than the criminals and felons for which it was intended. The Countess of Cathcart had been divorced by the Earl in 1921, and another titled gentleman, the Earl of Craven, had been named as corespondent. This scandal was dragged out of the past and retold on the front pages of newspapers all over this country and Europe. In the eyes of immigration officials, it constituted a basis for refusing Countess Vera the privilege of a month's visit to our "land of the free."

As a blizzard was raging when the boat docked, they kept her a prisoner for two days on the ship and then brought her to the Island, where she was haled before the Board. She answered the questions put to her with absolute candor. She admitted having lived with the Earl of Craven in South Africa while the divorce was pending in London. She did not seem to consider it a crime. She did not appear penitent.

"Is that the only indiscretion you have committed?"

"The only one, before or after."

The Board of Special Inquiry, sitting as a jury, immediately ordered her excluded and deported on admission of a crime involving moral turpitude, which, had it been denied, would not have served as a barrier to her entry.

Meanwhile a strange coincidence had occurred. The Earl of Craven, who had recently been visiting in America with Lady Craven, came up from Bermuda. The women of the country, reading of his arrival, flew to an attack on the "double standard" of morals that was evidently being observed by the Commissioner of Immigration and the Department of Labor. The case did not leave the front pages of New York newspapers for two months. Petitions flew hither and thither gathering names. Editorials stirred up the public, the Department of Labor, the women's clubs. Protests descended by the hundreds upon the head of the unfortunate Commissioner at Ellis Island. Letters of sympathy in the same quantity came to the Countess in her detention. Consuls moved about briskly. Cablegrams flew back and forth across the ocean. English editors dipped their pens in sarcasm and treated of American morals and purity of ideals.

Immediately following the order for deportation the Countess' loyal friend, Mrs. Carr, who had insisted upon staying with her on the Island, hurried to Washington with another friend, Horace Green, to put the case before the Labor Department. William A. de Ford, New York lawyer, was engaged to present the case at the department hearing.

Ralph Neale cabled from London to Secretary of Labor Davis:

"As fiancé of the Countess of Cathcart, I wish to protest against any reflection on her character and earnestly solicit your benevolent intervention in her behalf to enable her to carry out her business in New York."

Sir Esme Howard, British ambassador, called upon Secretary Davis and went away without satisfaction.

The editor of the London *Evening Standard* accused us of bad international manners. He remarked that it was not important to emphasize that this action would make our country ridiculous in the eyes of the world, as well as childishly inconsistent in American standards.

"America can well afford to be ridiculous," he wrote. "She is amazingly rich, exceptionally independent, and she can do with impunity all sorts of things that less fortunately placed nations would have to think twice about. It may provoke a smile to compare the moral standards of Ellis Island with those of Hollywood and to reflect that the land which permits so much freedom in matrimonial readjustment within its own borders should be so squeamish concerning the divorces of foreigners. But Ellis Island is not so much a question of international law as of international manners.

"If the United States government does really hold that being divorced by a foreign court of justice implies moral turpitude of a degree to make even a short sojourn a source of spiritual danger to American citizens in general, then its business is clearly to make it known that all divorced persons will be denied admission unless they have previously satisfied the American embassy or consulate in their country that special indulgence may be extended to them."

He said even more. He said that the dependence of divorced persons at present upon the caprice of immigration officials arose from an American superiority complex brought on by the flattery of Europe and of England in particular.

Sir John Foster Fraser, in an article called "The Billionaire Puritans" in the London *Illustrated Sunday Herald,* said some rather harsh things about our high standard of morals for other people. He discussed our divorce laws, our prohibition situation, and our crime statistics.

"We do not understand," he wrote, "why it is that in this land of a hundred and twenty millions of people, with hearts beating in righteousness, democracy and fraternity and 'doing to the other fellow what the other fellow would do to you and doing it first,' there should be such a calendar of hold-ups and sandbaggings and murders."

"Of all the remarkable innovations introduced by the United States," said the London *Daily Express,* "this decision of the Ellis Island tribunal is one of the most astonishing on record."

"How do Americans who get divorces in Paris get home afterwards?" inquired the *Westminster Gazette.*

Commissioner Henry Curran received many telegrams, both of commendation and reproach. One of the most remarkable messages came from a group of well known women who resented impartially the slight put upon women in the operation of the "double standard." They said:

We see in the daily papers that the Countess of Cathcart has been excluded from the United States on the grounds of moral turpitude because of her divorce in which the Earl of Craven, a married man, was the corespondent. We know nothing of this case except what we have read in the papers. We are not championing the case of Lady Cathcart. We are not acquainted with her. But we know that the Earl of Craven has been admitted into the United States and is at present here. The purpose of this letter is to ask why the woman is debarred for an act which has not barred the man, although he is admittedly as guilty as she, if the case is as reported. We protest against such discrimination against women.

This was signed by Mrs. A. Gordon Morris, Mrs. Raymond Brown, Mrs. H. C. Dreier, Mrs. John Blair, Mrs. Alice Duer Miller, Mrs. Norman D. R. Whitehouse, Mrs. James Lees Laidlaw, Mrs. James Russel Parsons, and Mrs. Lewis S. Thompson.

Lady Cathcart, from her little room at Ellis Island, demanded that the Earl of Craven be made to leave the country if she had to leave it. The Earl, who was much annoyed about the whole proceeding, said "the country is quite big enough for the two of us."

Commissioner Curran gave an interview in which he maintained that the inspectors were simply obeying the law when they took the Countess off the ship and were not disobeying it when they let the Earl in. The inspectors and other officials were not posted on all the scandals in high life on the Continent, he said, and the Countess was detained because her own statements provoked inquiry. The Earl of Craven, on the other hand, being a properly married man, had marked an "M" in the square on his sheet, and had entered unquestioned. The Commissioner expressed himself as willing to look further into the Earl's case.

The hearing was postponed at Washington for several days, while New York and London circles seethed, and the question of immigration laws rose to the surface of the public mind in America once more. The Countess murmured from her prison that adultery was not a crime in England; if it were, most of the nobility would be criminals. Lady Huntington sailed back to England to avoid further publicity, without making an effort to see the friend with whom she had planned a five weeks' visit. The Earl of Craven, followed a few days later by his wife, went to Canada and from there commented on the absurdities of the situation. Mr. Neale cabled President Coolidge.

The president of Carnegie Institute sent Secretary Davis an amazing telegram, which the newspapers reproduced:

A tragic and appalling outrage is being enacted at New York in the case of that poor woman who is being made by your men to tell her sins to the whole world. I hope you will realize that Christ is holding his sheltering arm over her head because she is the heroine of his most beautiful adventure. He would not accuse her, and her exclusion will put the stamp of a detestable hypocrisy upon our country.

The American Weekly and the *Graphic* went into court to discuss their respective rights to publish the Countess' memoirs, entitled "The Truth About My Love Affairs." Commissioner Curran got a warrant of arrest for the Earl of Craven after it was too late. The National Woman's Party marshalled a group of one hundred and fifty women, representing nearly all the states, to appear at the Washington hearing. Vera said the Earl of Craven was a coward. Mrs. Harriot Stanton Blatch, suffragist leader, headed a delegation of women who came to Ellis Island to condole with the Countess.

The matter at last reached the floor of the Senate, and the majority of senators were agreed that the immigration laws needed revision. The government began to consider the possible effect if European nations should retaliate. Secretary Davis hesitated, and the Countess obtained a writ of *habeas corpus*, to be used in case the hearing went against her.

Members of women's clubs, flooding the Island, suggested to Commissioner Curran that he resign. He was mightily embarrassed at the undesired publicity, and chafed because he could do nothing. "The whole thing goes by me like a trolley car in the next street," he remarked.

Earl Carroll bought the Countess' play and offered her the leading rôle in it.

The Earl of Craven sent the government a radiogram:

"Gentlemen, you must be a bunch of Godforsaken idiots."

The Department of Labor affirmed the decision of Ellis Island. The day of deportation was set for February 20. The day passed and she did not go, because the writ of *habeas corpus* had been granted the day before. Then suddenly a telegram came late on the night of

February 21, ordering the release of the Countess for ten days on her own bond for five hundred dollars. She had gone to bed, but rose and dressed and took the ferry for Manhattan. She was as gleeful as a small child at her release.

The case put the immigration laws under public scrutiny, and discussion of it continued unabated. The Countess, free under the grant of liberty, demanded through her attorney that a rehearing be held at Washington on the grounds that she had been held illegally, never having, according to her interpretation, come under the moral turpitude clause at all.

The law containing this famous clause was passed in 1917, and states that any person having been convicted, or admitting the commission of a felony or other crime or other misdemeanor involving moral turpitude must be barred from the United States. The officials said that the United States courts had always held adultery as a "morally turpitudinous" crime, and had deported two hundred and sixty-one persons under the same provision during the year 1925. The Countess came under the section involving those who "admitted" their crimes; she had, of course, never been convicted of anything.

The Countess' lawyer maintained that since adultery was not a crime in South Africa, or in England, his client had therefore never been guilty of any crime at all. He went into court and had her freed on the writ, thus discharging her from the custody of the Commissioner of Immigration, and technically limiting her stay in the country to six months. Judge William Bondy sustained the writ.

The Department of Labor asked an appeal, saying that the officials were anxious to obtain a more precise interpretation of the application of the immigration act as a basis for future decisions. If a person may enter our gates after committing an act that is a crime in our country but not in the country where it was committed, then the laws have been misinterpreted ever since they were first penned, Washington declared.

The appeal was not granted and the matter was dropped. Vera demanded an apology, which was not given. People said that Secretary Davis had killed his chances of obtaining the nomination for governor of Pennsylvania. When Sunday came round the pastors preached on the affair from their pulpits. The question of divorce in general got a thorough airing.

But it had gone on too long, and people were tired of the affair. When her play "Ashes" appeared in Washington, it got a definitely cool reception. Infuriated, the little Countess bought the work back from Mr. Carroll for twenty thousand dollars and presented it herself in New York a week or two later. The critics were not kind to her.

"'Ashes of Love' does not merit the serious consideration of any audience in the world," said the *Times*. "It is admittedly naïve, and recounts with quite an air of discovery a rather childish and undramatic story of a woman who elopes to South Africa with a lover. He deserts her, and she returns to her home in London. That is absolutely all there is to it. The fact that it duplicates events in the author's life is of no avail in the theater."

The reviewer went on to say, further, that the acting of the Countess was quite without theatrical effectiveness.

The play closed at the end of a week, and the Countess returned to England on March 31. She had pawned her necklace to get the money with which to pay Mr. Carroll for the play, and the play had failed. She did not love America.

The whole affair was, of course, a tempest in a teapot. There was no reason in the world why the Countess of Cathcart should not have been admitted to the United States to make a five weeks' visit and to get her bad play quietly on Broadway, where so many bad plays had been before. Nothing was gained by so interpreting the law as to prevent her. The newspapers which pointed out that immigration officials should be given precise and definite instructions as to the interpretation of our laws, were right. No repetition of the affair has occurred, and should such a decision be again required,

I believe it would be made more calmly and quietly, in the light of the memories of the Craven-Cathcart case.

A Spanish Prince was detained for four days on Ellis Island in the autumn of 1912 without excessive notoriety. He was the young Prince Ludovico Pignatelli d'Aragon, who made numerous trips to this country in the course of his wanderings and finally married a young American girl, and settled down here.

This Prince was noted for the repeated reports of his engagement to American society girls. He made good "news" on each of his arrivals, though he was haled to Ellis Island only once, on the occasion mentioned.

The officials held him because of reports that he had been sent out of France for operating a gambling establishment, which, as a foreigner, he could not legally do. After consultation with the Paris embassy and serious consideration of the case, Commissioner Williams concluded that the Prince did not belong to any of the classes of aliens which the law barred from the United States.

The suite of rooms occupied by Prince Pignatelli on Ellis Island—the Commissioner's own rooms—have been placed at the disposal of many a prominent personage whom the immigration ritual has detained against his will. In December, 1916, they were occupied very unwillingly by Baron Robert Emanuel Oppenheim of Paris, who was ordered deported on the ground that he had been convicted in France of a crime coming under that often-used category, moral turpitude. The fact that those rooms were the best on the Island and had been occupied by many notables before him, did not seem to reconcile the Baron to his fate.

The Baron's "moral turpitude" was of a financial nature. Commissioner Frederic C. Howe had received a cable dispatch while the questionable visitor was on the ocean, warning him that the Baron had been convicted in France for his part in some illegal financial transactions. The Frenchman could not believe his ears when denied permission to go ashore, and gazed through his monocle at the immigration inspector who had given the order.

I learned from the records that the Baron was eventually admitted on his promise to remain no longer than three months. Since he did not return to Ellis Island, we must assume that he kept that promise.

One of the most interesting stories connected with "barons" and "baronesses" in their relation to Ellis Island may be told about a young and beautiful Turkish woman taken as a spy in the last year of the World War. Her claim to rank was never established, but in the annals of the Island she is always included among the other baronesses who have made a temporary home there.

The chief of the Department of Justice Secret Service Bureau for the New York district announced on March 19, 1918, the arrest of four persons, two men and two women, whom he believed to be important members of an international spy system which had operated throughout the War in the interests of Germany.

Madame Despina Davidovitch Storch, known as the "Baroness de Beville" because of her established relationship with the young Baron Henri of Beville, was twenty-three years old, and had served throughout the War as one of the most important spies in the German service. Her success was due chiefly to her feminine charm, which attracted to her friends from the highest circles of New York and Washington. These friends were twisted to her own uses, and unwittingly helped her in the furtherance of her dangerous aims. She had incredible daring, and was described by the newspapers of that time as a "strikingly handsome woman".

Caught with Madame Storch in the spy net were the Baron de Beville, Mrs. Elizabeth Charlotte Nix, and a man giving his name as Count Robert de Clairmont, a Frenchman.

For a full week after her arrest the young spy matched wits with the agents, and, as one said, "could explain documents which on their face would bring her before a firing squad in France in fifteen minutes." She was trapped at last into an admission that she was "Madame Hesketh," and then the case was all set against her in France.

A deportation warrant was issued in the name of President Wilson on March 19, 1918, for all four spies, and they all, with the exception of the Count de Clairmont, who was ill in New York, were conveyed to Ellis Island. Once there, they began to realize the seriousness of the situation, and were no longer so defiant as when they were first taken into custody. They failed in all their attempts to get a hearing before a special immigration board.

Exactly ten days later Madame Storch died on Ellis Island. It was reported that she had contracted pneumonia soon after her arrival there. Deputy Immigration Commissioner Byron H. Uhl vehemently denied that she had committed suicide, as was of course rumored. Madame Nix became violently ill of appendicitis at the same time, and the Count de Clairmont in New York had to be removed to a hospital.

The parents of the Baron de Beville made arrangements for the funeral of Madame Storch, and the Baron was permitted to be present in the custody of an immigration guard. The services lasted only five minutes. Madame Storch was buried in Mt. Olivet Cemetery.

A day or two later her clothes, beautiful and brilliant enough for a princess, were auctioned off for a few paltry dollars at City Hall. Rich jewels went for a song. One of the famous feminine spies in history was quickly forgotten.

In the crowded and colorful history of Ellis Island, these blue-bloods have amounted to practically nothing in numbers, and nothing at all in their effects on our melting-pot. I have written about them because their experiences in our country illustrate one of the odd quirks of our American mind—we have taken a certain wicked little pleasure in holding them up. After they have languished a brief while in our immigration prison, we have pitied and forgiven them and opened our gates a tiny way to permit them to squeeze through. We are, after all, proud that they wanted to come. We are a democratic people, and we like to make democracy a potent force now and then.

II

From the same first class cabins that brought these men and women to our shores have stepped the pseudo-royal personages who have hoped to gain something—money, perhaps, or friends—by pretending to rank and title.

During my sojourn on Ellis Island one of the legends of America developed before my eyes. This is the tale of "Prince" Mike Romanoff, whose career to-day is still in the making.

Prince Mike will never be just a memory in the minds of Ellis Island officials, who through the years have dealt with him. He will become, unless I mistake, a twentieth-century legendary hero—or villain, as you will. He is one of our popular scalawags, like the great wild-west cowboys of a past century.

His paraphernalia are the walking stick and Dunhill pipe, rather than the six-shooters of the Jesse James era. He is the rascal of the big cities, rather than of the frontier which has vanished.

He has the same quality of lovable charm, the same ability to hatch mad and impossible stories, and the same careless disregard for facts that all legendary heroes of far-off days are reputed to have possessed. We do not require our heroes in America to be white knights or King Arthurs. Let them be as lawless and turbulent as they will; only let them do interesting and unexpected things, and never descend to cold-blooded cruelty or big-scale swindling. Then the American public will follow their antics with amused tolerance, and even defend them if prison bars loom too close, or the deportation ship is waiting in the harbor to take them out of our sight and life.

I was introduced to Prince Mike in April of 1932. He was brought to the Island—which he playfully calls the "Isle of Ellis"—as a stowaway from the *Ile de France*. He was always debonair and good-natured under detention. He affected natty English clothes, and his Oxford accent was impeccable.

I attended the hearing when he was brought up, and began an

investigation of his case that was to be continued from time to time through a full year. Though we were put to repeated inconvenience and trouble during that year, and had to bear the whole country's criticism and laughter at our expense because we could not seem to keep a firm grip on the slippery actor, no one at Ellis Island bears him a grudge.

To be frank, I was getting as much "kick" out of the Romanoff performance as anybody reading the story in the press—unofficially of course—though the papers kept trying to make it appear that he was getting on my nerves.

And I am sure that Prince Mike, still walking the sidewalks of New York on a three-year parole, bears us no grudge. I suspect he rather enjoyed his various sojourns there, where in his "palace on the Isle of Ellis" he sat clipping out the press stories about him and interviewing the reporters with whom, by that time, he was on familiar terms.

For Prince Mike's call upon us in 1932, when I met him, was not his first appearance on Ellis Island. Our little chugging ferry had brought him over a good many times before that, and I found that his record on the Island dated back many years.

He claimed from the first to be a citizen of the United States, but his memories were hazy and he could never recall in what part of New York State he had been born. He always said blithely that it was "somewhere around." Our records showed that he had been born in Russia about 1890, and it was on that basis that we continually deported him. I believe he really prefers New York to Paris or London, because Americans have shown themselves more good-natured after being fleeced and hoaxed and made fools of.

At the hearing in April, 1932, Mike told us how he got over. He did not risk his life in an airless cubbyhole, or pay an enormous sum to be smuggled in. He had travelled back and forth between the United States and the continent too often for that. He simply walked on board with the visitors, and by occupying different empty cabins each night managed to escape detection until the last day. During the voyage, witnesses told us, he chatted with prominent persons and drank at the bar on their invitation.

"How did you get caught, then?"

His ego would never let him tell the truth. He loved being considered the friend of prominent persons, and he had not been able to refrain from boasting of his personal acquaintance with the captain of the *Ile de France*. The captain turned him in.

So Mike, who answered to his proper name of Harry Gerguson when anyone remembered to call him by it, was ordered deported. He had an apartment in New York. He had to get his things.

I sent him over in charge of an immigration guard. Then I wrote an order to have him locked in the brig of the *Comte de Grasse*, the next liner to France, when she sailed four days later. I meant to make sure of his departure.

The guard turned up a day later and confessed to losing his prisoner. It seemed very funny to the press and Mike's admirers. But a guard who allows himself to get drunk under the table of the man he is guarding, however urbane and free-handed the prisoner may be, is no guard at all; so I dismissed him, and suspended three members of the staff involved in the escape.

Agents dove in and out of speakeasies on the upper East Side, looking for Mike. I was making a speech in Boston, when my wife called me on the telephone and said someone had "tipped her off" about Mike's whereabouts. Over the long distance telephone I gave the instructions which led to his capture. By the time I had finished my speech, the whole performance had been carried out and Mike was back at the Island.

Peering out from behind the barred doors of the ship's brig, he grinned and said he was reconciled to serving a jail sentence when he arrived in France. "But I'll be back," he promised.

When he got back just before Christmas he found proprietors and patrons of his favorite speakeasies secretly glad to see him, but a little nervous as to what their outward reception of such an undesirable scoundrel ought to be. If he entered through Ellis Island, we did not see him. The inspectors were on the lookout for him, too, as I had received word that he had been dismissed from his French jail a week or so earlier.

He was discovered in the company of a well-known lawyer in one of the better post-prohibition restaurants on the upper East Side. The lawyer, who had not met him before, was enjoying himself hugely, and so was Prince Mike, until the management suggested nervously that its decorations were a trifle shabby and scarcely suitable for the entertainment of royalty. Mike took the hint. When he got up to go, the patrons of the restaurant rose as one man and followed him to another establishment further downtown.

We got him again, but his friends who turned him in suffered qualms of conscience for weeks afterwards. The manager of a Dunhill shop, where Mike went to purchase his favorite tobacco at ten dollars a pound, had the painful duty of putting the policeman on his trail.

Before he was taken from the station house he graciously posed for photographs.

"Too bad they got you, Mike," said one of the photographers sympathetically.

He shrugged his shoulders. "It's all in the game. I've got nothing to fear. I'm a citizen of the United States, and I'll be a free man in a few days."

Mike always considered me his business manager, and would never see the newspaper men unless I were present. Once he came in to ask if he ought to sell his story for one hundred dollars.

I said, "Mike, since you've made a good story out of it, you might as well get what it's worth."

The government grew interested in Gerguson, and sent up Mr. Samuel Dickstein, chairman of the House Committee on Immigration, to investigate the case. Two lawyers offered their services in an effort to prove that the wanderer was an American citizen.

The whole case was reviewed. It appeared that he had many

records in many places. Once the thing got started, stories about him popped up from everywhere.

The most famous story concerned the 1923 hoax. Posing as Prince Dmitry Michael Alexandrovitch Obolenski, whose mother was a Romanoff, Mike fooled the most fashionable and wealthy circles of America's big cities for a year. Because he spoke so earnestly of his willingness to do anything—"work on a large estate where they have horses, or be a private secretary or a tutor, or even a department store floorwalker,"—they paid good money to hear him lecture on conditions in Russia. They even hired him as a floorwalker (that was in Kansas City) and made a business man of him.

Of his lectures Mike said: "I am getting death threats every day, but I am not worried. I know of no one I should fear."

Into their homes on Park Avenue and Fifth Avenue he went, and many free drinks he got along Broadway. He went down to Harvard for week-ends, and as a Cambridge man he was accepted. He borrowed too much money from the Harvard students, however, and left too many unpaid bills among the town merchants. These crimes were his undoing, and the Romanoff bubble burst when he was arrested in December of 1923. The records do not show that he was deported that time, and according to his own story he escaped from Ellis Island by swimming to the Battery, trailing his walking stick on a long string behind him.

The Island has an earlier record showing his presence there in the winter of 1922, when he arrived with a group of ex-service men who were bringing their German and French wives and children to America. He was then plain Harry Gerguson. He had just been released, he said, from ten years' solitary incarceration in a German dungeon; he had killed a high-born German youth in a duel. He could remember nothing about the first ten years of his life in New York, and imputed his loss of memory to the long term of confinement in prison. There is an order for deportation against him on this occasion, but no indication that it was carried out.

An investigation of his youth showed that he had come to New

York with his Russian parents when he was ten. After the father and mother died he drifted about the city, sleeping in pool rooms, selling newspapers, living for brief periods in orphan establishments, and being adopted by well-meaning ladies who later turned him loose again. It was the discovery of these childhood records that secured governmental sympathy. The assistant United States attorney, who attended some of the final hearings, described Gerguson as a "product of our own institutions." With this I am inclined to agree.

They finally released him from Ellis Island on bond, and tried him on charges of perjury and violation of the immigration law. At the trial it came out that he was appearing daily in a Broadway vaudeville show. The Judge was annoyed.

"I didn't want the vaudeville contract," Gerguson said. "I was urged to take it. It was a chance to rehabilitate myself, to earn some money, to live in peace and be left alone."

He added that it was not vanity which had prompted him to pose as a prince.

"It's not vanity. It's loneliness. What is more, I'm not lazy. I'd take a job if I could get it. It seems to me sometimes that we are just like ants, milling around and around. But for what? Nothing."

The Judge gave him ninety days in the federal house of detention, more than a public vote would have given him. He served the three months and emerged as suave as ever. He would live at the St. Moritz Hotel, though he would prefer a farm.

"I'd like to get a modest little farm and a horse or two, and actually work the soil," he told incredulous reporters. "Ireland, I suppose, is out of the question, because I must report to the probation officer every week for three years."

Despite these moderate desires, he said, celebrity-hunters would not let him alone. Some had even offered him jobs in the cinema.

The case of "Baron" Krupp, whose real name was George Adorgan Gabor, was somewhat similar, but not quite so tinged with dramatic quality. The "Baron" was rather more business-like. He went into the impersonating game for the profit that he could get out of it. Though he made friends almost as readily as Mike, he could not hold them after the fraud was discovered.

Gabor was a Hungarian. He imposed upon American gullibility partly because he enjoyed the sensation of the courtesies and deferences shown him, and partly because he had settled upon that method as the quickest and easiest way of securing ready cash. It is known that he treasured the newspaper clippings relating his exploits.

He played his first little joke on America in 1926. In the summer of that year, posing as the son of Germany's most famous manufacturer of munitions, he made a trip across the continent visiting manufacturing establishments all along the line and leaving behind a bad check at almost every one of them. He travelled with a companion in a *de luxe* Ford car presented to him by Henry Ford during his stop-over at the automobile capital.

In Los Angeles the fancy for a little publicity struck him. So on August 23 readers of the *New York Times* saw a sober little boxed story on the front page which read as follows:

Los Angeles. Germany's famous Krupp works at Essen probably will never manufacture arms again, in the opinion of Baron G. Frederick E. von Krupp, only son of the present head of the plant.

The young man, who recently completed his second year at Harvard, said his father was educating him eventually to take charge of the works. When he assumes control, he added:

We won't make guns, for I don't believe in war. The plant now manufactures steel.

Baron von Krupp arrived from the East in an automobile presented by Henry Ford. He and his parents will sail for Honolulu in a few days.

This little story was fatal. Almost immediately the "Baron's" house of cards fell in a heap. The Krupp secretariat in Berlin next day denied the announcement, saying briefly that the oldest son of the house, Alfred, was only twenty-one and at home. Moreover, as the family name was Krupp von Bohlen, there could not, obviously, be any Frederick von Krupp belonging to it.

People who had been fooled on the "Baron's" cross-country tour began looking out for him. He was wanted in a half dozen places. Henry Ford, indignant at being taken in, started to wire here and there in an effort to recover his automobile.

They arrested him at Albuquerque, New Mexico, where he had passed a worthless check for a hundred dollars on a Denver automobile agency on the strength of a letter purporting to be from Mr. Ford. Simultaneously came telegrams from police departments at Pittsburgh and Wilmington, Delaware, saying they held warrants for the arrest of the man posing as a son of the noted German family.

The prisoner was all innocence. He said he could not explain how a bad check charge had been brought against him, unless his father had withdrawn money placed to his account in New York. He had received a letter from his father while at the Grand Canyon, he said, notifying him that his allowance had been cut to twenty-five dollars a week, until he decided to return to Germany and enter the Leipsic Military Academy.

He was identified, tried and given nine months in prison; he was deported to Hungary in July of 1927. Before leaving he gave the federal officers a document entitled "How I Fooled Ford, Edison, Firestone, Four Governors, and New York's Four Hundred." Before this document could be read it was snatched out of the hand of the official holding it by a wayward breeze and carried into the bay. The immigration officials saw him off.

In January, 1928, he was arrested at the Harvard Club in New York City for offering a worthless check in payment for a suite on a Cunard liner scheduled to sail for England. How he had got back into the United States was a mystery to the immigration officials.

Rather proud of his exploits, the young "Baron" did not mind explaining. He had got to Rotterdam, he said, still posing as a member of the Krupp family. There he formed the acquaintance of Herman Schwartzenback, a member of a wealthy New York family.

He stole Schwartzenback's passport and birth certificate. On the strength of the certificate he obtained a duplicate passport from the American consul at Berlin. He arrived in September of 1927 on the liner *Arabic*.

So, after he had been tried, sentenced to five years and given a suspended sentence by Judge Knox in Federal Court, the immigration officials again saw him off.

In June, 1931, Gabor again stood before Judge Knox and told the court how he had returned to America illegally in the same year that he had been deported.

He had been brought to New York on this occasion from the prison at McNeill Island, California, where he had just completed service of an eighteen-month sentence for impersonating the "Third Solicitor General of the United States."

After arriving at Hungary on his second deportation trip, he went to London, he told the court. There he telephoned to Alanson B. Houghton, American ambassador, posing as W. C. Widener of Philadelphia.

"If my nephew, Taft Thew, Jr., son of the former ambassador comes round, you might keep an eye on him," he said he told Mr. Houghton. This led to his being entertained at the embassy and taken to a polo game in Surrey.

From London he went to Paris and registered at a hotel as "Thew."

"Thew?" asked Judge Knox. "I never heard of an ambassador by that name."

"You're quite right, your honor," said Gabor. "There never was such a person in the American diplomatic service."

"What saps we are!" Judge Knox remarked.

In Paris the "Baron" said he telephoned to Ambassador Herrick, posing as someone else, and explained that John W. Davis, "guardian of young Thew," was worried because the young man wanted to join the American legion. By this ruse he got acquainted with the ambassador to France, who not only bought him clothes and a first class ticket to Halifax, but wrote a letter stating that "the bearer is an American citizen in whom I am interested." On the strength of this letter he got his passport.

The judge gave him two years.

These stories interest me as sidelights on American good-nature and respect for—though not envy of—the little connectives that indicate rank. He who boasts a "de" or "von" can tell us many things we would not otherwise believe. We have not learned that blue blood does not always make men honest. And if the blueness turns out to be self-assumed, then we have an American farce that is often amusing enough to remember afterwards, but sometimes hurts our pride at the time.

One of the most picturesque persons ever detained on the Island was a young man who posed as the Emir of Kurdistan, claiming to be a direct descendant of Mohammed. He was deported three times before he finally proved to the satisfaction of federal authorities that he was, after all, an American citizen born in St. Louis.

The Emir happened to be in the United States when Balbo arrived, and he went out on the field to meet the famous Italian flier with all the dignity of his boasted Mohammedan ancestors. He had Balbo ruffled, until a policeman recognized him and locked him up again.

As an Emir he was fêted by high society in America, and while at the Island was literally venerated by the Mohammedans in detention.

Chapter V

STORMS OF THE PRESENT AND PAST

I

AUGUST KOSUTIC
THE CROATIAN PATRIOT

Occasional figures out of the caravan of immigration have provided international amusement; others have evoked protests which rang around the world. One case which aroused a great deal of international discussion was that of August Kosutic, son-in-law of the assassinated statesman Radic of Jugo-Slavia and the leader of the Croatian peasant party. His case was finally closed during my own administration at the Island.

Kosutic really wanted a very simple thing—only to be granted a few months' stay in America in order that he might speak to the Croatian population of this country, and collect from them what hard-earned dollars they could give for the benefit of their oppressed race at home. He had come because of the appeal of a group of Americanized Croats in Chicago, who wished to give their people an opportunity to learn the clear facts about the political situation under the military dictatorship in Jugo-Slavia.

When, in accordance with the Treaty of Versailles, the Serbian monarchical dictatorship had been set up and the order had gone forth that the Croatian flag should never be displayed and no Croatian should be spoken in the schools, the patriotic Kosutic had circularized the League of Nations in behalf of the oppressed Croatians. As many another patriot has had to flee his own country, so Kosutic had to flee from Zagreb; and again, like many another patriot, he had come to the United States for the benefit of his suffering people.

August Kosutic embarked from Europe on the White Star Line on July 23, 1930. The immigration officials first heard of his visit six days later from a Mr. D. M. Tsvetkovich of New York, who called at Ellis Island to protest against his admission to the country. Kosutic, he said, had been a Deputy in the Assembly at Belgrade. After Parliament was dissolved, and while he was a member of the board of directors of a bank in Zagreb, criminal proceedings had been instituted against him for mismanagement of bank funds. He had fled to Austria, then possibly to Germany and other countries.

So Ellis Island issued a confidential "lookout" for August Kosutic.

Then the Jugo-Slavian Legation at Washington issued a protest. They sent a memorandum to the State Department announcing the arrival of Kosutic on July 30 and his presence on Ellis Island, and asserting that his passport was irregular in addition to his being without the Jugo-Slav visa to this country. He had obtained his American visa from the American Consulate in Zurich. They repeated the bank charges, and stated further that Kosutic was coming to America primarily to rouse radical elements and raise funds that would be used for creating disturbances in Jugo-Slavia.

Therefore, said this dignified document, "it would be advisable and desirable that Mr. Kosutic be prevented from entering the United States that he may not be given the privilege of abusing the hospitality of the U.S. Government."

Radoye Yankovitch, Consul General for Jugo-Slavia at New York, wrote a series of letters to the Commissioner at Ellis Island saying that his government had specifically notified him that Kosutic's passport was forged, as to both signature and seal, and that he had obtained it in a criminally fraudulent manner. The Consul

General requested that Kosutic be deported immediately to Jugo-Slavia. He emphasized the necessity of maintaining excellent relations between his country and the United States, and intimated that these could not be maintained unless Kosutic was deported.

The Croatian patriot was denied admission to the country on that same day, August 4, and immediately appealed to the Secretary of Labor.

As soon as the newspapers carried news of his imprisonment at Ellis Island, the Croatian protests began to pour in. Evidently Kosutic was well beloved by his people. A lengthy telegram from M. D. Krupotich, President of the Croatian Republic League of America with headquarters at Kansas City, charged the Serbian government with attempting to bar him chiefly in order that Americans might not become informed of actual conditions in Jugo-Slavia.

"August Kosutic is a gentleman of high character and education," he said. "He fled from Croatia as a political and religious exile to find refuge in western countries. . . . Austria, Germany and England admitted him, why not America? Our country is a traditional refuge to political exiles. The Hungarian patriot Kossuth was admitted, why not the Croatian patriot Kosutic? . . . His intention on landing on the shores of the free is sacred—to work within the law for the freedom of Croatia from barbarian rule . . .

"The subjection of the Croats to Servia cries for revenge. . . . If America is blocking progress to the freedom of a nation, then the fathers of our country died in vain."

He said further that Servian spies in this country were accusing Kosutic falsely to prevent him from exposing to fair-minded and educated people the crudity of Servian rule over Croatia.

Mr. P. I. Tanin, President of the Macedonian Independence Association, wired the government that to keep Kosutic out meant that the United States was "supporting the abominable policies of the present despotic régime of Jugo-Slavia, which exists contrary to the historic pact of Corfu of 1917, as well as to the express provisions of the peace treaties of 1919 to which the United States is a signatory power."

So the struggle went on at Washington. The Jugo-Slavian diplomatic representatives pressed with all their strength for Kosutic's deportation, and members of Congress hastened to intercede in his behalf at the behest of Croatian-Americans.

An irate New Yorker sent a pertinent telegram to Commissioner Day at Ellis Island. Among other things he said:

"I plead for the executive action of President Hoover and yourself. Serbs have not clean hands. Will they deny that their accredited press agent to Washington, Birislav Jelinovic, is a convicted murderer, yet was thereafter Secretary of the Serb Legation in Paris and now in good standing at the Yugo-Slavian Legation at Washington? Should he not be deported rather than this patriot, Kosutic? Let us remember the unprecedented public and official reception America gave the banished Hungarian patriot, Kossuth."

Numerous attempts were made by Jugo-Slavian officials to get possession of Kosutic's passport, and that Consulate even sent him a new fifteen-day passport to be exchanged for his old one. The purpose was evidently to secure the old passport as evidence in the event of Kosutic's being deported to Jugo-Slavia and there brought to trial on a criminal charge. The solicitous Jugo-Slavian officials almost persuaded our immigration authorities at Washington.

At the hearing on July 30 at Ellis Island, Kosutic answered frankly, intelligently and quietly, all questions put to him. He said he was by profession a mechanical engineer. He had a wife and a seven-year-old child in Zagreb. He said he had not earned any money since he had left his country, and that his wife was in partnership with her parents in a book store in Zagreb. He had not visited his home since August, 1929, because his wife and relatives feared he would be in danger there. He disclaimed all knowledge of the bank charges, though he said that some of his political associates had been involved in some such business and had been tried. He had lived at home for a year after Radic's assassination, and had not been molested in any way. He said the money he brought with him had been sent by his wife.

He explained the passport, saying that when the paper became invalid a friend had taken it to Belgrade, where it had been extended. He had not dared to extend it in Zagreb because the police and officials were hostile to him. He expected to go from America to Switzerland, where he had already lived for several periods, working on a book and numerous magazine articles.

In spite of the good impression created by Kosutic at this hearing, at its conclusion he was denied admission on grounds that he was a quota immigrant not in possession of an immigrant visa. He appealed the case. A writ of *habeas corpus* was served at Ellis Island, and his deportation was stayed. The strain in Washington was too much, however, and on August 29 the writ was dismissed and Kosutic was deported on the *Europa*.

One can feel only sympathy with his telegram from that ship:

> Heartfelt thanks for such generous humane treatment.
> Kosutic.

The patriot's many friends here would not allow matters to rest however, and on May 28 of the following year Kosutic, then in Berlin, was advised that he might apply for admission to enter the United States within a year after his exclusion. On July 15, 1931, he arrived on the S.S. *Bremen* and was admitted to the country for a period of four months. On October 2 he applied for an extension until January 15, 1932, and that was granted.

The truth seems to be that the passport *was* forged, but solely because Kosutic's political enemies in Jugo-Slavia had prevented him from securing a legal permit to this country. When he sought to enter this country on a forged passport, his political enemies here not only had him deported but tried to secure his irregular passport as evidence against him. His uncontradicted and clear testimony that he had fled his country to save his life availed him nothing in the face of the technical irregularity of his coming.

On January 15, 1932, this patriot telegraphed me:

Commissioner Corsi:

While leaving American shores, may I express to you personally and your service, my deepest appreciation for your courteous treatment accorded me while a temporary visitor, which certainly enhanced my admiration for America and its government.

Kosutic.

II

GENERAL CIPRIANO CASTRO

Among the one million five hundred thousand and more cases on file at the Island are world-famous names and other names that are internationally notorious. The illustrious Premier of Italy, Il Duce Benito Mussolini, in his earlier and allegedly radical days, was thought to be about to seek refuge in the United States. The information was received by the State Department at Washington from confidential sources abroad and immediately communicated to immigration authorities at Ellis Island. If he had attempted to land in the United States, he would have been detained and examined by a board of special inquiry.

Premier Ramsay MacDonald's file tells much the same story. In recalling his recent visits to the United States, especially his visit to President Hoover and the conversations of the Rapidan, one cannot fail to be impressed with the shifting winds of political ideas. Mr. MacDonald was fêted and hailed by America as a messenger of good will and one of the most important and distinguished guests of our generation. If he had arrived a few years earlier, he would have been detained on Ellis Island and the conservative elements of the country would have demanded his deportation.

Soon after I became Commissioner, discussions with various members of my staff, who had been on the Island for many years, roused my interest in these numerous famous cases, because of points of law involved and the reaction of the country at large to their disposition by the immigration authorities, the Secretary of Labor, or the courts. I thought then that almost any political refugee could be admitted and find in the United States a haven from persecution. A study of the case of General Cipriano Castro, ex-President of Venezuela, revealed that I was mistaken.

That petitioning immigrant, who had ruled our neighboring republic in South America with an iron hand for eight years, was ordered deported from this country. Though he had long been heralded as the "bad boy" ruler of the world, the Napoleon of South America, the self-styled "Man of Destiny", the revolutionist extraordinary, there are men at Ellis Island to-day who saw General Castro break down and cry like a baby when he learned of his impending deportation.

A just review of his case necessitates a brief outline of the General's background.

Born in the wilds of the Andes mountains in the year 1861 of a negro mother and half-breed Spanish father, Cipriano Castro was an outlaw and cattle-thief during his late twenties and early thirties. In 1899, when he was only thirty-eight years of age, Castro entered Caracas at the head of an army, of which the nucleus was the twenty-three Andeans with whom he started. He was lashed to his horse because both legs had been broken in battle. His first act was to announce himself "Restorer" and "Supreme Military Leader." At the elections one year later he was made President and served for seven years.

The Castro administration was marked by affronts to foreign nations, confiscation of private property, complete disappearance of his enemies, and many deportations of aliens.

One day Castro wanted to borrow a large sum from the Bank of Venezuela. The bank regretted its inability to accommodate the beloved President. It really did not have the amount of cash the beloved President required. On the following day charges of appropriating bank funds were lodged against the directors, and a file of soldiers marched them, tied together, bare-headed, through the streets for incarceration in the San Carlos jail. At the railway station the directors held a meeting and proved their innocence by voting the loan to their beloved President. Of course their judges dismissed them in a perfectly regular court proceeding.

President Castro showed similar judicial irregularity when he confiscated the Bermuda asphalt lake property, the Orinoco steamship plant, and other concessions from Americans, the cable concessions from French owners, and the railways from the Germans. His audacity so provoked and bewildered the greater world powers that their warships were always at Venezuela's doorway.

Irate at the trend of Venezuelan relations with France, Castro learned that M. Tainy, French Chargé d'Affaires, was aboard the *Martinique* one night having dinner with the Captain. He sent orders to have the *Martinique* move away from the dock. He then announced that M. Tainy had left Venezuela and if he wished to return and be recognized, he must again be accredited by France.

History records that it was the psychological moment for an affront to France, because she was at the time deeply immersed in her Moroccan difficulties. But in Venezuela her fleet was expected daily. One day word came that the French fleet was off the coast. Castro suddenly ordered all French residents arrested and placed in exposed positions along the harbor walls and on top of the forts.

"Now," he said, "let the French ships fire."

During this turbulent period more than twelve thousand Venezuelan nationals were arrested. Many of them were summarily executed without arraignment or trial of any kind. Finally Castro was privately accused of the murder of General Antonio Paredes, and fled the country for the stated purpose of undergoing an operation in Germany, although he had still two and a half years to serve as President.

Such is the record of the man who sought to enter the United States in 1912.

Before he reached American shores, the case of General Castro, from the immigration standpoint, began at the direction of the State Department in Washington and was continued on Ellis Island and in the courts. It brought to light many chapters of revolutionary movements in South America both before and during the Castro administration in Venezuela, as well as in the year 1913, when his case was pending and it was alleged that he had come to America for the purpose of overthrowing the existing government in his native country.

For approximately five years General Castro had been living in exile, spending part of the time in Berlin, part in Spain, and the remainder in Teneriffe. Back in Venezuela he was under indictment for the murder of General Paredes. Most of the major governments of the world were advising one another of his movements.

On Christmas Eve, 1912, Ellis Island received the following telegram from the Bureau of Immigration in Washington:

State Department advises Cipriano Castro, ex-President Venezuela, sailed from Havre on *Touraine,* December 25. Has been ill and is probably still suffering from some contagious disease. Detain and examine carefully, not releasing in any event until Bureau has been communicated with.

A "lookout" order was immediately dispatched to the Chief Inspector of the Boarding Division, together with the information that his passage had been booked in the name of "Luis Ruiz." Details were soon forthcoming from Washington in a letter dated December 28, 1912. The contents of the letter were neither flattering to the exiled dictator nor conducive to his effecting an entrance into the United States on any basis.

"It is understood," said the letter from the Bureau, "that General Castro has for many years been afflicted with an incurable disease. If his examination by the doctors shows that the disease still exists, the case will be materially simplified. It is also understood that he is under indictment for murder in his own country although, having escaped, his case has never been brought to trial. Possibly he might admit the commission of some such offense. Everything that can be developed by the Board should be brought out, and *whether or not any specific reason is ascertained for his exclusion under the immigration law,* Castro should be *detained* until the case can be referred to the Department for consideration and decision."

In accordance with instructions, General Castro was taken off the *Touraine* by immigration inspectors on December 31, brought to Ellis Island on a government cutter, and given a special hearing. But in the midst of the hearing he became annoyed and expressed a desire that the proceedings be ended, stating through his interpreter that he would return to Europe on the first available steamer rather than submit to further inconvenience.

On the morning of January 2, 1913, however, Attorney Harold A. Content of New York presented a letter of introduction from George Gordon Battle in which it was stated that Mr. Content was calling at the request of Senator O'Gorman to investigate the case (which had been widely publicized) and would interview the General. And since it was reported that General Castro had left Venezuela originally with the tidy sum of nine million dollars, immigration authorities suspected that they were facing a long court battle in attempting to pull the chestnuts of the State Department out of the fire.

Their suspicions proved well-grounded. A writ of *habeas corpus* was sued out by George Gordon Battle three days later. Judge Holt of the United States District Court postponed decision upon the writ for one week. On January 11 he dismissed it. The entire case was reopened at Ellis Island, and General Castro was accorded a new hearing.

At this hearing he refused to affirm or deny any allegations of the immigration authorities that he had been the cause of the various crimes attributed to him in Venezuela. For example, he was asked by Inspector Moore:

"We are informed that the light company of Caracas went into bankruptcy as the result of your direction that the city of Caracas should not pay its bills. What have you to say?"

General Castro listened to his interpreter's translation, then replied:

"You know what you are talking about. I have nothing to say."

"Did you at any time acquire an interest in this light company at Caracas?" continued Inspector Moore.

"I do not," replied General Castro, "consider myself obliged to answer questions relating to matters of government or private business."

"Then you did have private business with this light company?" was the next question.

General Castro had become exasperated again. "I have told you two or three times," he flared, "and I repeat again that I will not answer this question. I do not think that my private affairs have anything to do with my right to enter the United States."

A determined effort by the government failed to elicit any admission from General Castro that he had ever been personally responsible for the confiscation or loss of foreign-owned property while President of the South American Republic.

"Who was General Paredes?" Inspector Moore asked suddenly.

"I do not feel obliged to answer who he is," General Castro countered.

"Is he dead or alive?" asked Inspector Moore.

General Castro replied: "I do not feel myself obliged to answer. If you want to know about it, you can inform yourself through the Venezuelan government."

The chairman of the board advised General Castro that he must answer all questions, and if he failed to do so he must take the consequences. General Castro retorted that he did not feel obliged to answer questions regarding the lives of other persons, but only with regard to his own.

"How did General Paredes die?" Inspector Moore demanded.

General Castro did not answer. Instead, he asked whether or not he was in a criminal court, and when told that he was not, he re-asserted that he was not responsible for the lives of others.

"You do not deny that you knew General Paredes?" he was asked.

"I never knew him," was his answer.

A member of the board read the following telegram copied from the files of the State Department:

From Port of Spain, 6:30 P.M., February 13, 1907.
Hon. Elihu Root, Secretary of State, Washington.

General Antonio Paredes and seventeen officers and men shot after capture by government troops near Barrancas, State Bermudez, about 13th; bodies seen floating in Maraceo river.
William W. Handley,
Consul at Trinidad, B.W.I.

The board introduced a letter from William W. Russell, American Minister at Venezuela, which stated that General Castro was indicted in 1907 for the murder of General Paredes and for the attempted assassination of General Gomez, who succeeded him to the Presidency.

General Castro denied that there was ever a criminal accusation for any attempt to kill General Gomez.

A few more efforts were made to connect him with the death of General Paredes, but with no success. The hearing was adjourned.

Meanwhile additional information was being sought by the State Department and on January 15th the hearing was resumed.

Telegrams supposed to be originals of messages passing between General Castro and a subordinate, Luis Varela, were introduced by the board. One of the telegrams purported to be an official report of General Paredes' death in an altercation between government soldiers and the revolutionists, while the revolutionists were attempting to effect an escape.

When they were read at the hearing, General Castro stated that he did not know Luis Varela. He was asked a few more questions and the hearing was closed.

The board retired, returning in a few minutes with a decision of exclusion which commented upon the evidence, and accused General Castro of perjury. The decision found that General Castro's failure to affirm or deny the allegations made by the board was equivalent to admission of the killing of General Paredes. General Castro signified his desire to appeal and the hearing was adjourned.

The case was reopened on January 22nd, and once more General Castro, the board members who had previously interrogated him, and official stenographers were assembled in the Ellis Island hearing room. They expected defiance but were unprepared for such spectacular opposition.

Chairman Eppler announced that the government had come into possession of new information and would offer it in refutation of any explanation the General cared to make. The official account of what transpired, taken from Ellis Island files, is as follows:

The alien became very excited and declined to participate in any manner in the hearing. He declined to listen or answer and was very discourteous to the board.

An effort was made to swear him, but he again declined to participate in the hearing, refused to listen to or answer any questions and left the room, retiring to his bedroom. The board, being desirous of bringing to the alien's personal attention the important telegrams hereinafter mentioned, followed him to the door of his bedroom.

Chairman: We have no desire to intrude on your privacy, but we must proceed with this hearing. At the hearing held January 15, the board caused to be read and translated to you a telegram dated Bolivar, February 13, 1907, addressed to you by Luis Varela, reporting the capture of General Antonio Paredes. The State Department now has on its files a copy of a telegram——

Alien interrupts, leaves the bedroom, goes to toilet and locks the door. Later he returns from toilet to his bedroom, slams the door and bolts it from inside in the face of board members, who conducted the remainder of the hearing in the room immediately adjoining the bedroom.

Chairman: The State Department in Washington now has on its files a copy of a telegram sent by General Castro which reads as follows:

Maouto, Feb. 13, 1907.

General L. Varela,
Ciudad, Bolivar.

You should give immediate orders to shoot Paredes and his officers. Advise me of receipt and fulfillment.

Cipriano Castro.

The State Department now also has on its files copy of telegram in reply to Castro's telegram to Varela of February 13, 1907, which reads as follows:

Bolivar to Maouto.
General C. Castro,

Received. Immediately.

L. Varela.

The board of inquiry proceeded to introduce additional evidence in the form of copies of State Department documents, which were alleged to be excerpts from the court testimony of persons in Venezuela having knowledge of the manner and time of General Paredes' death, while the hearing went on outside General Castro's locked bedroom.

A few days later Secretary of Labor Nagel reaffirmed the decision of Ellis Island, and ordered the General deported. Meanwhile George Gordon Battle obtained bail for General Castro, sued out a new writ of *habeas corpus,* and appealed to the Federal District Court for a reversal of the decision and order of deportation which held up proceedings.

On February 15, Judge Ward ordered that General Castro be admitted to the United States. On learning of the decision the diminutive revolutionary leader said:

"Liberty, which has been enlightening the world, will continue to do so. I am much gratified for I have always honored and respected the United States, and had a warm feeling for the people of this great country."

He expressed contempt for the Taft administration and informed newspaper reporters that he expected to be present when Woodrow Wilson was inaugurated.

During the time General Castro was out on bail, about one week before the court decision which officially admitted him to the country, he made a trip to Albany. The New York *Times* of February 7, 1913, has the following account of his visit:

Castro was lionized by Governor Sulzer and was his luncheon guest, but was hardly treated as a hero in any part of the Capitol outside the Executive Chamber. He came into the Senate Chamber while the Senate was in session, accompanied by his Secretary and a local cicerone. He received no official recognition and left after glancing furtively at the splendors of the Chamber's onyx adornments.

When Castro and his party reached the Executive Chamber, they were received by Major Schermerhorn, the Governor's military aide. Governor Sulzer was busy in the "People's Corner" talking to the press. As soon as he caught a glimpse of the Venezuelan, he began to praise him.

Castro, after he had been escorted to a seat, got rid of his big fur coat, and disclosed a finely tailored frock coat of quaint brown material, with trousers to match. He wore a magnificent pearl pin and a brilliant diamond ring.

Castro went to the Assembly where he was rushed into the room of Speaker Alfred E. Smith. When Castro was told of Smith's title and that he bossed the entire assembly, he nearly fell prostrate on the red carpet of the Speaker's room. Speaker Smith bowed stiffly and addressed his visitor in the harsh, rasping voice which he has acquired in calling down Progressives and telling Republicans in the assembly their real place. Castro looked at him in wonder, but did not understand a word of what he said.

"I have met your Governor," he told Smith. "I think he is a most notable statesman. And now I have the happiness of placing myself entirely at your disposal."

"All right," said Smith. "I am glad to have met you. If I should go down to Venezuela for a vacation, I will hunt you up."

It was not until General Castro was sailing out of New York harbor on March 15th that his own inner reactions to, and private version of the treatment accorded him in the United States became public knowledge.

In an exclusive interview to the New York *Herald,* he told an inside story which bitterly assailed the authorities and called the United States a tyrant, at the same time declaring that he had been treacherously insulted.

"Since the day I was kidnapped from the *Touraine,*" he said, "I have been made the object of a ridiculous farce and have been vilely treated. I did not at that time protest as strongly as I might have against the imprisonment because I thought I was serving an ideal, one which would be of service to humanity and would redound to the credit of the American people. I did not think of myself.

"I was actually buried alive as if I were a great criminal. If this is the inheritance which the great Washington left, the American people ought to weep bitter tears or give up Imperialism. Unless the imperialistic government of the United States gives a satisfactory reason for such iniquitous conduct, it stands convicted of being a tyrant and having forgotten the past glories of America.

"I was insulted treacherously. They even descended to crime. I refer to that terrific night of December 31. After a very bad voyage of ten days, I was thrown into a dirty, small room, and at six o'clock in the evening I threw myself on the bed and tried to sleep. Vain illusion! At a quarter past six somebody knocked on the door. I got up and opened it. In walked a man of about twenty-seven or twenty-eight years. He approached me with such a menacing air that I did not know what to think. As I do not understand English, I did not know what he was saying, but it appeared to me that he was looking for the keys to my baggage although it had already been examined by the Customs House officers. I by signs tried to make him understand this.

"Finally when I understood the magnitude of this aggression, I saw clearly that they were trying to provoke me into committing a crime. As this passed rapidly through my imagination, I took the only step which could save my life in this dire circumstance.

"The man was walking around the room like a wild bull. I, without showing my uneasiness in any way, turned my back on him and lay down on the dirty bed which they had placed for me. The man suddenly took off his overcoat, threw it on the floor, took off his coat and finally took off his gloves. Then he looked at me as if he was going to strike me. I preserved a stoical attitude, still lying on the bed. Who was this man? Where did he come from at such an hour? What had he to do with my baggage which had been examined time and again by the Customs House officers? How did this man get past the official who was guarding my door? All these questions will have to be answered in court proceedings.

"The man seeing my stoical attitude, put on his coat and overcoat and went out. He forgot to take his gloves with him. So I picked them up and gave them to the guardian at the door, so that he would have no reason for coming back and bothering me.

"Fifteen minutes later another knock came at the door, and a young man smaller than the other came in. He repeated the actions of his predecessor, without, however, taking off his coat. He also spoke English, which of course I did not understand. At seven o'clock two other men and a woman came in and repeated the performance of the others. They all spoke at the same time. They were gesticulating wildly, and finally they picked up my baggage and left the room. I locked the door and said to myself, 'Let it be what God wishes.'

"I could not sleep all that night. What a terrible experience! The next morning when I opened the door, I saw my baggage outside. The tragic blow which they had prepared with unequalled cynicism more like highwaymen than government officials did not succeed.

"I have kept silence until to-day because I understood that in that way alone could I save myself, being in the clutches of the 'Black Hand' which was directing the attack on me. In view of the grave nature of the attempt any indiscretion on my part would have meant certain death.

"I hope the American people will appreciate these facts, which are nothing but the truth, and I hope that the judicial authorities will immediately order an investigation of them. While the American government is responsible for these insults, the real responsibility lies with the asphalt companies of Venezuela, who have never failed to work harm for Venezuela and for me, because I defended the interests, which had been confided to me as President of Venezuela, for spending large sums of money to organize the Matos revolution, in which I conquered those enemies of my country after two years of war."

It is extremely doubtful that anything occurred which might have been taken as a basis of fact for General Castro's allegations. An exile immersed in bitterness, uncertain about the outcome of his detention, and brimming with the consciousness of some of his own political edicts which had brought him widespread enmity, he doubtless suffered from a fear complex which imputed malicious motives to all who approached him. There is also the vague possibility that his state of mind was such that he dreamed the entire story.

Later he received an anonymous letter, obviously written, not by a crank or lunatic as might be implied from superficial analysis, but rather by some former citizen of Venezuela, who cherished a deep-dyed hatred for that country's former dictator. The letter which is herewith reproduced could scarcely be termed a piece of "fan mail:"

January 17th, 1913

Mr. Cipriano Castro,
Ellis Island, N. Y.

My dear sir:
I have seen in the daily papers of the respectable press of this country, several articles that refer to your detention as a criminal, political transgressor of Venezuela, of which country you made a joke by your acts as an arbitrary dictator, causing numerous criticisms from foreign nations while you governed the country during the years of 1900 to 1909.

I don't think you have stopped to turn over in your mind the cause of your arrest, so take a few seconds to search your memory for that which you did in Caracas in the days of your arbitrary power, banishing Ministers Extraordinary and Plenipotentiary and Diplomatic Ambassadors. You must remember, Mr. Castro, of the arrogant manner by which you appropriated the asphalt mine called "Guanoco," belonging to an American company, whose contract you broke by your despotic power, and knowing this, did the same with other foreign countries established in Venezuela, all of which had the same luck as the "Guanoco" or the "Bermudez" Asphalt Co., belonging to some North American capitalists and now, you expect these gentlemen to recommend you.

No, Mr. Castro, you cannot enter New York, because you are and always will be an enemy to the peace of Venezuela and to the country of the great George Washington, i.e., the United States of America.

Mr. Castro, if you had been a citizen well-born and educated in practical ideas and had had the forethought and practical intelligence to know the pitfalls in the road you were travelling in those days of your executive power, you would not have trampled the laws, mistreated peaceful citizens of Venezuela and outraged foreign residents. Also, Mr. Castro, there is a criminal court in the city of Caracas in which you are charged with the attempted assassination of the present President of Venezuela when you were President and dictator.

You assassinated and shot in a criminal manner, General Antonio Paredes, F. Marrero, Mr. Racamonde, and many others died in the "San Carlos" prison in Maracaibo and the "Castillo del Libertador", prison in Puerto Cabello.

All these crimes in which you are steeped are still fresh in the memories of all Venezuelans, and no one can serve you in any manner except to work against such a person as you, who caused terror as an assassin and criminal, and as such you are now prohibited from entering New York.

A man such as you, Mr. Castro, deserves the numbered coat of a convict and condemned to life imprisonment on some island far removed from human contact, because you don't deserve to be dressed in the clothes of a gentleman on account of the abuses and horrible crimes you have committed, you should be removed a greater distance from the country. Anyway I am here on guard and taking precautions of your treacherous audacity through which you expected to place your feet in this country.

Do you remember the interview you had with Gen'l Reyes of Colombia where it was decided to take passage to the U.S., you were to come first and Mr. Reyes immediately afterwards in order to plot the overthrow of Venezuela and Colombia and placing them both at the same time at the mercy of an interior war? You now understand, Mr. Castro, that I know why you have come to the United States.

Here you can buy arms, ammunition and explosives of war and load a ship or several with men who make a business of volunteering for pay and these will be the main beginning of a revolution when you arrive at a seaport. I would have you know, Mr. Castro, that I have been watching you since your arrival in Europe, and I must have been very near you to learn all about your diabolical plots. I am more powerful than you with all your money, though mine was never so much that it would not enter my pocket, but in diabolical arts, I have great power accorded me by "Lucifer" and I can transform myself into different persons like the great "Tregoli" used to do, but more rapidly as I fly with an aeroplane. I have been with you, Mr. Castro, at all hours of the day and night, face to face in the seclusion of Ellis Island and I have heard your conversations when you talked to yourself. I have been at the head of your bed listening to your mouth expressing terrible maledictions in that dark garret where they have you secluded and guarded. There in your dreams I have read your thoughts and plots and your bloody intentions which you have given out in moments of desperation and discouragement. I have also learned through your dreams, the manner in which you expect to invade the territory of Venezuela and Colombia with your friend General Reyes.

Mr. Castro, you should be ashamed to come here and expect protection under the standard of George Washington which you wanted to destroy in a moment of bloody craziness at the time the foreign nations blocked the ports of Venezuela in those memorable tragedies of national dishonor, like a Nero, and had you gone a few more steps in your arbitrary conduct, Venezuela would have lost her independence and owed it to your character as a mule-driver and Cacique (Indian Prince) of the robbers and assassins of the Andes.

When did you have millions, Mr. Castro? Never! Never! These millions belong to the people of Venezuela and you are a robber of the national treasury. This is how you became rich, Mr. Castro. For when you arrived at Caracas, the capital, you didn't have twenty cents in your pocket and entered the city through the most criminal treason that is registered in the national history of Venezuela. Though I say it and not the press or society of Venezuela, one of your acts which was contrary to law and truly criminal, was that of making an officer of one of your lowest servants, who was formerly a servant of Mr. Ignacio Andrade, as Minister of War, Mr. Diego Baustiste Ferrer, the Traitor.

Mr. Castro, tell me what infernal monster gave you birth and placed you on earth? You should go and hide in some cave away from all civilized human kind as your person infects harm through the least contact.

In closing these writings that I am making too long, I wish to give you some useful, lucrative and glorious advice, as follows: Arrange your next trip to Turkey. There they are in need of men like you, of criminal ferocity, the bravery of a rat and skill of an Apache, and when the hour arrives for your body to rest in the wild forest may the soles of your feet be surrounded by vampires.

Yours truly,

A Spy.

"R"

Following his voluntary departure in 1913, General Castro went to Havana, where he was seen frequently in the company of other former South American revolutionary leaders. Since it was believed by the State Department at Washington that his manoeuvers contemplated the overthrow of the Venezuelan Republic, he was meticulously watched. Finally he left for Trinidad, remained there almost three years, and again returned to the United States. This time the board of special inquiry interrogated him on the ship and again ordered him excluded.

He was brought to Ellis Island despite the fact that he had answered all questions freely and unequivocally, asserting with much emphasis that he had been critically ill in Venezuela during the time General Paredes was said to have been summarily executed. He disclaimed any acquaintance with General Paredes and reiterated his total innocence in the matter.

The government had never appealed from the original decision of Judge Ward, in the *habeas corpus* case, who held in 1913 that failure to affirm or deny on the part of the General had not constituted the admission of a crime involving moral turpitude. Consequently General Castro was admitted to the country two days later on advices from Washington.

He remained a short time, returned again in November of 1917, went back again to Trinidad, and finally died in Porto Rico. Thus ended more than a decade of exile and constant battles with immigration authorities throughout the Americas and outlying insular possessions of the United States and Great Britain. His spectacular career had been followed by the entire world from the day in 1899 when, with two broken legs, and lashed to his horse, he had made his dramatic entrance into the city of Caracas.

III

EMMELINE PANKHURST

Most of the major mass movements of a political nature, wherever they occur in the world, have a common characteristic in that sooner or later Ellis Island receives their repercussions.

For more than a hundred years, stifled minorities in European countries seeking furtherance of their causes have sent representatives to America. Sympathy has been asked from the lecture platform, funds have been solicited by popular subscription, and direct support has been requested of the United States in countless instances. As a result, the United States has always been regarded as a fertile field for the political crusader—partly, perhaps, because of our traditional guarantees of freedom of speech and freedom of the press, partly because of our reputation for wealth, and for many other reasons.

Few, if any, crusaders from abroad during the brief period of our history have proven to be such storm centers as was the diminutive militant suffragette, Emmeline Pankhurst of London, who paid her first visit to these shores during the summer of 1919.

The treatment she had been accorded in England—public ridicule, scorn and imprisonment—and the attitude with which she was confronted by thousands in the United States upon her arrival here, seem to-day as far a cry from our present liberalism towards women as did our earlier ignoble epoch of Salem Witchcraft to nineteenth century church liberalism.

That she was able to enter the country both on that first visit in 1909 and again in 1911, despite the bitter protests registered against her, may be attributed to the liberal disposition of Ellis Island authorities. That she was twice subsequently detained and ordered deported argues the opposite. However, higher authorities, President Wilson among them, intervened, and the fervent little lady, who has been honored since her death with a marble statue at Westminster—erected on the very scene of her most violent resistance—was spared the ignominy of a prisoner's passage back across the Atlantic.

A glance at her record in England during the ten years before the World War, together with the story of her relations with Ellis Island, throws considerable light upon the American attitude toward that once burning topic—the right of a woman to cast the ballot. It may also, as in the case of prohibition, cause some of us to exclaim, "How we Americans contradict ourselves!"

At the time of her arrival here in October, 1913, Mrs. Pankhurst had behind her some nine or ten years of active rebellion against the British government. She had visited America twice previously without causing any upheaval either at Ellis Island or in Washington. This time, however, she came fresh from a prolonged period of rather sensational revolt against the continued refusal of the Liberal government, then in power in England, even to consider the question of Woman Suffrage.

She was approaching fifty, and this, together with her small feminine stature and gentle, motherly smile, gave her the appearance of anything but the virago, the wildcat, the turbulent anarchist and dangerous misleader of youth she was reputed to be. She had a refined and intelligent face, clear eyes wide apart, gray hair drawn softly back, and firm, rather thin, determined lips.

Remembering the matronly and all-enveloping garments prescribed by feminine fashion in that day, I think she must have looked harmless enough as she marched down the gangplank of the liner *Provence,* escorted by the immigration inspector detailed to bring her to Ellis Island. She was, I have been told, a trim neat figure of a woman, attractive, friendly, and pleasant in her approach to people.

Mrs. Pankhurst was probably the most hated woman in England at that time. As the leader of the feminine militant movement to

THREE FAMOUS VISITORS.

Left. Vera, Countess of Cathcart, who stirred up a tempest in a teapot over the interpretation of "Moral Turpitude." *Center.* Mrs. Emmeline Pankhurst, a small person of international importance, vilified in her lifetime but eulogized after her death for her heroic fight for Women's Rights. *Right.* "Prince Mike Romanoff," né Harry Gerguson, world-famous impostor, who crashed our gates with a debonair smile and kept on smiling when deported.

win the ballot, she had kept London in a ceaseless turmoil for some eight or nine years. English women under her guidance had been waging a destructive war against the government, employing as weapons arson, riot, and pitched battles with the police—a program which they purposed to continue until the fight was won and political privileges for women were legalized.

She was born into the suffragist movement, and had always been surrounded by a family that was constantly taking up the cudgels in defense of women's rights. Her father and mother were both ardent champions of the vote for women, and her courtship and honeymoon were conducted over the drafting of a bill to promote property rights for married women. At the time she made her momentous visit to America, Sylvia, one of her two rebellious daughters, was exposing herself in the hottest part of the English political furnace, engaging almost daily in physical struggles with the police, who had orders to suppress the revolt with retaliating violence if necessary. Another daughter, Christabel, after a fierce resistance had escaped to France and was conducting the printing operations of the movement from there.

Mrs. Pankhurst's own stormy career had included a long series of passionate speeches made from soap-boxes, in front of the Parliament houses, in halls and private homes. She had been thrown into prison eight times on various charges—for attempting to present petitions at government sessions, which they called in England "obstructing the police in the performance of their duty;" for inciting her followers to riot, to break shop windows, burn property, blow up telegraph poles, and attack the prime minister, Mr. Asquith, and other officials. She served her first prison sentence of six weeks in 1908, submitting to the almost inhuman treatment then accorded English criminal offenders. Later in the same year she was arrested for helping to prepare leaflets which urged the women suffragists to "rush" the House of Commons and demand a hearing, as they, in due time, did. Four years later the destructive campaign began, and although she personally broke no windows and set fire to no houses, she was accused of conspiracy with the mobs and was given first a nine-months' and then a three-years' sentence. She actually served only a small portion of each sentence.

During her prison periods Mrs. Pankhurst had gone through several hunger strikes, first against the policy of refusing the status of political prisoners to women agitators, and later because she alone was transferred to the political group while her companions suffered the indignities of ordinary prison routine. In this process of hunger and thirst striking she had broken down her health. Many of her followers were put through the torture of being forcibly fed by tubes inserted through the nostrils, and though she herself was spared this because of a bad heart condition, she was repeatedly revolted by the news of its increasing infliction upon her friends and disciples.

At the moment of coming to America in 1913 Mrs. Pankhurst was out of prison under what was known in England as the "Cat and Mouse Act." This had been passed to permit the release of hunger striking women until they should have regained their health, when they were again liable to arrest, at the will of the authorities, to continue their sentences. Mrs. Pankhurst had served only a few days of the three years' penal servitude decree.

In 1913 the rebellion in England was at its hottest, and American papers had for a long time been carrying stories of the feminist activities. When it was casually announced that the leader of this "Votes for Women" movement intended making a lecture tour in America for the purpose of refinancing her cause, Ellis Island was deluged with letters and telegrams of protest.

"This creature who should properly be in an English jail at hard labor is infinitely more dangerous to our country than Castro or others whose entrance has been disputed," wrote one of our more conservative citizens. And from that bulwark of conservatism, Boston, came many enraged, pleading and puritanical cries. Men and women wrote that they were praying she would not be allowed to set foot in the country.

"America has no place for a public or private worker whose mistaken idea of martyrdom does so much harm to her race," said Gloucester, Massachusetts.

"It was a great mistake not to allow her to starve to death in jail in London, instead of letting her out to commit more crimes. The women over there proved they were not fit to vote," said Long Beach, California.

"Mrs. Pankhurst is a faker. There has been no more blatant anarchist in any country than she, and she should be excluded just like Herr Most and Emma Goldman," said wealth and commerce in Albany, New York.

"It has come to my notice that the notorious criminal, Emmeline Pankhurst, is coming to America to realize money to help her and her two daughters and an army of 'hangers-on' to live in luxury, ride in automobiles, and spend the summer and autumn at the most fashionable French watering places. I trust that the Immigration officers will do their duty and give her the 'right about face' for England or France or anywhere the steamship company may see fit to land her. She is a living disgrace to womanhood, and the women of America should not be defiled by her," violently protested Philadelphia.

How vexed we Americans do get over other people's morals! How concerned we become that the soil of our country should not be smirched by contact with those of whom we disapprove! During the weeks previous to her arrival Ellis Island officials waded through hundreds of such letters advising them how to dispose of this "anarchist and criminal," this "fanatical suffragette, evidently insane."

"If ever there was a criminal, she surely is one, and a sneaky, cowardly, deceitful one. Keep her out! Keep her out."

A letter from New York City predicted that Mrs. Pankhurst intended to burn down many American homes. An English moralist advised Ellis Island that she was a convict on leave and had caused much trouble, more than many a murderer who had been hanged.

The most scurrilous protest of all came from a resident of Utica, New York. He wrote:

"Under another cover I send the three most recent issues of *The Suffragette,* the official organ of the militant suffragettes, which in themselves furnish adequate evidence on which to exclude that wild anarchist, Mrs. Pankhurst, from this country. The pages devoted to praise of incendiary fires is enough to exclude a whole regiment, while the prurient stuff contained in the articles on the dangers of marriage, written by the daughter of this woman, shows that the mother is not fit for the society of prostitutes."

Purity spoke, as well, from political position. Mr. William H. Dodge, who in 1933 was elected prosecuting attorney of Manhattan on the Tammany Hall ticket, sent a letter to Ellis Island in which he stated that American doctrine demanded Mrs. Pankhurst's exclusion as an ex-convict.

Meanwhile metropolitan newspapers were flooded with letters of protest, many of which were published and served to fan even higher the fires of wrath that burned in the breasts of good American citizens against the frail little woman who was so soon to rouse the admiration of so many of them by her magnetic personality and her eloquent speech.

In the news columns, our press took an amused attitude, printing much sensational material that was later denied vigorously by Mrs. Pankhurst's American friends. Reporters said that she had decided to enter the country in disguise; they said she had threatened to hunger strike if she were ordered deported, and had predicted that such a measure would cause her death within forty-eight hours.

In England, editorials discussed the possibility of her exclusion here, one editor going so far as to say that America ought to consider her international relations in making so momentous a decision. "To prohibit her entry there would seem almost to be required by the comity of nations," said his paper, the *Standard.* "It would be in strict accordance with the understanding by which one country declines to harbor the condemned criminals of another."

An expatriated Englishwoman, living in New York, wrote the

Times that to admit her would be a deliberate insult to all English-women residing in this country.

Members of New York suffragist societies were divided in their attitude. Mrs. O. H. P. Belmont, President of the Political Equality Association, whose guest Mrs. Pankhurst intended to be while in New York, and Mrs. Harriot Stanton Blatch, head of the Woman Suffrage Party, were making elaborate plans to welcome the rebel, and had arranged for a huge meeting in Madison Square Garden soon after her arrival. Members of the six other suffrage organizations shied off from the preparations, saying plainly that they believed her lecture tour would be a distinct detriment to the suffrage cause in America. Mrs. Carrie Chapman Catt and Dr. Anna Howard Shaw, two of the most animated workers in the history of the woman suffrage struggle in America, declined to take part in the proceedings. They objected chiefly on the grounds that the tour was to profit financially only the English movement, and lamented that American money collected for the promotion of woman suffrage should not be used to push the American cause in Congress.

While all this was going on, Mrs. Pankhurst, recovering from her last hunger strike, was sailing peacefully towards our shores, accompanied by her friend, Mrs. Rheta Childe Dorr, who had gone abroad to meet her. The tempest aroused by public knowledge of her coming, appears to have petrified activities at Ellis Island, so that little action was taken before the boat docked. Then inspectors felt themselves obliged under the law to detain her, upon her free admission of the prison sentences at home. The acting commissioner at Ellis Island, upon learning of her prospective visit, had, it is true, requested a ruling from Washington as to whether her newest offenses in England could be construed as "morally turpitudinous;" and the Secretary of State had requested data from abroad and from Washington concerning her alleged crimes. In connection with this it is interesting to note the reply of the English Consul General, Mr. John L. Griffiths, who explained frankly her criminal record and cited offenses of which she was later to be completely exonerated in the eyes of the public. He said that opinion in this country as to whether or not her offenses involved moral turpitude necessarily depended upon whether the persons expressing the opinion believed or did not believe in militant suffragism.

The Commissioner General of Immigration was much blamed afterwards for not having arranged a settlement of the matter while Mrs. Pankhurst was on the ocean. Records at Ellis Island show that his special instructions were to treat this alien in exactly the same manner as all other alien applicants under the law, and to pay no particular attention to mere newspaper articles with regard to her.

Not a single defender came to the aid of the suffrage leader before her landing in America, so far as Ellis Island records show. After her exclusion many letters and telegrams protesting the act of the immigration officials were received.

Upon arriving at Ellis Island, Mrs. Pankhurst was put through an hour and ten minutes of "special inquiry" before a board of three members. She was quiet and collected, and answered the questions simply and without the smallest sign of vexation.

"Do you admit that the nature of your speeches was such as to incite to riot and rebellion and to the destruction of property?"

"I have made speeches urging women to adopt methods of rebellion, such as have been adopted by men in every revolution."

"Did you advise women to destroy property or life if necessary?"

"I have never advised the destruction of life—but of property, yes, if necessary."

"What is your purpose in coming to the United States?"

"To tell the true story of the women's fight in England, and to get sympathy. I come exactly as Parnell and Redmond and other revolutionary leaders have come."

"Is it your purpose in this country to advocate the tactics that you use in England?"

"I do not come to interfere with the business of American women, for it is their business to get the vote for themselves."

Mrs. Pankhurst had already told reporters, on landing, that she considered the position of American women entirely different from that of the women of her own country. American women were in the minority, she said, and consequently had a greater social value; they were not so cheap as in England, where they were in the majority and had to perform drudgery and bear the contempt of men in general. Fifty years of non-violent methods had borne no fruit whatever in her country, she said.

The outcome, of course, as is well known, was an order for her deportation, which drew from her the remark that she had always looked to America as the home of freedom, and regretted exceedingly the destruction of that ideal. She appealed the case to Washington, and spent what she afterwards described as an interesting two and a half days on Ellis Island, gazing at the Statue of Liberty from the roof of the building, receiving prominent and cultured visitors, reading floods of telegrams, and preparing for her speech in Madison Square Garden.

President Wilson took decisive, if a little tardy, action, and she was ordered released without bond at his personal request. Hordes of photographers and reporters flooded the Island, taking dozens of pictures and congratulating her enthusiastically as she boarded the ferry for Manhattan in company with her friends. The assistant commissioner at the Island said courteously that he was glad that the matter had ended as it had; she is said to have considered this an indication that he favored woman suffrage.

After her release the newspapers again took up Mrs. Pankhurst's case, this time accusing the immigration officials of insufferable stupidity. The *Times* asked plaintively how the dignity of the law had been upheld at all. Fingers of shame were pointed at Ellis Island by editors from every corner of the country. These editors remarked that there was no reason in the world why a country which had been for five generations a refuge for the oppressed of the world should now be blocked by a bastille. They reminded the nation that Mrs. Pankhurst had come only to make us a visit, and would not in any case be in this country long enough to blast the morals of a

single American. They said that the American people were rather
tired of being made the laughing-stock of Europe by the priggish
and pedantic literalism of the immigration authorities. They advised
a revision of the "moral turpitude" clause, since the officials could
not be trusted to interpret it with ordinary intelligence and common
sense.

The tour had a financial success due largely, many papers said,
to the valuable publicity the Ellis Island episode gave to her cause.
She spoke in all the great cities of the East and Middle West. She is
said to have been a born orator, speaking with eloquence, gradually
effecting an increase in spiritual feeling, climbing naturally from
peak to peak until at the end she had the entire audience with her,
even those who had come to hiss and heckle. She used choice and definite language and spoke without bodily movement, except that necessary to send her voice to the farthest parts of the hall.

But she had not seen the last of our American prudery when she
bade a smiling good-bye to Ellis Island on her release from detention. She had yet to meet our Anthony Comstock and learn of the
activities of our Society for the Suppression of Vice. Mr. Comstock
condemned copies of the English suffragist organ, *The Suffragette,*
which Mrs. Pankhurst had brought to sell and distribute to American believers in the movement. He actually swore out warrants
against the girl helpers selling the magazine at Mrs. Belmont's headquarters. He threatened Mrs. Pankhurst with five years' imprisonment and a five-thousand-dollar fine for bringing the offending
papers into the country, and another year and another one-thousand-
dollar fine for putting them on sale. The articles objected to were discussions of the double standard of morality and the white slave traffic,
which Mrs. Pankhurst considered a direct result of women's depriva-
tion of the weapon of the ballot. The magazines were voluntarily
withdrawn from sale, so no action could be taken. Mr. Comstock then
announced that he would arrest the employees at Mrs. Belmont's
suffrage headquarters for selling Christabel Pankhurst's book,
"Plain Facts about a Great Evil." Mrs. Belmont insisted upon being

arrested if anybody was, and this was too much even for the Society for the Suppression of Vice; so their leader again ungraciously withdrew.

These were several occurrences which kept Mrs. Pankhurst in the limelight during her entire visit; and these served, in the opinion of some, to vindicate the original judgment of Ellis Island. The press made much of Mrs. Pankhurst's attendance at "The Lure," a play dealing with the white-slave evil, which underwent a continuous process of investigation during its run here. Mrs. Pankhurst spoke between acts, commending American frankness in permitting an expression of such a theme in drama. Another event which offended her deeply was the request for her hand by a certain Dr. Henry S. Tanner of Los Angeles, dubbed the "champion faster of the world."

On her return to England in December of 1913 Mrs. Pankhurst was snatched from the ship two miles off-shore and incarcerated in Exeter jail. This move on the part of the police circumvented a demonstration planned by her Amazons, who meant to serve her as a bodyguard from the moment she stepped off the boat, and to prevent her re-arrest if it were attempted. The detention did not last long, however, as Mrs. Pankhurst immediately started a new hunger and thirst strike and in a day or two became so enfeebled that the authorities grew frightened and granted her parole.

It is unnecessary to describe at length Mrs. Pankhurst's final contact with Ellis Island on her last visit here in 1916, as it resembles in most details the detention, inquiry, and ultimate release of the 1913 visit. One would suppose that a repetition of this fiasco might have been avoided, had the authorities acted in advance and with precision. As it was, Mrs. Pankhurst arrived on the S.S. St. Paul on January 15 and was sent to Ellis Island, where she again faced a Board of Special Inquiry. The same questions were put to her by another inspector, the same decision was given by another board. She filed an appeal, as on the first occasion, with the Secretary of Labor at Washington, and was immediately released on the order of President

Wilson. The Labor Department protested that they had not known she was coming and so could not have arranged in advance to have her passed on shipboard. Frederic C. Howe, then Commissioner at Ellis Island, protested in a letter to the *Times* that the law rather than the immigration inspection was at fault, and that Mrs. Pankhurst had to be automatically detained as soon as she confessed to a jail sentence. One wonders why they had to bring up that jail sentence again, in view of their memories of the first occasion.

So greatly had Mrs. Pankhurst's world-wide prestige increased in the three-year interval that only one protest was registered in 1916 against her admission.

She came this time not in the interest of suffrage, but to make appeals for the destitute and starving Serbian refugees. She was accompanied by one Chedomyl Miyatovich, a high Serbian official, who was admitted. The militant suffrage campaign had been abandoned at the beginning of the War, and for two years Mrs. Pankhurst had led the women of England in war relief work, for which she was highly commended by the British Government.

It seems a pity that, for the prestige of the country, the two visits of Mrs. Pankhurst just described could not have been handled with the dispatch and ease which attended her two initial visits in 1909 and 1911. She came the first time to lecture under the auspices of the Equality League of Self-Supporting Women, and her sponsors in this country were informed before she sailed that she would be permitted to land. No effort, furthermore, was made to detain her in 1911, though a number of protests had been mailed to Ellis Island. Of course, if all her entrances had been made so tamely as those first two, some of the most colorful annals of Ellis Island would have been lost to the world forever.

It would not be fair to end the story at this point. One must go on to say that Mrs. Pankhurst's efforts were partially rewarded in 1918, when the British Parliament, urged on by Mr. Asquith and Lloyd George, passed the Representation of the People's Bill, which conferred complete franchise on all women who were on the list, wives of all men on the list, and all university women thirty years old; other women were permitted participation in local elections. This did not satisfy the suffragettes, though militancy was never resumed.

Mrs. Pankhurst devoted herself thereafter to various reforms, making her home for a time in Canada where she cared for half a dozen war orphans. Shortly before her death she had been chosen as a Conservative candidate to represent part of London in Parliament. After she died she was compared with Joan of Arc, and many extravagant eulogies were printed in England and America.

English women did not win full political enfranchisement until 1929, a year or two after Mrs. Pankhurst's death. About 1914 she published a book called "My Own Story," setting forth her defense of the militant methods she had advocated.

Universal woman's suffrage was won earlier by peaceful methods in the United States. An amendment ratified in August, 1919, gave all American women the right of the ballot. As in England, their devotion and heroism during the War period were largely responsible for the change in the male attitude toward the suffrage question.

PART V

CHAPTER I

LITTLE TALES OF FLOOD-TIDE DAYS

THE stories I have told concerning General Castro, August Kosutic and Emmeline Pankhurst were of international interest. The travails of Ellis Island with these three personages were flashed around the world.

At the very time these international dramas were being enacted, hundreds of other stories developed every day on the Island which never went beyond the files of the station. I have always been as interested in the pathetic and comic stories of these obscure aliens as in the doings of the powerful rebels who were judged by the immigration service.

Among the welter of those undesirables who had to be turned back to their native countries, there came thousands of sturdy and intelligent families who have put their strength and intelligence into every county of every state in our union. I have already paid tribute in a general way to this steady stream of fine citizenship which has so impregnated our country.

It would have been better if, during the growth of this nation, more publicity had been given to some of the desirables who chose us for their fellow citizens. I am sure there must have been many a family like the de Jongs, for instance, who came here in 1920.

This Dutch family was termed the model immigrant family of that year at Ellis Island. It was headed by Jacob C. de Jong, a sturdy ship chandler from Holland. He was accompanied by Mrs. de Jong and eight healthy, rosy-cheeked children,—Marrigue twenty, Gerrigue eighteen, Johannes seventeen, Johanna sixteen, Neeltje fourteen, Cornelia twelve, Mengo ten and Pilter eight.

When asked for some cash guarantee that his family would not come to want if admitted, de Jong produced five thousand dollars in American money and a great deal more than five thousand dollars in British currency and foreign checks. With a broad smile he explained that he had come to buy a farm and wanted to see his children grow up with the country.

"We believe this is a great country," he said, "and as I have been successful at home, I purpose now to invest my money in America and live here. We are all anxious to buy a farm and knuckle down to hard work."

The de Jongs were not the only family to bring money into the country. An amusing story is told about Mrs. Margaret Moraitis, an English woman, who came here to live with her daughter in 1922. She was bringing over three thousand dollars in cash and seventy thousand dollars' worth of titles to real estate. On the boat she met a gentleman who said he was an "English detective," and who cautioned her against speaking about her wealth at Ellis Island.

"Don't, whatever you do, tell them about your German real estate," he said. "There is a very deep hatred for anything German among the Americans."

A week after landing she left the Island, laughing at herself for her credulity in taking the "detective" seriously. She had declared herself practically penniless, and had been obliged to wait a week until her daughter in San Francisco could wire affidavits of support. She was a gay little old lady, with dimples and curly grey hair, and after finally confessing her wealth to the Island officials, she went away convinced that the joke was on herself.

We received a band of Russians, once, who boasted of untold wealth, but would not let Ellis Island inspectors see it. They were gypsies, about fifty in all including the women and children, and they intended to found a colony in Louisiana or Kentucky. They

Chinese youngsters waiting with their mothers for the examination and deportation.

CHILDREN OF MANY LANDS.

Left. A stolid Russian peasant mother with her brood of three little ones. *Right.* A protective young Dutchman escorting a damsel in distress and her rag baby down steep steps.

brought a huge chest, tightly locked and bound and guarded, which they said held over one hundred thousand dollars in treasure and money. Some of the gypsies sat on the chest night and day, and doctors and inspectors had to examine them there. I believe this was about 1897.

The leader of the party was a big, fine looking fellow who acted as spokesman for the whole group. He had been in America some ten years before, and spoke fairly good English. His wife wore a necklace of United States twenty dollar gold pieces and large pearls. The whole party held themselves aloof from the other passengers on their ship, and seemed to shun publicity.

The various races who have come here have been proud of their contribution to our country, as indeed they may be. I am told that an Italian priest, glowing with pride, once headed a group of eleven men, mostly laborers from Pennsylvania, who were waiting for the arrival of a ship from Italy. When the boat had docked and her passengers had been examined and passed, this group met with rough dignity another group of eleven shy women who had come over to be the wives of the laborers. The priest ushered his charges importantly down to the Marriage License Bureau, and afterwards to the chapel of St. Raphael's, where he married them. These weddings were culminations of war romances.

Some "picture brides" from Greece, who arrived in the same year, (1923) were not so fortunate. A group of these brides, who had been chosen from their photographs by their future husbands in America, had landed. A few evidently did not measure up to their photographs, for they were left unclaimed. They wept bitter tears into their handkerchiefs, while Island officials sent telegrams to the obviously unwilling bridegrooms.

It is said that in order to acquire the pale complexion and plump figure essential to Greek beauty, these girls lived on figs, Turkish delight and rose leaf jam for weeks before setting out on their journey to New York. Such a diet made them ready victims of seasickness, of course.

I have heard of many strange things that have happened to these would-be citizens of ours between their embarkation and their landing in America. Officials on Ellis Island heard of the case of Ng Kuen, though he arrived at our San Francisco and not at our New York port. This young man, when he sailed from Hong Kong, was twenty years, ten months, and twenty-six days old, and confidently expected to be admitted to this country without a certificate, as a minor, since his father was a California business man.

But on the way the steamer's propeller got out of order and the ship lost six days in Nagasaki harbor, with the result that young Ng Kuen celebrated his twenty-first birthday at sea. When he arrived here he was an adult, and as such was denied admittance to the country.

Our immigration officials have not always been as humane as they might have been in dealing with the problem of deportations and divided families. In the last decade of the past century, when big families were certainly more fashionable than they are now, Abraham Leiba, a paper-box maker and father of eight children, came here from Russia. He saved his money and in a short time started a shop for himself. After eighteen months he had saved enough money to send for his wife and eight children. So he rented rooms and furnished them for his family. He then heard that they had arrived on the steamer *Paris,* but were detained at Ellis Island because they had too little money.

Leiba appeared before the board of inquiry and asked that his family be released, as he was able to support them. The board was unmoved, and the family were sent back.

It seems to me that exclusion under such circumstances is unwarranted. There are occasions, however, when the law requires exclusion on grounds which even the victim himself cannot refute.

A nineteen-year-old Lithuanian girl, Miss Hamel Weshner, was ordered deported in 1906 because her medical examination showed that she had trachoma. She was a first-class passenger who was coming to live with three naturalized brothers, one a priest, in Pittsburgh. The brothers had had her educated abroad; when her school-days were over one had gone across to bring her to this country.

Before sailing the brother obtained a certificate from a physician stating that she had no disease. It was believed she had contracted the illness through attending to several of her countrywomen who were sick in the steerage. Federal authorities could find no way to help her, as she had the disease in a malignant form. Her two brothers in Pittsburgh were broken-hearted when told that she would have to return.

Ellis Island once deported a preacher, serving a warrant of arrest on him in his rectory in Brooklyn and bringing him up before the Board of Inquiry which proved that he had served two prison terms in England for a crime involving moral turpitude. Under the laws of this country any person who has been less than eighteen months in the United States must be deported if it is proved that he was convicted abroad for something which comes under the moral turpitude clause.

The Rev. Alfred Hart had taken over his pastorate about six weeks before, and had remained a mystery man to his congregation. At the time of his arrest none of them knew anything about him.

The immigration officials had information that Hart was born in a Whitechapel slum, and had been found and educated by a wealthy woman who sent him to Oxford to prepare for the ministry.

The Church of England, with which he claimed affiliation, repudiated him after his arrest.

About 1880 our country was deluged with numbers of fakers belonging to a group called "Maronites," followers of Maron, a supposed saint who lived in the fifth century. These people spoke Arabic and came here from Lebanon, in Syria.

They began coming in small groups in the garb of mendicants. They wore red fezzes, short open jackets, short baggy blue trousers to the calves of the legs, and ill-fitting shoes. As soon as they had passed the immigration authorities they would at once go out into the streets to ply their trade. At the end of his first day in America the whining Maronite would have added five dollars to his hoard, while the Irish or German immigrant would be bustling around trying to find work to enable him to earn a dollar.

The first comers returned richly laden with spoils, whereupon their admiring friends began selling their land and possessions in order to come also to America. They arrived in droves until about eight thousand were living in New York City alone.

Soon they were a nuisance, and the policemen were ordered to arrest all those caught begging in the streets. The story goes that a policeman arrested one of them for this offense, but before reaching the police station the expert mendicant not only had persuaded the officer to let him go but had actually got a quarter out of him. Upon returning to his friends he boasted about having got the better of that "goat" of a policeman.

An entire family of Maronites, landing at Castle Garden, remained there a week pretending to have no money. Sufficient funds were raised to send them to a southern state. Then it developed that they had twenty-four thousand dollars invested in sheep and railroad bonds.

After they were arrested for begging the fakers would produce little rosaries and trinkets to sell whenever a policeman was watching them.

Gradually the padrone system was organized, and professional Syrian tramps were hired and shipped to this country, the principals taking mortgages on their property and paying their passage. They printed a directory of American cities and towns, giving the population, together with the names of priests and clergymen, who could be easily deceived. The country was divided into districts and a definite gang went to each district. An alphabet of signals and signs was invented. Inscriptions in Arabic chalked on the fences often informed members of the gang, "We have begged this village thoroughly," or "Don't waste time here." Two always travelled together, the padrones depending upon one tramp watching the other.

When the inspectors learned of the racket and tried to keep the beggars out, they came dressed as Greeks or Italians.

An amusing sight that it is now no longer possible to see, since the immigration tide has turned backwards, was the scene at the Battery when the Ellis Island ferry-boat landed with its human freight. Many people have told me that half an hour after the boat came in, the dressing rooms in the adjacent ferry-houses, the bushes at the lower end of Battery Park, and even the gutters along the sidewalks presented the appearance of a junk shop. Queer headgear of women lay about, the familiar black-visored caps of the men and boys, waists and skirts or coats and trousers that undoubtedly went well in the outlying districts of Moscow but would not go far in Manhattan without causing comment and ridicule.

American friends and relatives hurriedly dressed the newly arrived immigrants to disguise the fact that they had come in the steerage. Modern American clothing and luggage were handed to the arrivals as soon as they stepped off the ferry-boat, and they were forced to put it on in the nearest convenient place, before meeting anyone in America. Typical immigrant valises and bags were discarded in the street, thrown overboard from the ferry-boat, or abandoned in public dressing rooms. Such are the ways of vanity!

A costly illustration of native vanity occurred in my time, when two Moroccan chiefs refused to discard their robes and fezzes and stepped off the ferry-boat at the Barge Office in all the glory of their regal raiments. They were bound for the World's Fair in Chicago. An enterprising taxi driver, on the lookout for business, lured them into his cab and sped them on to the Windy City. The trip cost $143 and proved that Chicago was not around the corner.

CHAPTER II

THE CARAVAN'S MOST AMAZING CHARACTER

IGNATIUS TIMOTHY TREBITSCH-LINCOLN has the reputation at Ellis Island of being the most amazing character ever detained there.

Scotland Yard and the New York *American* both called him the "most elusive man in the world." United States Marshal James M. Power said in 1922 that he was "just an ordinary thief." Among other things he himself claimed to be a Buddhist monk and a former member of the English Parliament; and he revelled in the appellation, as applied to himself, of "international spy." He was called other things—"one of the striking features of the war's aftermath, a picturesque relic of the great struggle . . . a Jew who became a Presbyterian minister . . . a curate in London . . . an Anglican rector."

His first official recognition in the United States is recorded in the 1915 police files. He was arrested on a charge of forgery and was demanded by the British Government. He effected a melodramatic escape from a deputy marshal in a Brooklyn restaurant in 1916, but was soon captured again and sent to England where he served a sentence. Since it was assumed by most of the Allied governments that the prisoner was accepting pay from Germany, and that he was serving in the capacity of spy, it was hoped that the British action against him would effectively remove him from the international stage.

Trebitsch-Lincoln was a Jew, but I do not know of what nationality. No epithet could better fit him than the out-worn one of "wandering Jew." In some of his correspondence with the United States, which I shall quote, he speaks of himself as a former subject of Great Britain, and expresses hopes of being reinstated as such. He expressed deep love for many countries, particularly our own.

The man was of a fairly well known type, though few of those belonging to his particular psychological group get themselves as internationally noticed as he did. That was the key to his personality —the necessity of being noticed. He was extremely egoistic, and whether or not he took himself seriously it was necessary to his health and well-being that other people should do so.

He reappeared in America on November 4, 1921, walking into various newspaper offices in New York and Brooklyn, effectively disguised, and announcing his return to the United States.

"I must and do acknowledge that I landed here in violation of the immigration laws, but I meant no deception or offense to the United States. I will petition the Government to allow me to stay here as a political refugee. If I am refused, I will slip out even more mysteriously than I came in." After this statement he was arrested.

His announcement came to the eyes of United States Marshal James M. Power, who wrote at once to the Commissioner of Immigration at Ellis Island protesting Lincoln's entrance. The Marshal complained that Lincoln "is a person unfit to be in this country, since he is not only a thief but his morals border on degeneracy, as can be verified from the reports of the Department of Justice made in February 1916."

He said further: "This man has been obtaining notoriety through the various newspapers through the allegation that he was an international spy. This spy allegation is nothing more or less than 'pure bunk'. Lincoln is just an ordinary thief who violated a trust and took his employer's money, and it was on this charge of grand larceny that he was heretofore extradited from this country, and not for any political offense."

They held a hearing for him on March 1, 1922, at which he made one of his amazing, extraordinarily lengthy speeches, explaining his pure purposes and outlining some of his political manoeuvers in Europe.

Lincoln based his right of entry on what he called his "rendition to this country of services of great value." He said his entry was made with the active assistance of members of the diplomatic corps in Europe, who had assured him personally that once here he would be free to remain. He dismissed the convict charge with the statement that his conviction in England during the War was simply a cover to secure his detention for political reasons during that period.

Forcible deportation to either England, France, Italy, Germany, Austria or Hungary would, he said, place his life in actual jeopardy, and he requested that if he might not remain in this country he should be allowed to leave the United States voluntarily, having his bond cancelled upon satisfactory proof through one of the American consuls that he had actually left the borders of the country.

His connections with the State Department of the United States began, he said, about September, 1919, when he called repeatedly upon Mr. Wiley, Secretary of the United States Legation at The Hague, and "gave him the benefit of my intimate knowledge of European politics."

About a year later he made application to the State Department through the United States Embassy in Vienna for permission to come to this country. Mr. Halsted, then Commissioner, asked him, he said, for his opinion and information on "the Upper Silesian question, the Monarchistic movement in Germany, Austria and Hungary, the Anschlussbewegung in Austria, the restoration of the Hapsburgs, the Russian situation in regard to both the Bolshevists and the Monarchists, and other matters."

"I most willingly rendered him and his government this service, since I was desirous of becoming an American citizen, if I were granted permission to come to this country," the statement continued. "Mr. Halsted so thoroughly appreciated the valuable information I gave him, that, later, when the State Department refused to

give me permission to come to the United States, he personally renewed the request in his own name in an official cable."

Then he launched into a long discussion of his relations with Mr.
Shoecraft, at one time Chargé d'Affaires of the Vienna Embassy, to
whom he had rendered further services and who had assured him of
the gratitude of the State Department. Among other things, he gave
Mr. Shoecraft secret information concerning the presence of the Russian Social Revolutionary leader, Kerensky, at Prague, and informed
him of the Russian Revolutionary Conference which was to be held
at Riga. While on a mission to Czecho-Slovakia he kept in constant
touch with the American Chargé d'Affaires by private telephone. For
all these services he persistently refused to accept money, saying that
he would expect from the United States in payment only permission
to come here. Mr. Shoecraft, he said, accepted the gift of his secret
documents on those conditions.

He had been advised by a gentleman of the United States Diplomatic Service simply to come to this country and notify Washington
of his arrival, after which he would find everything "all right." The
false passport had been necessary because the French government
refused to allow him to travel through France.

He admitted to a list of about a dozen aliases, stating that there
had been others which he couldn't at the moment remember.

On March 28, 1922, the Secretary of Labor issued a deportation
order for Trebitsch-Lincoln but permitted him thirty days in which
to leave the country voluntarily. Five months later this astonished
official received a telegram from Los Angeles requesting "an immediate, definite and unequivocal decision in my case". He was notified
that if he did not leave immediately the deportation order, which
was to Hungary, would be executed. On September 4 of that year he
turned up at the American Embassy in Tokio.

This wandering Jew seems to have been at home wherever he
hung his hat; and the multiplicity of his escapades must have given
him contacts everywhere. Two years before his American adventure
the American Commissioner at Berlin had reported by cable that Lin-

coln was taking a prominent part in the reactionary movement at that time going on in Germany. In a dispatch dated November 16 of the same year, the American Commissioner at Vienna enclosed a memorandum received from Lincoln, purporting to be the story of a Monarchist plot to overthrow the existing governments of Austria and Germany, for which information Lincoln had admitted that he hoped to gain permission to live in the United States or be allowed to cross the country en route to China. A month later the American Commissioner at Budapest had sent a dispatch reporting an interview which a member of his staff had had with an individual regarding Lincoln's supposed activities in Germany and in Hungary; that report stated that the Kapp revolution in Germany "was practically organized by Lincoln and the programme worked out by him." When the movement failed and the new government ordered his arrest with others, Lincoln obtained "legitimation" papers from the Russian Bolshevist agent in the name of William Ludwig and stated that he was in close connection with Lenin, that they were organizing an expedition of German officers to Asia, near Thibet, that they were to receive arms and munitions from the Bolshevists and intended to form a state there among the tribes; after raising an army, they would attack India.

It is safe to assume that so resourceful an adventurer was not without money, for he had accumulated secret information concerning this government and those of Europe and was not at all above selling it to any purchaser.

For instance, on February 10 of the previous year, Budapest had submitted a report of his having received an advance of fifty thousand crowns from the French Legation in Vienna for "a military tactical work" written by Colonel Bauer; and, in October, going to Prague with a Bavarian passport in the name of Karl Lamprecht, Lincoln "sold his report to the Czechs for five hundred thousand crowns, receiving an advance of two hundred thousand crowns." He may have been a man of "hopeless devotion to an ideal," for it was reported that he intended to present a copy of this same much-used report to the American Legation at Prague in the hope of being allowed to come to the United States.

But, in spite of all his "good intentions," Austria wanted him for travelling on forged passports, and on October 11, 1921, our Department of State had been advised that the German Government had a warrant out for him with a price on his head of fifty thousand marks. Europe being thus too hot to hold him, he had turned gladly to tranquil Tokio.

In 1927 he was back again and had further dealings with our State Department. All this manoeuvering is in itself of no particular interest, as he apparently had no dangerous motive on this trip. He did, however, write the State Department one of the most amazing letters which that department of our Government has ever received. I should like to quote this letter in full, since more than anything I could myself say it reveals his character and personality. In itself it makes most interesting narrative and psychological reading. The letter was dated May 17, 1927, and reads as follows:

Your Excellency,
There are few persons to-day in the world about whom so much has been written in the Press of the whole world as about my poor self; few men who have so persistently been calumnied as myself; few, if any, who have had such a varied, not to say checkered, activity as myself.

I have been called the International Spy, Adventurer, Traitor, Charlatan, Arch Conspirator, the Confidant of ultra-Conservative German Monarchists, Adviser of Marshal Wu Pei Fu of China and many other things. That I have been connected with all of these and others, I do not deny.

But who can tell in what capacity, from what motives, for what ends? If there were any desire for unbiased truth in the world, everybody would have to admit that they do not know the real inner story of my life, nor are acquainted with the influences that prompted, nay, impelled, me to do those various things *the surface and apparent meaning of which alone is accessible to writers and readers alike.*

A few years ago, the *Neue Freie Presse,* the leading newspaper of Vienna, Austria, referred to me as the "belated relative of Cagliostro and Count Saint Germain". I am quite content to leave it at that. These two illustrious personages whose real identity and purpose of activities is known but to the few have always been referred to as Adventurers and Charlatans.

But I will not bother you with biographical details of myself; this task has been undertaken by Dr. Ritter Gustav von Kreitner, a retired Austrian Judge and who has the facilities of consulting the secret archives of some Governments. I await his conclusions with placid composure.

When a few years ago, I once more disappeared, as so often in the past, from the arena of public activity, I was said to have died, to have been shot, hanged and what not. Great was then the surprise when it was discovered that I had been living quietly as a Buddhist monk in a Buddhist monastery in the Island of Ceylon.

Of course, immediately, all kinds of surmises and stories were fabricated to try and explain my supposed or real retirement into the complete seclusion of a monastery and which fact was taken as a further proof that I must, indeed, be an adventurer. The fact, however, is that having finished with political work forever, which, however, was not undertaken with a purpose of affecting the political conditions of the world only, I retired into a monastery to fit myself for the remaining task of my life.

What that task is the future will show. The presentation of the Teachings and Philosophy of Gotama, the Buddha, since undertaken and successfully pursued, is the first step in the carrying out of that task.

I beg to ask you not to think of this my act as a "conversion", as the act of one who turned his back "upon his former evil deeds and tries to efface their effects by real or pretended religious gesture"—as newspapers would describe it.

I have not been "converted" at all; I offer no explanations or apology to anyone in the whole wide world for anything. I have been more sinned against than sinner. Let everybody look into himself, examine his own thoughts and actions instead of sitting in judgment upon his fellows, of whose motives and secrets (and we all have secrets) he is in total ignorance. As a Buddhist monk I have learned not to allow thoughts to arise in me that:

> "any are better than I,
> "Or equal to me,
> "Or less than I."

Few persons living to-day have had such a varied and eventful career as I have had; few have had so many unique opportunities to contact life with all its sordid and sublime realities, with its shame and fervent seekings of truth, as I have had. Few men have had the opportunity to stalk and live behind the scenes of political plots and counterplots in many parts of the world, being, indeed, one of the principal actors in many of them.

At one time I was Member of the British Parliament, during the War I became known as the International Spy, I was put into an English prison for forgery, kept there after the expiration of my legal residence until peace was signed in 1919. I then went to Berlin and completely disappeared from public view till some newspaper correspondents discovered me in Amerongen, Holland, on a visit to the ex-Kaiser to whom I was sent by Col. Bauer and the German Monarchists. A few weeks later I was detected visiting the ex-Crown Prince on the Island of Wieringen. And then I disappeared so completely from public activity that once more my death was published with all circumstantial detail. But when the Monarchist anti-revolutionary armies of the ill-fated Kapp Putsch marched into Berlin in the spring of 1920, it was found that I marched at the head of them and the amazed foreign correspondents found that they had to submit all their cables to me to be passed before they would be accepted at the chief telegraph office in Berlin.

Later I was discovered "plotting" with Ludendorff in Munich, with Admiral Horthy in Budapest, with the Monarchists in Vienna. Then I once more disappeared as completely as if the earth had swallowed me up. And, of course, once more I read the obituary notices in the press about myself. After two years I was discovered in China as an intimate and trusted friend and advisor of Marshal Wu Pei Fu. On secret missions to Europe, back to China, back to Europe, back to China—I finished with politics and retired into a Buddhist monastery. A very tragic occurrence in my family forced me prematurely out of my retreat and I hurried to Europe.

Since then I have been travelling about clandestinely as no other possibility existed for me. Many times during the past few years have I been arrested, have had hairbreadth escapes; I lived in palaces and hovels, contacted intimately the high and the low, know most parts of the world as few people do, have been in parts of Asia where no foreigners venture, have seen, heard and acquired many strange things, have seen and looked through things and persons, not merely at them. And I am sheer overwhelmed by the lies, wrongs, humbugs, sufferings and misery of the world.

Hence, consistently and in strict harmony with the aims I have pursued for many years (though the choice of the means has been often wrong), I decided to devote my remaining years to show a way out of all this mess of misery. Please, do not shake your head incredulously, do not smile. I have been travelling about the world during the past fourteen months silently, unknown, unheralded, scattering seeds here and there. The result has been more than remarkable. There are individuals all along the way I covered whose mental attitude, nay, whose very lives I have changed. With many of them I am corresponding. What a remarkable and cheerful commentary on all the cheap lies and calumnies that have been published about me.

Last fall, after my arrival here in New York, I have called at the State Department in Washington to find out whether I could remain openly in this country for a period of six months or a year in order to deliver lectures on Buddhism. Mr. Benham of your department received me kindly and treated me very courteously. But I have entered the United States (acting under necessity) in violation of your immigration laws. I could have been arrested and a deportation order might have been issued and enforced against me. That it was not done was an act of supreme kindness for which I shall always be duly grateful. Mr. Benham pointed out to me that being in this country illegally, it was impossible for me to come out publicly. That was correct. I therefore decided to leave the United States, return to a certain monastery in Asia and end my days there. With this fixed determination I left New York for San Francisco, intending to take ship there for a certain port in Asia whence I hope to be able to go to Tibet. Before leaving New York, I applied to the British Government to allow me to travel openly to Calcutta and thence to Tibet. Unfortunately this my request was not granted. Still, I decided to go to Tibet by a roundabout way.

On the 11th day of January, this year, I arrived in San Francisco under the name of Ruh, which in German means "rest". I lived under this name in the Japanese Hotel Ebisu, 1645 Buchanan Street. On the day of my arrival I met Mr. Nyogen Senzaki, a former Buddhist monk in Japan and who came to this country some twenty years ago with his Master Sojen Shaku, who was well received in this country including Washington, D.C.

Mr. Senzaki remained in this country when his Master returned to Japan and has been quietly working as a teacher in San Francisco. He invited me to speak at his monthly meeting on Buddhism and which happened to fall on the 15th of January, a few days after my arrival there. I, of course, consented. As a result of my address there, I was invited to address other meetings in private houses. I never intended to remain in San Francisco. I and those who invited me to speak to them on Buddhism merely asked me to defer my departure a few days. The first days became another few days and still another few days. Out of such beginnings there grew up spontaneously and without planning or intention a Buddhist Center in San Francisco, the first of its kind in the Western Hemisphere. Three times, halls which had to be hired to accommodate the hearers had to be changed for larger ones, such interest was manifested in my lectures which were solely on Buddhism. On the

24th of March this year we moved into hired permanent quarters in 234 Haight Street, San Francisco.

One remark before I proceed. I want to declare that though the students were willing to pay almost any price for my lectures, I have not made any money, either directly or indirectly out of this, my work. I am a Buddhist monk, vowed to a certain rule of life, and though I am not now living in a monastery, still I conform to the monkish rule of life, one of which is not to accept any money for spiritual work. I only drew twenty dollars a week to cover all my expenses.

Thus I lived among my ever increasing number of students being the recipient of their loyal and loving attachment.

I am telling your Excellency all this with perfect frankness because I have nothing to hide; because by so doing I hope to convince you that I did not deliberately stay in this country, but the thing developed out of itself. During the whole of this time I refrained from publicity, though the newspapers in San Francisco were after me when they heard of the new Buddhist Center. A paragraph even appeared in the *San Francisco Examiner* on Sunday March 20th, page 13, under the caption, "S.F. Growth of Buddhism Held Certain". That interview was not sought by me at all but a reporter came to me not knowing of course that I was I.T.T. Lincoln. They asked for my photo which I declined to supply or to allow myself to be photographed.

On Sundays I used to speak in a public hall of the Native Sons Building and there were always some three hundred people present. Thus the work grew. I now faced a very delicate situation: I was illegally in this country: I gave my word to Mr. Benham that I would not publicly lecture; but now I had to expect the fact of my being there to leak out sooner or later, which would place me in the wrong light with the U.S. Government, the last thing I desire. I, therefore, decided to leave San Francisco, to come to New York and to lay the matter before you, as I am now doing with all frankness.

What shall I do now?

The reasons which mitigated against my public activity last fall when I visited the State Department still hold good,—I am fully aware of this. Yet I should like to remain in this country a few months longer until the Center in San Francisco is well established and possibly others started for which there are many opportunities placed in my way. But I cannot do it, I, intending all the time to leave next week, and again the next week. The San Francisco Center just grew without my planning it. But if I were to undertake similar work under an assumed name, I would feel that I am abusing the kindness and forbearance which has so generously been shown towards me by your Department when I called there last fall. The San Francisco work cannot condemn me in your eyes as you can find out by careful and unobtrusive inquiries that it just grew spontaneously. Were I, however, to go on with similar work here, as I am asked to do, I feel I would place myself in a wrong position with you and, therefore, I am not going to do it.

I have made application during the last few days to the British Government to be reinstated as a British subject and to be allowed to travel freely and work openly as a British monk. What the outcome of my application will be, I cannot, of course, tell; in any case it will be many weeks before I shall get a reply. Would it be possible, Sir, meanwhile to carry on my work;

1) either as Mr. Ruh,
2) or as Mr. Lincoln?

Perhaps the difficulty of the Immigration laws could be circumvented by leaving for Montreal, making application to the U.S. Consul there for a legal and open entry into this country for, say, six months. During the interval I may receive a favorable reply from London and could then depart for Europe or Asia. But even if no favorable decision would reach me from London, I would leave the United States at the expiration of six months. And, possibly, the British Government might allow me to live in Burma in a monastery even without granting me the privilege of restoring my British Citizenship and later go to Tibet.

Your Excellency, there remains but one more consideration which I want to urge upon your kind and favorable consideration. Very great things are happening all over Asia. The political ferment and concomitant national aspirations, battling against foreign restrictions and limitations are merely the outward symptoms of deeper lying causes and which are of religious and cultural nature.

The upheaval now going on in Asia, and I am not referring to China alone, cannot be met by political means alone.

The powers, and particularly America and Great Britain, must align themselves with the spiritual forces which cause all the turmoil.

May I point out to you the ferment which is going on in British India, drawing over widening circles? The British Government has met this movement in liberal, conciliatory and far seeing measures, the most notable of which is the Chelmsford-Montague reforms. Yet, what has been the outcome? More unrest. Why? Because political measures alone will not be able to deal with the complex problems now emanating from Asia and disturbing the whole world. Due regard should be paid to the totally distinct mentality of the Asiatic races and their attitude toward life. It is the pressure of Western Civilization, cultural, religious, which is unwelcome to Asia more than gunboats.

It is only on cultural and religious grounds that they can be met; that the West and the East can find a formula of peaceful and harmonious coöperation.

I know of certain things along these lines which are being prepared and will come more and more to the front.

There is a great Buddhist revival going on in Japan to such an extent that the opposition of the Buddhists there prevented the Japanese Government from appointing a duly accredited Minister to the Holy See. Similar work is going on in China, Burma, Ceylon and even India, sponsored by the powerful Maha Bodhi Society in Calcutta.

Why not recognize these things, trying to understand them and cooperate with them for the benefit of all? The Buddhist revival in Germany is simply phenomenal; there is a Buddhist House and Temple just outside Berlin in Frolmau, a similar institution will be built in London this very year by Mr. Anagarika Dharmapala who is there now and who visited America last year. Thus, I have not done such a bad service to America by having started a similar work and Center in San Francisco, the Gateway of the Orient. I know that that Center will in days to come become a great force and power for good in many ways. Were I permitted to work openly, I could extend its activities and increase its usefulness.

Your Excellency, the Government of the United States has always and consistently proved herself a friend of Asia; she has repeatedly rendered great service to China and to other Asiatic countries; she is looked upon as the champion of their just aspirations among the western nations. I think the present moment is the most auspicious to allow this Buddhist work to go on in this country. But there is another aspect to this matter. No matter how powerful and sincere the United States is, she cannot deal successfully with the problems in Asia alone. Needless for me to point out to you the reasons as they are, I am sure, well known to you. One of the many Asiatic questions alone is sufficient to prevent you dealing with it alone; the Manchurian question which will come up again and again and which Japan will prevent finding any solution except in accordance with her policy which is being pursued with marvelous tenacity.

Great Britain and the United States must and will coöperate there as in other parts of the world; in their keeping is really the peace of the world. And Sir Austen Chamberlain's program for China called the Christmas program proves that they are fully alive in London to the great changes that are and have taken place in Asia and that they have the wisdom and good will to meet them in a spirit of liberal conciliation.

But I am not interested in politics, I am merely alluding to these matters to show that I am fully alive to them, and that even as a Buddhist monk doing spiritual work I shall watch them and make them serviceable to the ends I have in view; a friendly coöperation between Great Britain and America for a harmonious and real coöperation in

Asia in order to allay the destructive tendencies that are gathering force there.

I appeal to Your Excellency to find a way and to permit me remaining here openly for six months in order to establish other Buddhist Centers and then go, with the anticipated permission of the British Government as a British subject to Asia and continue my work there openly and in full view of all men.

Permit me to express to you my profound thanks for past kindnesses and to express the hope that my humble request may be granted, and to sign myself,

Your Excellency's
obedient and humble servant
(SGD) I.T. Trebitsch Lincoln

I am acquainting Sir Harry Armstrong, his Majesty's Consul General here with this letter.

I.T.T.L.

P.S. I just beg to add that in the Japanese Hotel Ebisu I only stayed two weeks, moving into the Hotel Willau, 161 Ellis St., San Francisco, where I remained uninterruptedly till April 12th on which day I came East. Nobody in S.F. knows my real name.

I.T.T.L.

Comp. by ro.

After that he left America and disappeared for a while. Later he turned up in Europe, bearing the twelve-point brand of the Buddhist religious leader on his skull—those scars, according to Buddhist rites, being reminiscent of the twelve spokes of "the wheel of life." He was now Abbot Chao Kung, the Buddhist monk.

About two months ago I read about him again in the newspapers. He had been shipped from Canada to England and back to Canada again. When last I heard, he had reached the Pacific Canadian coast on his way back to the Orient where alone, it seems, he is still received. He now avoids all extremes and eats only one meal a day. He wants to be on friendly terms with all the world. Perhaps he will one day fold his wings in a monastery and really pass into obscurity, but I doubt it. I see him as a Buddhist itinerant preacher, passing still from one country to another with appropriate publicity.

Chapter III

WHO SHALL APOLOGIZE?

It is an inspiring sight to watch a mighty parade, to hear martial music, to view the gorgeous costumes and note the uplifted chins beneath eager determined eyes. But how different, and what a contrast is an army in retreat! The broken ranks, the maimed and wounded, the dying, the desperately struggling, proceeding anywhere but toward the original objective. Such is the contrast between the caravan of immigration to America, and the exodus of those hapless ones who, old and broken, defeated, discouraged, the better parts of their lives spent in vain, often turn in refuge toward their homelands after disappointments in America!

And how filled with pathos are the annals which reveal the cruelty, the swindling, the merciless exploitation of thousands who came to our shores with high hopes and ideals of American citizenship.

Both lanes of humans—the incoming and the outgoing—converged at Ellis Island. The incoming were often buoyed as much by false promises as by high hopes; the outgoing frequently bore the earmarks of human treachery as well as the shadow of shattered illusions.

In the corridor which leads to the Commissioner's office at Ellis Island, there hangs overhead the following framed notice:

ORDER CONCERNING TREATMENT OF IMMIGRANTS
"Immigrants shall be treated with kindness and civility by everyone at Ellis Island. Neither harsh language nor rough handling will be toler-

ated. The Commissioner desires that any instance of disobedience of this order be brought immediately to his attention."

By Order of the Commissioner
May 1918.

I read this sign the day after I took office, but, being preoccupied with so many responsibilities, not until I had walked beneath it day after day for some time was I led to wonder what conditions had brought about its issuance and display.

Interpreter Martocci and others in and out of the service had already informed me concerning some of the ruses and rackets that were perpetrated upon the incoming aliens in the days of old. I heard from the lips of immigrants themselves many tales of exploitation. And one of my prime resolutions was to do everything that lay in my power to humanize the Service. I determined to investigate thoroughly the treatment received by the immigrant—both past and present.

In dealing with people it is always difficult to measure accurately where the blame really rests. A system involving thousands of illiterates at the mercy of organized routine is one thing. Illiterates at the hands of wily scoundrels and sharpshooters is another. Criticism and complaint are inevitable, and are bound to combine an essence of truth with an element of bias. It is difficult indeed, even after years of experience, to determine what is truth and what is prejudice.

It is natural for individuals to air personal grievances over conditions where individuals cease to exist. It is natural for society at large to shout about abuses of which they hear only one side or mere fragments.

However, in all this mass of evidence there was a challenge. I listened and learned first-hand—and from the stories of abuse and fraud I tried to select the false from the true—and then, to the best of my ability, suggested modifications and changes to correct the situation as far as possible.

Professor Edward A. Steiner of Grinnell College, a leading authority on immigration, interviewed a group of returned immigrants a few years ago in an inn at Cetinje, Montenegro. This is what he found:

Cheated by employment agencies	80%
Cheated by Austrian boarding-house keepers	60%
Money lost by giving bribes to Irish-American bosses who promised jobs never given	36%
Rough treatment by bosses	72%
Robbed by railroad crews in Montana	80%
Shanghaied—made drunk and railroaded from St. Louis to Southern Kansas	15%
Robbed of money and tickets before departure for home	40%

The press accounts of those days abound in stories of vice syndicates, steamship exploitation, unsavory conditions in the steerage, padrones, white slave rings, shyster lawyers, and bankers who embezzled funds entrusted for dispatch to relatives in foreign countries; of cheating, robbing, beating and "shaking down" of every variety.

Frequent investigations were conducted in the years when immigrants were received at Castle Garden. These dealt with dishonest money-changers; railroad "pools" which handled the transportation of immigrants across the continent at the will of the railroads and not of the immigrants themselves; baggage rackets, labor rackets and boarding house rackets.

Pictures of the time often show a boarding house runner, heading a line of bewildered arrivals, himself carrying the baby of the family to be sure that the rest will follow. This snatching of the baby or of a valuable piece of baggage has been a favorite ruse since the beginning of immigration to this country.

There are many stories of immigrants bringing over American gold dollars perforated with holes in England or France before they were sold to the traveller. The fine dust thus drilled out made a handsome extra profit for the unscrupulous broker.

After immigrants were received at Ellis Island, the same conditions prevailed and investigations of the same swindling tactics were constantly in progress.

In February, 1902, it was charged that immigrants were forced into the Island barber shop and compelled to pay for haircuts and shaves for the purpose of swelling the receipts of the concessionaires, and that some newcomers were made to work in the kitchens or dining rooms. The charges were promptly denied by Ellis Island authorities, but President Roosevelt ordered another official investigation in April of that year. Commissioner Fitchie immediately countered with a statement that there had been no cruelty to immigrants, but rather a vigorous effort on the part both of New York police and of Ellis Island authorities to protect the immigrants from "sharks."

"It is not the immigrants," he said, "that the police and guards are driving, but the hordes of hotel runners and idlers who gather at the Barge Office to rob them by one scheme or another.

"The officers must use force, and sometimes they need to use plenty of it. They no sooner drive one bunch back than another crowd rushes forward at a different point and has to be similarly handled. It is these crowds of hangers-on and idlers that the police use their whips on, not the immigrant.

"In several instances the 'sharks' have drawn knives and attacked the officers. A man whom detective Quackenbos arrested a few weeks ago made a slash with a knife, and cutting him through his coat and other clothing just missed disembowelling him."

But throughout those early years, with each successive administration the immigrants charged cruelty and ill treatment against the immigration officers as well as the "sharks". There were frequent dismissals and many investigations and outcries that reached even to the floors of Congress.

It would require a special volume to fully chronicle the investigations at Ellis Island and their repercussions across the nation. Each was a modified version of the same old story—employees of the government accepting, even demanding, tips and bribes. The outcry usually started in the press and ended in Congress, after some ambitious Senator or Representative with immigrant constituents obtained the authority of his colleagues for the investigation. If guilty, the employees were discharged, but human nature being what it is, and the tide of immigration being what it was, there were always recurrences.

Nineteen hundred and five was the year when protests against the vicious aspects of immigration echoed around the world. There was a debate in the British Parliament reminiscent of American Revolutionary days. In this English controversy the policy of the United States, as reflected by Ellis Island, was scathingly excoriated.

About this time John Redmond, the Irish leader, speaking at Killarney, declared it was time to stop emigration from Ireland. "One cause of emigration that ought to be removed," he said, "is the exaggerated prospect held out to Irish boys and girls if they will go to America. The poorest laborer we have in Kerry is happier than the majority of the Irish working men in the United States."

In that same year the Collector of the Port of New York caused the arrest of the masters of the steamship *Citta di Napoli* of the Italian Line and the *Erny* of the Phelps Line, for violating the United States passenger laws for immigrant steamships. The Crown of Italy became incensed, not at the arrests, but because of the treatment of immigrants *en route* to America in the steerage, who were fed from cans and made to sleep spoon-fashion in smelly bunks filled with vermin. It finally became necessary for a representative of the Royal Italian Government to accompany each immigrant ship on its way to America, to see that such practices and cruelty were stamped out.

Tales such as this were all too frequent for many, many years. In spite of conflicting evidence, there was undoubtedly basis in fact for dismay at the profiteering methods aimed at those powerless to protect themselves.

When the S.S. *Red Sea* arrived at Ellis Island as far back as July

1893, her indignant passengers gave forth a roar which was heard on the Jersey shore. They had no sooner landed than they began in many tongues to protest against the treatment on the tramp steamer. They made affidavits to all sorts of cruelty and abuse, stories such as were once told of life on African slavers.

Captain Buston, Commander of the *Red Sea,* countered with the excuse that the immigrants were vexed because they were made to bathe, and because they were not permitted to eat up the *Red Sea's* stores. He denied the charges categorically.

It appears from these records that four days out of Bremen a bread riot broke out on deck. Most of the immigrants had recovered from seasickness by that time, and were ravenously hungry. At meal times many would request second and third helpings of food. The stronger would crowd the weaker passengers out of line, causing suffering among the women and children. Captain Buston changed the procedure in the issuance of rations. The new system did not suit any of the passengers, and one day a crowd of burly men, armed with knives, rushed the galleys and brandished their weapons at the cooks.

The frightened cooks appealed to the Captain who ordered the crew to place two of the ringleaders in irons. After that a semblance of discipline was maintained.

But upon their arrival at Ellis Island, nearly every passenger of the *Red Sea* had a complaint to register. They alleged that the food served was insufficient, that they had been compelled to live on crackers, bad beef and worse barley soup. Schlome Seligson, one of the first passengers to be inspected by immigration officers, told that he had paid sixty-four dollars for his passage, supposing that he would receive at least second class accommodations. Instead, he said, he was shoved in a narrow bunk between decks. According to Seligson most of the passengers almost starved on the way over. He, himself, had to pay sixty dollars extra for food for himself and family.

Six Russian Jews made an affidavit that they had seen a man

knocked down and struck between the eyes because he had asked a steward for more food.

The human cargo of this vessel numbered more than one thousand, six of whom were stowaways. The stowaways had been set at work as stokers, and were said to be as "slender as fire bars" when they reached Ellis Island. Commissioner Senner told New York newspapers that all the immigrants ate like hungry wolves after their arrival.

Commissioner Senner must have spent many turbulent and troublous days at Ellis Island, for his administration was constantly attacked by the Press, immigrant aid societies, prominent citizens of New York and even members of Congress.

In December 1895 he had to defend his administration against the charge of immorality.

A young girl from Germany, Lena Grimmer, had landed from the S.S. *H.H. Meier* on November 15. She was accompanied by a man, Curt Foster, who she admitted was already married. Both were detained, but Foster was finally permitted to land.

While Lena Grimmer was in detention, she insisted a guard had approached her. Her story was corroborated by the Polish woman beside whom she slept. Both made affidavits that the report was true. The newspapers learned her story and the New York press flared into flames. Commissioner Senner finally dismissed a number of guards and transferred two watchmen to day duty.

In April 1896, the Commissioner discovered that the Island was being overrun with shyster lawyers. He had the following notice tacked up to be read by new arrivals:

Immigrants and their friends are warned that it is not necessary, in order to secure justice, to obtain the services of any paid attorneys. The Commissioner of Immigration is always ready to listen to any reasonable application for rehearing on the part of detained immigrants. Should immigrants be desirous of conferring with the Commissioner, the officer in charge is instructed to bring the matter to the attention of the Commissioner, and no charge of any kind for such services will be permitted under any circumstances.

Commissioner Senner also learned that many immigrants had been charged counsel fees amounting to as much as one hundred dollars. The following advertisement was appearing regularly in an Italian newspaper:

To the parents of the fifteen thousand Italians who are about to arrive in New York. By calling personally on [a name and address] whoever has an interest in an immigrant detained at Ellis Island (except that the latter is not under contract) may avail himself of his rights; and that the immigrant will be restored to his liberty will without fail be the end. The compensation will be small and much lower than most lawyers.

During the War years, when immigration dwindled to inconsequential proportions, the public forgot about Ellis Island, but with the end of hostilities in Europe, and the imminent passage of the Act of 1921, once again the cavalcade from overseas swelled to record proportions. The final week before the new law became effective saw a mad dash of thousands to American shores. Imagine the ships, bulging with human cargo, racing through the Narrows and into New York harbor, actually colliding with one another in their hurry to be at Ellis Island before the last minute of grace.

The *Saxonia* of the Cunard Line was one of the last of the immigrant ships to get under the wire. But there was no more room at Ellis Island. Guarded by Customs officials and Cunard Line detectives, her eight hundred human souls were landed on Pier 53, North River, at the foot of West Thirteenth Street, where they camped on the floor for four days.

Neither camp beds nor cots were available, but mattresses were supplied, and it is reported that the last-minute newcomers were well fed and comfortable.

While the immigrants, many of whom were Irish, were encamped on the pier, some waved handkerchiefs from the windows to a group of their former fellow countrymen who were working at the Gansevoort Market. The workmen yelled, "Throw us a line, we'll give you some fruit." This was done and the Irish immigrants received enough bananas to supply every alien in the shed.

However, there was again a storm of protest against the detention of incoming aliens in such an unbecoming manner. This criticism was further accented when customs officials assured the press that a squad of Immigration Inspectors and two physicians could have passed two thirds of the persons held on the pier in less than five hours. Once more fuel was thrown on the flames of opinion, which for nearly thirty years had raged at the mention of Ellis Island.

At the same time this renewed rush to America revived all the canny wiles of the swindler.

There is an account of a banker who was arrested for swindling fifty Russians out of an aggregate of one hundred and sixty-eight thousand dollars. He loaned cash on jewels and other valuables to immigrants who wanted a start in business. When he had garnered most of the possessions of the fifty Russians he left the country, but was apprehended on a ship at sea.

Another banker was convicted of taking large sums of money from immigrants for the supposed purpose of bringing their relatives to America. Of course the relatives never arrived. After several months this banker also disappeared but was finally caught and convicted.

Over in Cherbourg, France, in November 1920, two hundred and fifty immigrants, including women and children, were left on the pier because they had bought worthless tickets.

During 1922 and 1923 the British were seriously concerned about cruelties and insults their countrymen were said to be suffering at Ellis Island. Our immigrant station got a thorough trouncing in the House of Commons. Viscount Curzon, the Foreign Secretary, rose and stated that he knew personally of two English women who had been treated like dogs on Ellis Island, and fed on bread and water. The British press wrote long articles about the inhumanity of keeping English citizens in "cages" with people of dirtier and inferior nationalities.

One British paper printed the story told by a lace-maker from Nottingham, who said he had been persuaded to emigrate. The blessings of America had been painted so rosily that he had sold his house and taken his wife and children with him. Though he had the proper passports, he was taken to Ellis Island and herded with men of lower habits than his own. Here he was kept for six weeks, and was lanced so often for specimens of his blood that boils broke out all over his body. Inspectors, he said, had finally detected a slight cyst in his daughter's eyes, and had thereupon sent back the whole family with papers marked "likely to become a public charge."

The furore grew with each story published by a British citizen concerning the terrors of Ellis Island. Miss Louisa Vidler, an English immigrant then living in Boston, came forth with the tale of the tragic dénouement of her journey to America in 1921. She came with her father, she said, who was not well and was making the journey partly for his health. They had world passports and were first class passengers. The immigration officials ordered her father detained for observation, though he had already been passed by the physicians. At Ellis Island, she said, she was separated from him, and found after a few days that he was receiving almost no attention and had fallen ill from the continued neglect. She insisted thereafter upon being with him during the day, but when shortly afterward he died during the night, she was not called.

Feeling ran high in both England and America as the discussion continued. Finally Sir Auckland Geddes, British ambassador to the United States, went to Ellis Island and made a thorough personal investigation of conditions. He said that officials at the Island frankly admitted that often one hundred and fifty people of various races were housed in one dormitory. As he could see it, what we needed was a new and gigantic building with separate quarters for each race. This, however, was impracticable because of the small size of the Island.

About the same time the government of South Africa took diplomatic action against the United States on the complaint of Mrs.

DOUBLE DECKERS IN THE OLD DORMITORY FOR MEN SHOWING THE GREAT NUMBERS HUDDLED IN ONE ROOM.

Mark Glenville, an English woman who had come here with her family. After failing to gain admission to the United States under the South African quota she wrote, while *en route* to England, one of the most scathing criticisms ever made about Ellis Island.

Thank God, we are free again and away from the horrors of Ellis Island. Every night I awake in terror, dreaming that we are back again in prison.

The details of our life there were so horrible I feel too stunned still to describe them. It was such a shock that it will leave a mark on one for life.

Our poor innocent baby suffered. There were no baths, no fresh air, nor a sleeping place for it except in my arms. It was terrifically hot, and the stench was abominable. I felt my strength ebbing fast, and the life would have killed us had we remained a day or two longer. I really felt like committing suicide to get away from the horrors of cruelty and disease and the terrible filth. We were herded with thousands of foreigners.

We were yelled at, pushed and cursed from morning to night, and driven from one cell to another for unknown reasons.

I could not believe that such a hell existed on earth, or that free British subjects could be treated so.

Our only means of escape was begging to be deported to England, on which plea we succeeded after four days of these horrors.

In that year (1922) the *Times* commented editorially on the too delicate sensibilities of the British, and said truly that what most offended England was our failure to draw any line at Ellis Island between immigrants of more or less gentle nurture, and those whose sensibilities are supposedly blunted by poverty. The editor maintained that such a line ought not be drawn at a place like Ellis Island, which was admitting all immigrants alike to the most democratic country in the world.

It has always seemed to me that British criticism of the American immigration system was the cry of the aristocrat coming in close contact with those less cultured and dainty in their taste and habits. Ellis Island doubtless is to them unendurable torture. They failed entirely to see the other side of the picture—the hope and the promise of its inner meaning.

Such outbursts on the part of the English naturally drove the democratic United States almost to a frenzy of wrath.

There is also another side to the story. While many of these revelations and rumors of inhuman treatment of the immigrants at Ellis Island doubtless had a basis in fact, many were political diatribes directed against the commissioner in charge, or else deliberate revenge taken by some of the victims.

In 1923, during the commissionership of Henry Curran, a Russian baroness, Mara de Lillier Steinheil, was detained on the Island for three days. After she was released, she repeated far and wide that though she had been in Soviet prisons she had found nothing to equal the filth and squalor of Ellis Island. The dirt was so thick that it stuck to her shoes, she said.

The Commissioner denied it. He said it was impossible to provide a Tsar's suite for every immigrant, when as many as fifteen thousand arrived in one week, but he insisted that decency and cleanliness were provided for all.

During the same administration, a young German nurse, Miss Anna Hans, who was not allowed to enter under the contract labor law, charged that she was subjected to inhuman conditions during her detention on the Island. She was forced to sleep with a negress, she said, and she witnessed the birth of a baby in the dormitory.

Commissioner Curran accused her of being one of the many who are all smiles when they want to enter the country, but when refused admittance, leave a trail of lies and abuse behind them.

Philip Hotinguer, son of the German baron, was detained by us that same year on his way to one of our large universities. He departed from Ellis Island insisting that he had been forced to sleep on the floor and had been brutally kicked in the back. Curran replied that he would not have been permitted to sleep on the floor even if he had wanted to.

Many complaints stated that those detained were not permitted to communicate with their friends and relatives.

But these instances of abuse at the Island seem trivial when compared to the real exploitation by bosses and clever swindlers, who mercilessly exacted tribute from illiterate immigrants by a variety of "shake-down" rackets then in vogue.

By 1901, petty racketeering was practised so openly by those seeking to prey upon the arriving immigrants, that Commissioner Fitchie requested additional New York policemen to help prevent aliens from being robbed of their money and baggage.

One of the most common games of the swindlers was to pretend to be armed with the baggage checks of the aliens; then they marched off with luggage and disposed of it.

On April 18, 1901, Detective Grogan of the New York Police arrested Pasquale Sentico on this charge. Sentico walked into Grogan's trap by attempting to secure the baggage of a poor Italian woman, whose checks he had held for several days, until he supposed that she had despaired of ever seeing her property again.

In England, the newspapers were so aroused over reports from the steerage and Ellis Island, that the London *Express* sent a representative to report conditions first-hand. This is his account of a supper on the Island in 1901:

We passed in a long line around the room. A man with filthy hands filled our hats or handkerchiefs with mouldy prunes. Another thrust two lumps of bread in our hands. Supervising the distribution was a foul mouthed Bowery tough, who danced upon the tables and poured forth upon us torrents of obscene, blasphemous abuse. I saw him drag an old man, a long-bearded Polish Jew, past the barrel of prunes by the hair of his face. I saw him kick another immigrant, a German, on the head with a heavy boot.

Individual cases of petty annoyances and unpleasantness have, of course, the value of any first-hand report. They must, however, be judged as such. That an English reporter, of a class far removed from steerage, should object strenuously to what an immigrant might consider part of the day's work is scarcely important in the face of real and vital abuses practiced on aliens.

No matter how strict the contract labor laws, there was always a way of getting around them. The steamship companies had agencies in every village of Europe. Competition was terrific. Every inducement was offered the peasant to go to the country where the streets were paved with gold. And in America's boom days no immigrant needed a contract for a job. Jobs were plentiful.

I remember hearing of a swindling ring that operated in 1887 to obtain free labor for American farmers. A large jobber in farm labor had an office in Northampton, Massachusetts, through which passed hundreds of Poles, Hungarians, Danes, and Swedes. The ignorance and credulity of these new arrivals were exploited to force them to sign papers promising their labor for a full year with little or no salary. They were literally "bought" by the farmers, who came in from the countryside to look them over and choose the huskiest and most innocent. A New York office lured these men from the legitimate labor bureaus established for the new arrivals by promising immediate work at higher salaries.

The deception and cruelty which recurred with the great rush of immigration before the gate was finally closed by the Quota Act of 1924 continued up to my own term of office, and have not yet been completely wiped out.

But I, too, have been swindled and cheated. Even my vast experience with the foreign born has not made me immune to mistakes. The human element is notoriously uncertain, and with all my practical knowledge of the situation, I have often been deceived by the very individuals I have set out to help. It is not always possible to avoid the disappointment of a mistaken kindness or a misplaced confidence.

One day a woman came to see me. I recognized her name because I had received and answered several of her letters, all pleas that I intercede with the Governor of a nearby state where her husband had been in prison, to prevent his deportation. She told me the sad story of her struggle to keep the wolf of poverty from the door during the years she had been without her husband's support.

"Two of my babies are sick", she said. "I have a job for him, if you can only get him back to us. I've carried on about as far as I can go. If they send him away—out of the country—I don't know what will become of us."

After serious consideration, I had the Catholic Welfare Council take up the matter with the Governor in question. A few weeks later I received a letter stating that the case was being considered. A month later her husband was pardoned. Her gratitude was unbounded. She came to see me, bringing him with her.

In talking with this former convict I urged him, for the sake of his wife and family, to atone for his past by making an earnest effort in the future. He assured me, with every possible vow, that he would certainly do so.

Some weeks later he came again, this time to inform me that he knew of a number of criminal aliens who were in the country illegally. Since he, himself, had reformed, he felt it his duty to aid the government in every possible way by furnishing information.

I have never personally favored such activities by persons outside the Service, but the man before me spoke so convincingly that I listened to him and made some remark that the country would well be rid of alien criminals who could never be reformed. He left me and I heard no more of him for several weeks. Then came the news that he was posing as an Immigration Inspector, a friend of the Commissioner, who could save aliens illegally here, on payment of money intended in part for me. He was finally indicted and convicted in Federal Court. I appeared as a witness against him.

These impostors who victimize the alien in our midst, and abuse our patience and confidence, constitute a very serious problem. We arrested and convicted many of them during my term of office.

But on the whole, the crimes committed against the immigrant undoubtedly far outweigh his own offenses against society.

Chapter IV

THE NEW DEAL

I

ELLIS ISLAND is, first and last, the main entrance to America. In its half century of existence, passing on the right of approximately twenty-five million foreigners to enter this country, its errors are understandable in the face of its enormous achievements.

An island too small and inadequately equipped for the work confronting it, has made the best of its limitations and, in spite of its handicaps, accomplished one of the biggest and most trying jobs in the whole history of our country.

It has gone through a period of changing attitude toward the foreigner, and changing attitude of Americans toward the Island and its function, and to-day, thanks to a sympathetic administration in Washington, is in accord with the liberal policy I so earnestly set out to pursue.

Many mistakes blot the record of Ellis Island and great have been the hardships, the humiliations and the exploitation suffered by the immigrant. Yet, I am sure, there have also been instances of exaggeration in which the vitriol of the public and the press has been unwarrantedly directed at a Service which, in a last analysis, has been more sinned against than sinning.

Such blunders as came to light in the examination of the Cathcart and other cases narrated in this volume, were due more to the inflexibility of the legal system, and the want of discretionary power, than to wilful abuse of authority by the enforcing officials. They arose from the assumed necessity of those in the Service to enforce the laws to the letter, whereas public opinion invariably views individual cases from a more practical point of view.

Because I, too, felt the need of justice tempered by mercy, it was this public point of view that I sought to interpret from the very outset of my administration at the Island. One of my first official utterances was: "Let us carry out the intent of the law, but let us do it as humanely as possible." My emphasis was on the spirit and not the letter of the law, and because I had been given a free hand by both the President and the Secretary of Labor, whose confidence I enjoyed throughout my term, I found it possible to carry out my program of humanization.

I mentioned earlier that an attitude of suspicion and fear pervaded the Island when I assumed office. A few days convinced me that I could rely on my staff for the kind of cooperation I needed if only I conveyed to them the thoughts that were in my mind, and the policies I wished them to pursue.

With this idea uppermost I sought to have the human touch emanate from the Commissioner's office, I, myself, setting the pace as I carried on.

The key men of the Ellis Island contingent had been there for twenty, thirty and in the most important case, that of the Deputy-Commissioner, forty years. They knew the languages, the customs and the psychology of the immigrant. Their wholehearted response to my announced desire to humanize the Service was encouraging. That attitude was just what they had long wanted.

If I had any doubts concerning the ability of these men with whom I was to work, such doubts vanished rapidly. Nothing in the laws or regulations, and little in the history of the Island had escaped the watchful eye of my assistant, Byron Uhl. A hostile press, sharp shooting at details over which he had no control, had surrounded him with a legend of sangfroid which was entirely unsupported by the man's underlying character. Working with him daily, and availing myself of his wide experience and ripe judgment, I came to admire him as I do few men whom I have met in my public career.

I would also add a word for Percy Baker, Superintendent of the Island and second in command to Uhl, a Brooklynite, for thirty years in the service and an expert on Island affairs. His grand sense of humor stood him in good stead in handling the plant, the food, the equipment, etc.

Edward J. Zukor, Chief of the Registry Division, had formerly served in the Consular Service at Vladivostok. He knew the immigrant first-hand, having come in personal contact with thousands who fled Russia after the World War and the revolution there. For several years he has been President of the Immigration Inspectors of all Immigration Stations in the United States, and those detailed to the vast Border Patrol which vigilantly protects our international boundaries.

Among the last of these men I can never forget is Inspector John Montgomery, Chief of the Boarding Division. Passing through his room at the Barge Office going to the ferry in the morning and returning at the end of the day, I never ceased to enjoy our conversations together. Years before, Montgomery had been in the Border Patrol near Montreal. He delighted in reminiscences of his experiences with smugglers, but in recent years had transferred his interest to transatlantic stowaways.

Inspector Connolly, another descendant of old Erin, reflected the good humor of his chief, Inspector Montgomery.

The guidance of Inspector Dwyer in charge of detentions, of Pat King, the good Irishman who had charge of incoming immigrants, and especially of Ed Barnes, head of the Law Division with whom I always discussed deportation cases, became a pleasure and a necessity. Inspector McIntosh knew the history of radicals individually and collectively in every country of the world. Inspector

Brophy, liaison officer with the various prisons incarcerating alien criminals, knew when the bad characters of the old world would arrive at Ellis Island. And even among the guardsmen there was a celebrity. Guard Costello had served on the ship which took Woodrow Wilson to Europe and later acted as a bodyguard to President Harding.

Certainly it would be gross negligence on my part to mention all these capable key men of the Island without saying a word about Captain Matthew J. Munster of the ferry boat. His enviable record for making the fifteen-minute mile to the Island in perfect time and without fatality endeared him to all who made the daily journey.

I know too that soon after we became acquainted, these men were happy and self-confident again. They knew their jobs, and what they desired more than all else was to be themselves. By my permitting them to exercise their best judgment, the spirit of the Island waxed into one of enthusiasm, and even the old interpreters, men speaking every language in the world, who had perhaps grown bored with the lull in immigration, actually appeared to take on new life.

Happily, my relationship to my job was peculiarly personal and direct. While former Commissioners of Immigration had been men of unusual ability in their fields, able administrators and executives, none of them had a foreign background or a personal approach to the problem of the immigrant. They, in most cases, saw their position in terms of administrative duties, while to me the situation of the alien was an identification with myself. I was bidding for consideration for the immigrant by my own attitude of respect for him. I myself was cooperating to prove the validity of this attitude, rather than ruling with an iron hand. I found that my attitude toward my assistants was reflected in their treatment of the alien.

"Can you make a speech—I mean an inspirational talk?" the Assistant Commissioner General in Washington asked me, on one of my first official visits to the Capital.

I explained that my work in the past had frequently made it necessary for me to deliver addresses on various topics.

"The Island is in bad shape," he continued. "What you need to do is herd that gang into a room and tell them you mean business."

I said nothing. But that speech was never made. We had many round-table discussions, but no speech. It did not seem necessary. Instead I tried to convince by example.

II

Conscious of all to which the aliens of other days had been subjected, I felt that every effort should be made to liberalize the restrictions surrounding their stay in government custody.

In my own mind Ellis Island was not a prison, not even a prison for the deportees, who had served their prison terms and presumably paid their penalties to society. Accordingly it was wrong to treat them as prisoners.

It was obvious that one of the things they most wanted was more freedom. Another was the right to receive visitors. Previously they had been allowed to have their friends and relatives only on Tuesdays and Thursdays. This regulation was at the discretion of the Commissioner. I rescinded the old ruling and issued an order that friends and relatives might come to the Island any day in the week, or every day if they chose.

Another drastic ruling was the ban on the use of the telephone. Detained aliens were allowed to write letters and to telegraph. It was foolish to forbid their telephoning. We discussed the matter at a staff meeting and I subsequently had telephones installed in the detention rooms. All guards were instructed to act as interpreters and to assist the aliens in obtaining their desired numbers.

At that time the aliens spent but an hour or two a day outdoors. The reason for this limitation was the lack of sufficient guards. A request to Washington soon produced the necessary number of officers, and the immigrants, weather permitting, now spend most of the day playing games or walking in the sunshine.

We granted deportees the privilege of going out under guard to visit relatives or to attend to business. The only person who took advantage of this leniency was my friend, Mike Romanoff. He probably would never have endeavored to escape had the guard been armed. In earlier days no alien was permitted to go off the Island, even for the purpose of visiting his consulate to get a passport, unless handcuffed and accompanied by an armed guard. In contrast to the Romanoff episode, I once permitted an alien, who was about to be deported, and whose mother was dying, to visit her for two days without a guard and purely on his own recognizance. He returned punctually. Many similar instances of our confidence in aliens to leave the Island and report at a given time proved that we could well afford to depend on their honor. We had the satisfaction of many proofs of our good faith.

Perhaps my greatest success in striking a responsive chord in the heart of the alien and in the foreign-language press of New York came with the opening of the Commissioner's door to the aliens themselves.

Having abandoned the older practise of keeping aloof and leaving all contacts to subordinates, I had a discussion with Inspector Forman of the Deportation Division, a son of Interpreter Forman who was of foreign birth and had been in the service many years. An outgrowth of that conversation was the Commissioner's mail box in the detention room. No person save my secretary could open that mail box, and all immigrants or deportees were free to write letters and post them to me in this manner.

More than anything else it revealed to me the aliens' side of the picture. They frequently asked for appointments, and I saw them as soon as possible. Perhaps I spoke their languages, and if so they were immediately at ease, unburdening to me their grievances and difficulties. Many made valuable suggestions, and often those talks were responsible for the prevention of injustices.

An Arab, Hussan Bey, one day wrote me a pathetic plea, stating
that his life was in danger and he desired to talk with me immediately.

In the interview which followed, he told me a strange story.

"My enemies," he said, "have written to the tribe at Yemen, telling
my tribesmen that I have been drinking liquor and eating pork in
the United States. If I am deported to the tribe they will kill me."

The man spoke with such apparent sincerity that I believed him,
but decided to investigate further so that I might have independent
information upon which to change his deportation order. An inquiry at his consulate was not satisfactory.

"I doubt if they would kill him," the Consul said. "It depends
entirely on how near he lives to the desert. I think the worst they
might do would be to cut his ears off."

Further inquiry of the editor of the Arabian newspaper in New
York was no more reassuring. The editor practically confirmed all
that the deportee had said.

"There is one place where they would not touch him," he finally
advised, "the capital city of Aden."

We deported him to Aden, with a special request dispatched to
the British government urging his protection.

Curious indeed were some of the developments originating from
that mail box. A German boy, whom we shall call Hans Muller,
had escaped from the Island by climbing the fence and swimming
the long mile of waves to the Battery. On the following day he was
captured and returned to us. A few hours later I received his letter.
I was astonished, because usually the recalcitrant in such cases hates
the thought of having to face the Commissioner. Inspector Forman,
however, brought him to my office.

"I want to apologize and explain," he began. "I did not run away
to stay away, merely to see my two-year-old daughter."

The youngster had never married, but his agitation over the
child's welfare was strangely impressive.

"They are sending me out to-morrow," he said. "I hope you will promise me to look after the child." I did make inquiry, and found that the mother and her relatives were able to care for it.

In this constant desire to humanize the service and the attitude toward the alien, I witnessed many pathetic scenes.

A criminal, released from the Atlanta penitentiary last November, was on his way under guard to Ellis Island. A day or so after we had received news of his impending release, a letter came from his wife, requesting a ferryboat pass so that she might visit him before his deportation. She arrived at my office at my request, and brought along her five-year-old child, a little girl whom he had never seen. When the visit was over, and the guard had come to escort him to the detention room a few hours before the cutter was due to transport the deportees to the New York wharves, he kissed his wife good-bye. The tiny girl sidled up to him and said: "Come on, Daddy, we're going home now. It's nice to have you back with us."

One of my most frequent visitors was an Irish communist. He seemed to enjoy writing to me. It was not enough that he had made a red flag out of the cloth given to the deportees by the Daughters of the American Revolution for occupational amusement, but under pretense of various grievances and suggestions, he made repeated visits to my office. Each succeeding visit ended the same way. He sought to convert me to the "Utopian" plan. On his last call, he said: "I won't come any more. I had hoped you would see it. But my efforts are useless. You have missed the vision."

A young Chinese boy also wrote frequently. This was mainly because he enjoyed merely coming up to shake hands with me.

But intense agitation marked some of those interviews. A Hindu who had fired in self-defense, killing two shakedown artists who had milked him for years, did not mind being returned to India; all he wanted was my promise that the government would convey no official account of his crime, for if so, he would lose caste in his home land.

Fully as interesting as any story I heard was the one of the famous Auburn prison riot. The leader of the riot eventually reached Ellis Island.

"We received movie reels every week," he said. "On nights when we had no movies we listened to the radio. It was fixed on the outside that the guns were to be hidden among the movie reels. On the night before the reels containing the guns were to be shipped, the signal for all the prisoners was the Cotton Club in Harlem playing the 'Merry Widow Waltz'."

My greatest pleasure at the Island was the sight of joyful reunions among the immigrants. Perhaps it was a mother coming, or possibly a son or daughter, for in most cases the father had been longer in America. But in a great many instances they had not seen each other for ten or fifteen years. When they met in my office I frequently had to introduce them.

Occasionally we encountered problems which were difficult of solution because the immigrants spoke tribal languages and the interpreters could not make out their desires. Wrapped in towels, the Chief of the Ubangis, that weird tribe of the elongated lips, arrived at the Island with five women of his clan. Polygamy in these United States and at Ellis Island has ever smacked of moral turpitude. It was several days before Chief Woki made it clear that only one of the women was his wife, the rest merely friends.

The deportation laws with all their rigidity have been enforced more humanely in recent years. I had occasion to intercede in the case of a young Italian, Massielo, whose entire family was being deported. The youth was a senior in the Jersey City High School. I was requested to stay deportation until his graduation, and the boy was graduated with high honors. Mayor Frank Hague of Jersey City sat on the platform and presented him with his diploma. The case aroused so much sympathy among neighbors and friends, that finally we were able to get the Department at Washington to change the deportation order to one of voluntary departure. This injustice was prevented by Secretary Doak himself. And in that same year ten thousand deportation orders were lifted by the Department at the request of Ellis Island to prevent separation of families.

The lifting of a deportation order meant that the deportee was free to leave the country voluntarily, and reenter on application to the Secretary of Labor. Secretary Doak had the reputation of being "hard-boiled," but in many specific cases, he proved very soft-hearted indeed.

The Commissioner's mail box often held suggestions for improving the food. Some were adopted, others were impossible. On first going to the Island, I had hoped to be able to have the menus arranged so that all nationalities might in turn be fed native diet. But an inquiry revealed the amazing information that in one day we were entertaining no less than thirty-seven different varieties. It was impossible to satisfy all, but we did the best we could with so many tastes and preferences. If we served spaghetti to please the Italians, all the rest went hungry, and if we did not have spaghetti, the Italians complained. Likewise with corned beef and cabbage for the Irish, and rice for the Chinese. The solution was a "least common denominator" of wholesome food. Immigrants were well fed. In fact, Mrs. Roosevelt was astonished when she visited the Island and learned that it cost about $1 a day to feed each immigrant on Island rations.

It was about this time that I received a letter from the spokesman of two hundred Chinese who had been several days in the detention room. They had arrived with boxes of food and boiled eggs five years old. I went down to see what he wanted. The two hundred were grouped for my reception. Their faces were impassively oriental. Not one stirred while the spokesman arose and made a long speech. When he had concluded, one of my staff, a Chinese graduate of Harvard told me what he had said.

"They want the rice a little drier."

Such conferences brought about a reduction of complaints to a minimum. But there were other problems besides food. The Island was overrun with "Jersey" mosquitoes, and these insects seemed to take quite a fancy to the children who came from Europe. We had all the buildings screened and made a new drive for sanitation.

In all this work, there was an ever-ready cooperation from Social Service agencies. They reported unseemly conditions and helped in handling the problems. Frequently I turned over cases to them for investigation. On occasion they secured pardons for deserving deportees. They gladly performed countless services for the immigrants and deportees, running errands, obtaining their baggage, writing letters and otherwise getting in touch with their friends and relatives.

The annual Christmas concert became a permanent institution with the help and cooperation of the Social Service workers, who arranged and procured the best available talent. Sunday afternoon entertainments, conducted alternately by the various New York settlement houses, became accepted as a regular feature of Ellis Island amusement. No one wanted to miss anything, so everyone attended everything. All the immigrants attended all the concerts, and also appeared at religious services of all creeds and denominations. In fact religious services once became so popular that instructions were issued requesting the immigrants to select whatever religion they cared to, and then to stick to it. Otherwise we found Jewish festivals attended by large congregations of Catholic, Protestant or even Mohammedan believers, with space at a premium for the Jewish worshippers themselves, and similar situations for other groups attempting to follow out their ritual and ceremonies.

The social workers procured equipment for games and directed the recreation of the detention cases. An East Side settlement house bought a set of Bocce (bowling on the green) for the Italians. But after the Chinese learned the game, the Italians were forced to stand on the sidelines and watch.

Such liberty and intermingling gradually built up a spirit of fraternity among the immigrants. When the great Balbo air fleet zoomed across the Island, the immigrants rushed outdoors to greet it. There was fully as much enthusiasm among the others as there was

CHRISTMAS PARTY AT ELLIS ISLAND IN 1933 WITH COMMISSIONER EDWARD CORSI DISTRIBUTING GIFTS TO LITTLE ONES OF ALL NATIONS.

among the Italians. It was one of the most impressive spectacles I have ever witnessed—this fervor of the Europeans for those who had flown from their side of the Atlantic.

And what was true of the adults held good in the case of the children. In the little kindergarten school in the top of the administration building, I saw tiny Italians, Chinese, Serbs, Roumanians, English, French, Germans and a host of others playing together in tender comradeship.

This program for humanizing the Service was my dream from my first day on the Island, in fact from the day I had talked with President Hoover, who devoutly declared that Ellis Island had to have a new deal and that he would back his appointee to the limit.

The success of my intention to acquaint the public, especially the foreign public most concerned with the affairs of the Island, was illustrated touchingly and beautifully when I sailed abroad during my term of office. Foreign-language newspapers had apparently done their work so well that Ellis Island and its officials were being eulogized instead of vilified. That my program's accomplishments paralleled its ambitions, and that Ellis Island's New Deal was reaping its reward in widespread good-will, it was my good fortune to find in living illustration on my way to Europe.

I sailed on the *Conte Grande*. On the second day at sea the Captain informed me that he had one thousand former immigrants travelling third class. "Come down and see them," he said. "I'd better not," was my reply. "The deportees couldn't feel very kindly toward the man who had signed the orders which sent them away."

"They won't know you," he returned. "Not a chance that you'll be recognized." He persisted and I finally agreed to accompany him.

They were eating when we arrived below. Some of them appeared to be in excellent spirits. He told me that only one hundred of them were deportees. The others were fleeing the depression. I was standing behind the Captain trying to keep in the background. I wondered how they might have received me had they known my identity when suddenly one of them spied me. Forgive the personal allusion, when I say that he shouted: "Viva Corsi!" The welcome which followed was perhaps the greatest I shall ever enjoy as long as I live.

III

Living down a bad name is never an easy job. When I went to the Island I determined to remove the air of mystery with which it had been surrounded. My first step was to unmuzzle the press. With this end in mind I proceeded to hold three meetings of major importance.

First I called the New York reporters to my office. I had them to lunch, explained my policy and intentions, listened to their suggestions and invited their cooperation. I told them that henceforth they might have free entry to the hitherto forbidden ground. They might hold interviews with aliens, with me, and with the Chiefs of my Divisions. Practically overnight their attitude changed from one of hostility to one of friendliness.

The second meeting was a luncheon tendered to the correspondents of foreign newspapers—European and South American. For years these correspondents had been giving the United States a bad name in their native lands because of the actual or imagined conduct of the Immigration Service at Ellis Island. Their opinion changed radically when they saw with their own eyes how humanely aliens were being received, and their attitude toward their foreign-born readers reflected our new spirit of fair play.

The third meeting was with the Consuls of foreign nations who were located in New York. Being diplomats they naturally gave no outward indication of past feelings, but I am sure they left the Island with a more friendly attitude.

The sum total of these three meetings was incalculable. Favorable publicity of our government spread throughout Europe and among our neighbors to the southward. Previously every account of Ellis Island had been one of pointed criticism.

Following up this program of selling a once poison name to the world, I made numerous radio addresses and platform appearances, urging my men to do likewise.

"We have nothing to hide!" I reiterated many times.

This new spirit and the publicity it evoked brought many visitors to the Island, and all departed as walking advertisements of good will.

We had already declared war on racketeering and had made long strides toward its annihilation. The mail box in the detention room brought much valuable information which helped us. My settlement work in New York had resulted in many contacts with the foreign-born who readily came forward with information and offers of help.

Such wholesale raids as that of the Finnish dance hall were stopped. The Washington special agents, untrained and overly ambitious, were gradually cleared from the Island. Raids were canceled; arrests were made in orderly fashion and on warrants as provided by law; third-degree methods were strictly prohibited; agents abusing aliens, severely punished; hearings on warrants of deportation were orderly, fair and strictly in accordance with law. All this was in direct contrast to conditions which the public had protested vigorously.

I believe that the records will indicate that our relations with the Bureau of Immigration reached a record mark for amity and cooperation. There had previously existed a strained relation regardless of administrations. Washington's contact with the Island is mainly through a record room, a court of last review for the cases that are appealed. Their cooperation made possible our humanity, and emphasized our success.

I realized that no improvements or appropriations could be expected unless friendly relations existed. I invited Secretary Doak to the Island, and he came on several occasions. He watched the games of the aliens, mingled with them and gradually changed his attitude.

These satisfactory relations made two more changes possible:

First, in dealing with cases more humanely we often prevented unjustified deportations through an arrangement, in special cases, for voluntary departures.

Secondly, they secured the money and authority for physical changes.

Soon after I went to the Island we obtained three hundred and fifty thousand dollars for its improvement. We cleaned it up and dressed it up. We built a new Record Room. We tore down the old marquee or canopy in front of the main building, and built a beautiful plaza adorned with flower beds. On my further recommendation, one million one hundred thousand dollars were appropriated by the Roosevelt administration. Added together these amounts represent the largest sum ever expended for improvement of the Island.

Practically all the changes advocated have now been adopted and adequate appropriations have been made. It was my pleasure to confer with the Department of Labor's committee for three months upon these suggestions.

As a part of the New Deal begun by the new administration in Washington the committee of prominent citizens selected by Frances Perkins, Secretary of Labor, undertook a complete analysis of Ellis Island—its past and present conditions, and recommendations for future improvement. This committee, in conjunction with experts in various fields qualified to conduct such an investigation, worked hard and diligently. I consulted with them freely and gave them the benefit of my first-hand experience, and the conclusions drawn after long consideration and practical application. It is with profound satisfaction that I found embodied in the Ellis Island Report practically the whole body of my own conclusions and recommendations for improved physical conditions, reforms in deportation laws, and an educational scheme for considering aliens not purely

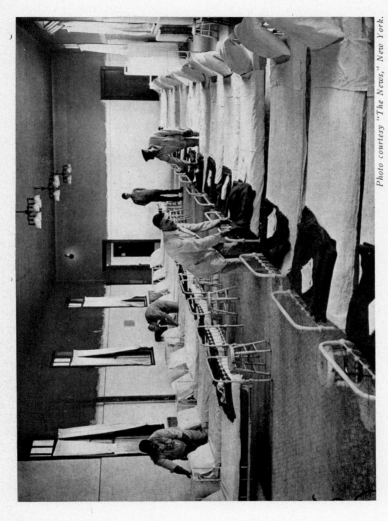

THE NEW DORMITORY FOR WOMEN AND CHILDREN, GIVING EACH A NICE CLEAN BED IN A WELL VENTILATED ROOM.

as so much labor hazard to the American workman, but as future American citizenry, whose assimilation into our lives and ideas was our responsibility.

I had myself made a preliminary step by the organization of all national associations dealing with the foreign born into a working group. The purpose was to cooperate with the Department of Labor in preventing exploitation of the foreigner, and to explain to the foreign born the "what" and "why" of the American immigration policy. I had carried the idea so far that delegates had met in Washington and conferred on the matter with the President and the Secretary of Labor, and had expressed their intention of drafting the foreign press for their purpose, but in the course of future events this campaign was lost sight of and left to die out.

I had myself thrilled with the new vision of the Administration in its attitude toward the alien, through the leadership in the Department of Labor. I had endeavored, during all my time at the Island, to consider the immigrant as a whole rounded human being in his relationship to his new country, from the time of his landing to the inevitable time of his citizenship, and had worked out a plan for his training in our language and customs that would naturally lead to his acceptance of our ideals and hopes as an American. As a ward of the Federal government I felt our responsibility to the alien to give him its protection against exploitation by swindlers, and to act as his guide and teacher on his way to citizenship. I was always urging upon my subordinates this new view in relation to the foreign-born—our responsibility as an Americanizing influence— a view which, I rejoice to state, is shared by the present Department of Labor.

It was with pride and satisfaction that I noted in the finished Ellis Island Report, dated March 13, 1934, the following tribute to my services:

"The spirit and policy at Ellis Island depend chiefly on the ability, humanity and disinterestedness of the Commissioner in charge. The

Committee trusts that for the future the high standards of the past year may be resolutely maintained."

The new program for dealing with the alien in the United States, which was finally recommended by the Ellis Island Committee Report, was almost in toto the plan for dealing with the immigrant that I had devised and followed out as far as possible within the limitations of the law. I had myself urged such legal change as would permit more leeway in future to those dealing directly with the foreign-born.

Besides my continued desire for the physical improvement of the Island, which finally bore fruit in the newly planned building schedule now under way, I had advocated from the very beginning of my office the need of publicizing and humanizing the Island in the eyes of the entire world.

As it is the port of entry to the largest city in the largest country of the Western World, it seemed in keeping that the physical appearance of that port should bear witness to the importance of the city and country whose door it opened. That Ellis Island should be to the immigrant, as well as to the American, an inspiration—a tribute to our physical development as exemplified in adequate buildings, well-planned grounds, satisfactory sanitary and housing conditions —was to my mind the first, but by no means the only or the most important, consideration.

My more insistent and persistent effort was toward the realization of the alien as a human being, to be considered from humane standards and treated not as a potential contestant for American labor, but as a potential citizen of these United States, sharing its life and adopting its customs. We, therefore, with whom he came in contact as representatives of his new government, could best shape his future attitude toward this country and its laws. We had our chance with him first, and were responsible for giving him a sympathetic understanding which no subsequent contact with less scrupulous individuals could alter.

Besides the many changes other than the completion of sea walls and improvements to buildings and the humanizing of rules which I urged, I pointed out also that the gateway to America was practically closed for the time being at any rate.

"What greater service," I asked, "could the Bureau of Immigration now render America than by helping to assimilate the more than six million aliens who already live among us? Many are illiterate, many need adult education and information as to how they may become citizens and why they should seek naturalization. Many do not know, and fear its imagined obligations."

This suggestion of expanding the Bureau to a government arm of usefulness and worthy purpose was embodied in the committee's final report.

Paradoxically when my attitude on some of these matters became known, the American Civil Liberties Union which had ever been hostile to Ellis Island in former years, invited me to serve on its alien committee. But of course I could not do so while holding an official status in matters pertaining to the alien.

I had been held over by a reappointment of the Roosevelt administration, recommended by Secretary Frances Perkins with whom I had had social service contacts many years before, and whose enlightened leadership was partly the result of years of experience in immigration work in New York.

Mention was made editorially in the *New York Times* of August 11, 1933, which said:

"Commissioner Corsi's background of experience and his own naturalized sympathies give him a special fitness for the position which he has been urged by Secretary Perkins and Commissioner McCormack to retain. Though born abroad himself, he is 'American-minded.' He is the good illustration of those who continue to come of the fine type of citizenship which may emerge from the alien population."

With the almost complete paralysis of immigration, the routine at the Island was so well established that there was little need for me to do more than sign my name to letters and documents. Aside from overseeing the functioning of the job, my daily duties were practically nil. My work there was finished.

Meanwhile, within the country a whole new panorama of need and poverty and suffering was taking shape.

Fiorello H. La Guardia, who had once served as an interpreter at Ellis Island for seven years, had been elected Mayor of New York. The problems that he faced in the City government had captured the public imagination.

The depression, the need for relief, evidenced in my own neighborhood and at every hand, was compelling. When offered the post of Director of Relief in New York City, I eagerly accepted the challenge. Here was an opportunity to return to my first love, active social service, in command of the largest program for public relief the world has ever seen.

Yet with the approach of my last day at the Island, it was with a heavy heart indeed that I faced my farewells.

My time was up on January 31, 1934. That was a hard day for me—breaking away from a routine of several years' contacts that had come to mean much to me, from satisfactory accomplishment and dreams realized. It was in a sense a fitting breaking-off point, but uprooting is always hard and not a little sad.

The thought of leaving my big room in the administration building forever—my last hours with two faithful secretaries and a staff whose memory I shall always cherish—made my heart ache. Even my last look at those unfortunate souls in the enclosure, who had failed in America and would soon be shipped back in disgrace to the lands of their origin, brought a lump to my throat.

My thoughts wandered to that distant October morning long ago when the shadow of Liberty had welcomed the arrival of the Corsi family in America, and of all that had come to pass in the many intervening years.

Ordinarily I left daily on the four-forty boat, but to-day I could not bear it. I looked up at the clock—I had time, if I ran, to catch the three o'clock boat. I wanted so much to ride back for the last time with all my old staff, but I could not face it. Cowardly, I fled the goodbyes I could not say. A solitary figure, I left the Island of my Destiny behind in the shadow of Liberty.

INDEX